Table of Contents

Acknowledgements

We are indebted to:

- The young women who took time to openly and honestly share their stories. We trust that these stories and this research will go on to have a positive lasting impact for other young women.

- The Young Women's Working Group who spent much time and effort taking the research and making it accessible to their peers.

- The Research Steering Group for their input and direction during the life of the research and for the doors they will, no doubt, go on to open for future dissemination opportunities.

- Kate Moore, Peer Researcher, for her work on the development of the ECHO magazine, her work with the Young Women's Working Group and her involvement in the field work aspect of this project.

- The community groups and organisations who granted us access to young women.

- The Gender Equality Unit of YouthAction, especially Eliz McArdle, for their feedback and input into the research and for taking these principles forward in their work with and for young people.

- YouthAction for the drive in taking this research forward and their commitment to equality and work with young women.

- Those who spent endless hours transcribing and proof reading the final document.

- The Big Lottery Fund for supporting this project throughout.

Glossary of Terms

AEP – Alternative Education Provision
AVC – Advanced Vocational Course
BTEC – Business and Technology Education Council
CAB - Citizen's Advice Bureau
CCEA – Council for the Curriculum, Examinations and Assessment
CDT – Craft, Design and Technology
CEDAW - Convention on the Elimination of Discrimination Against Women
DE – Department of Education
DENI – Department of Education Northern Ireland
DETI – Department for Trade and Enterprise
EDI – Equality, Diversity and Interdependence
EMU – Education for Mutual Understanding
EOC – Equal Opportunities Commission
FCO - Foreign and Commonwealth Office
FE – Further Education
FPA – Family Planning Association
GAA – Gaelic Athletics Association
GNVQ – General National Vocational Qualification
HND – Higher National Diploma
HPA – Health Promotion Agency
ICR – Institute of Conflict Research
JRF – Joseph Rowntree Foundation
LGBT – Lesbian, Gay, Bi-sexual and Transgender
MLA – Member of Local Assembly
NEET – Not in Education Employment or Training
NHS – National Health System
NIAYC – Northern Ireland Association of Youth Clubs
NICCY – Northern Ireland Commissioner for Children and Young People
NIHE – Northern Ireland Housing Executive
NIO – Northern Ireland Office
NVQ – National Vocational Qualification
OECD – Organisation for Economic Co-operation and Development
OFMDFM – Office for the First Minister and Deputy First Minister
PSE – Personal and Social Education
RCM – Roman Catholic Maintained
RSE – Relationships and Sexuality Education
STI – Sexually Transmitted Infection
UNCRC – United Nations Convention on the Rights of the Child
UVF – Ulster Volunteer Force
YCNI – Youth Council for Northern Ireland
YLT – Young Life and Times
YWCA – Young Women's Christian Association
YWWG – Young Women's Working Group

Foreword

Since its inception in 1944, our organisation has been deeply concerned about the quality of young women's lives. Indeed the foundation of YouthAction was laid through the establishment of the *"Federation of Girls' Clubs"* by women radicalised by the experiences and suffering of war, who made progressive social reform and the improvement of professional practice their ambition.

During the 1970s and 80s the focus of our work with young women was supporting them to find their voice, make informed choices and take control of their lives. But it became increasingly evident that young women were not fully making use of Youth Service provision or benefiting from resources. The Youth Work Committee for Northern Ireland (1987-89) supported our concerns "out of a knowledge that despite numerous policy statements and commitments to the needs of girls and young women in the Youth Service, the reality was that girls were absent from many youth service facilities at 15 years and often felt peripheral to mainstream provision" (Derek Wilson – Chairperson).

"Equality of Opportunity" (1990) investigated these concerns and confirmed fears that young women from age 13 were not participating in, or benefiting from, mainstream youth work interventions. This quantitative and qualitative research shaped YouthAction's strategy for many years, especially in reaching out to vulnerable and marginalised groups of young women. It also made us rethink the type of provision required to penetrate to the heart of young men's lives.

Almost twenty years after the *"Equality of Opportunity"* research project began and having journeyed through periods of major social change; including 30 years of equality legislation, a government agenda of inclusion and participation and a move towards a more stable civic society; it was time to reconsider. We asked ourselves "what is life like now for young women in Northern Ireland?" Has the equality agenda resolved many of the barriers constricting young women's lives?" "What stories do we need to take account of to shape youth work policy and practice over the next twenty years?"

From its title, *"Still Waiting"* immediately alerts us not to be complacent. Those of us who have championed gender conscious youth work practice may feel disappointment at the findings. Many of the stories will concern and perhaps shock the reader. At YouthAction we believe that young people's stories should shape youth work practice, training and policy. The findings of *"Still Waiting"* go beyond the scope of Youth Work policy. There are significant messages for all who have a commitment to or a responsibility for young people.

The strength of this report lies in the poignancy of young women's stories told within a robust research framework. One which was shaped, designed and advised by young women themselves. There is also a second story to be told concerning the development of valid and robust research methods underpinned by inclusive youth work principles and practice.

I congratulate the research team of staff and volunteers under the leadership of Eliz McArdle and Ann Marie Gray on this reawakening of the complex issues facing many young women in our society. I would encourage the reader to listen carefully to the voices in this report and take action.

I am reminded of the challenge set down by our founder member, Mary Gilmore in 1944:

"We must realise that it is we who control what Government departments do in the matter of progress and make it our ambition that 12 months hence we shall have some progress to show".

In 2007, with a new devolved administration in place, I too expect progress for all young women "12 months hence".

JUNE TRIMBLE   MBE
Director YouthAction Northern Ireland

Chapter One
Introduction

INTRODUCTION

"... there's so much media and so much literature about the fight for the woman going back hundreds of years and look how far it's come, then has it really? ...//... it's quite confusing when you're led to believe that you can do anything, but then when you try, you get knocked down and you think to yourself 'what's it all about?' (Young woman in Derry/Londonderry focus group)

This report sets out to offer a holistic view of the lives of young women living in Northern Ireland at the beginning of the 21st Century. While there has been much research on young people in general, rarely is this disaggregated by gender or has it had a specific focus on young women. The past 30-40 years has seen many local and global changes which have impacted upon all young people today – a widening of education and employment markets, the ratification of the UN Convention on the Rights of the Child, the Good Friday/Belfast Agreement and the 30 year anniversary of sex discrimination legislation in Northern Ireland. Within this context of change, and agenda of participation and inclusion, how have young women faired and have equality issues been subsumed into broader issues? These are some of the questions that this research set out to explore.

As a follow up to exploratory focus groups with 48 young women across the country, the reports draws on in-depth interviews with 43 young women aged 16-25 years, in which they offered accounts of many areas of their lives. That is, their attitudes and experiences of family and home life; education training and employment; free time and leisure provision; community life; sex, sexuality and related services; health and well-being and Northern Ireland politics. Across all of the issues explored, three cross-cutting themes clearly emerged: the impact of the conflict in many areas of young women's lives; continued gendered attitudes, perceptions and inequalities and the lack of visibility of young women's voices/participation.

As a team we struggled with a title for the report. There were, for example, no obvious quotes from the young women that were reflective of the views of all and despite team meetings and consultation with a group of young women, we were at a loss. The decision was finally made to call the report 'Still Waiting', because as will become clear in the forthcoming chapter, in many areas of young women's lives they are effectively still waiting. Still waiting to be heard, still waiting for equal representation in politics and positions of authority, still waiting for full and impartial careers education, emotional and sexual health advice, still waiting for equality of opportunity in many respects. In 1978 after a conference on work with young women in youth clubs, NIAYC (now YouthAction Northern Ireland) produced a resource specifically dedicated to programme ideas for work with young women. This was entitled 'Waiting Our Turn' and was a direct response to what many viewed as the low participation of young women in youth clubs based on existing provision and a lack of understanding of the lives and needs of young women. While this report moves beyond an exclusive focus on youth provision and the place of young women in it, over a quarter of a decade on the title still reflects that young women are 'Still Waiting' for equality of opportunity and provision.

When discussing the proposed title with various people, one comment fed back to us was that it was felt to be 'a little passive'. This is true in many respects and in fact does reflect the mood of the young women's accounts. When asked specifically about gender inequalities for example, many did not fully see or acknowledge these, yet their accounts were full of examples of gendered assumptions and inequalities within their everyday lives. In response to a direct question on whether they felt men and women were equal today, we were more often than not greeted with statements like:

"It's gettin' there" (Kim, aged 21)

"What does it matter? ...//... You just have to get on with it ...//... if you want to, you can get on and do whatever you want " (Jill, aged 17)

"There's more opportunities today than what there would have been years ago" (Pauline, aged 23)

"It's looking good" (Ruth, aged 17)

"There's a lot more opportunities" (Victoria, aged 22)

"It's not as though there still is that difference in equality" (Nicola, aged 20)

"I just think it's like all kinda equal" (Oscar, aged 17)

In many of the young women's responses to this question there appeared to be a kind of 'passive acceptance' of continued inequalities, often based on their knowledge of how things were in their mothers and grandmothers time and of the advancements made by women in education, employment, child care and equality laws. In light of the messages young women are receiving from parents, schools and the media in terms of the opening of opportunities, it is of little surprise that young women are not fully recognising the persistence of gender inequalities.

Inequalities may indeed be different to those in the past, or at least less obvious, but this report demonstrates through the experiences of young women that they are no less pervasive. We have taken a thematic approach to the report and presented young women's attitudes and experiences in relation to various areas of their lives, and while we point to continued gendered messages, lack of responses, deficits in information and structural inequalities we have also endeavoured to highlight areas of good practice throughout. Furthermore, we have made great efforts to keep the voices of young women at the heart of the research through retaining their words and dialect and ensuring that their voices speak through in the chapters that follow. This is in line with the overall approach we took to the research in terms of its design and methodology, which is outlined in detail in chapter 2.

While we acknowledge that the report is lengthy, this is in recognition of the complexity and multiplicity of young women's lives and in tune with keeping their stories at the heart of the report. Read in full, it offers a holistic account of young women's lives but each chapter has been written in such as a way as to be 'stand alone'. A context/background is offered to each themed chapter whereby related literature, research and policy is reviewed in order that the research findings may be set in the context of these. Furthermore, key recommendations relating to each theme are presented at the end of each chapter rather than at the end of the full report. The concluding chapter of the report, therefore, pulls together the inter-related nature of all of the themes discussed in the separate chapters and discusses issues which cut across all of the themes. Written in this way, we hope that those working in specific areas can dip in and out of the report and easier refer to the sections of most relevance to them.

Our aim is that at an agency level this research will inform and re-direct the work YouthAction Northern Ireland carries out with and for young women. But we feel it holds great potential beyond this. As a research report, it gives voice to the lives and experiences of young women in Northern Ireland and this fills a long-standing gap in research. In this respect, it will be of interest to academics within Northern Ireland and beyond. It is also our hope that it will inform the knowledge and practice of those who work with young women in a range of settings including schools, youth clubs/programmes, health services and communities. Further, as Northern Ireland enters a new period of devolved administration, and as social policy issues gain priority, the mechanisms but also the atmosphere exist to re-energise and politicise fundamental issues such as gender equality. It is vital that young women's voices inform and shape change. In the words of one young woman:

"... if you stop now, it'll probably go backwards." (Victoria, aged 22)

Dr. Ann Marie Gray, Vice Chair YouthAction Northern Ireland

Dr. Siobhán McAlister, Lead Researcher

Gail Neill, Research Co-Ordinator

May 2007

Page 15 Footnote 1: Six young women did not provide their ages and three did not provide details on their religious background

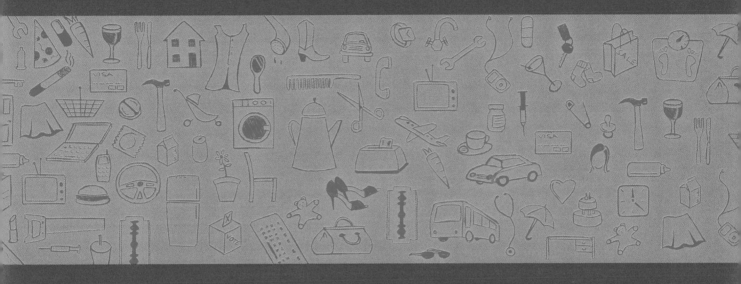

Chapter Two
Research Design and Method

Research Design and Method

2.1 A FEMINIST APPROACH TO RESEARCH: KEY PRINCIPLES

As young women were the focus of the research and it was about their lives, their views and their experiences, the aim was to ensure that they were at the heart of the research from start to finish. It is for this reason that a feminist approach was adopted. Not only does feminist research take women as its starting point in so far as it recognises women's stories as legitimate sources of knowledge, the way in which these stories are collected, analysed and disseminated is done with an ethic of "respect, collaboration and caring" (Campbell & Wasco, 2000: 775). It is the "motives and concerns" of feminist research which make it unique and relevant to this study (Brayton, 1997: 1).

While there is no singular feminist methodology, five principles which guide feminist research have been identified (see Brayton, 1997: 9-10). Firstly, women and gender are the focus of analysis. Secondly, it is about consciousness-raising at an individual level for both the participant and the researcher. Thirdly, there is a rejection of the power imbalances between the 'researcher' and the 'researched', and recognition that the researcher is an inherent part of the research process. Fourthly, there is a concern for ethics in terms of responsibilities to individual participants and the wider use of research findings. And finally, it is about the empowerment of women and changing gender inequalities in society as a whole. We have sought to implement these principles in all aspects of the research process.

2.2 FEMINIST ACTION RESEARCH

At a basic level it could be suggested that all feminist research is action research as a key feature of it is to affect change at an individual, group and societal level - "Change happens both by empowering women in the research and by distributing information which changes the actions of others" (Gatenby & Humphries, 2000: 90). This, however, does not adequately convey the nature of feminist action research in that it is not merely about a particular set of changes, as in an end result, but that the process of change is continuous (Reinharz, 1992).

Action research is when research, action and evaluation occur simultaneously throughout the duration of the research project. As such there were various stages to the research process: carrying out research with young women in order to gain a better understanding of their lives and needs; working directly with young women to inform needs led programming; designing and delivering pilot programmes of work on these areas and evaluating and amending them as appropriate and rolling them out to other groups of young women. While this provides an idea of the structure of the research project, it conceals and oversimplifies the various steps in the research process and outlines only the overall pattern. Table 1 provides some further examples of how the process of research, action and evaluation was continual throughout this research project. It not only illustrates some of the many ways that research, action and evaluation were built into this research project but the nature of action research more generally in that the research can be "transformed by emergent findings, which, in turn, impact upon the research process itself, and subsequent outcomes" (Todhunter, 2001: 1). Further, it more clearly illustrates some of the other key components of feminist action research – "inclusion, participation, action and social change" (Reid, 2003: 7). Here research participants were clearly involved in the 'change process' and empowerment was gained through this participation (see section 2.5.2 for further discussion).

Table 1: Components of the Research

Research	Action	Evaluation
• Review of literature • Consideration of methods of data collection • Consultation with young women to consider key themes of research • Discussion with young women about how best to run focus groups	• Compile focus group interview schedule • Design format for focus groups discussions	• Pilot data collection instruments with young women and amend
• Organise and run 7 focus groups with 48 young women	• Report initial findings of focus groups to young women and Research Steering Group for feedback • Decide upon, design, plan & deliver 'taster sessions' on theme of stress	• Analyse feedback from 'taster sessions' • Analyse feedback from young women and Research Steering Group
• Consult with young women about interview themes and format of interviews	• Compile draft interview schedule	• Pilot interviews with young women and amend interview schedule
• Organise and carry out 43 in-depth interviews with young women	• Report initial findings from interviews to young women and Research Steering Group for feedback • Report initial findings to Women's Sector & Government body for feedback and early dissemination • 5 week pilot programme set up and run on some interview themes	• More focused analysis of research findings • Evaluation of 5 week pilot programme • Young women and research team consider key issues to focus developing resources for other young women
• Young women and research team research ways to present information and run sessions for other young women	• Young women design four magazines as resources for working with other young women	• Evaluation of young women's role in designing magazines • Young women & research team pilot resources • Resources and delivery of programmes evaluated and amended

2.3 GENERATING AND ACCESSING A SAMPLE

With the existence of Section 75 of the 1998 Northern Ireland Act (which requires public authorities to have due regard for promoting equality of opportunity irrespective of religious belief, political opinion, age, racial/cultural grouping, sexual orientation, martial status, gender and disability), a variety of research and consultation with more marginalised or vulnerable groups in Northern Ireland exists (Davey et al., 2005). As a result of this we may know a lot about particular groups of young women, or particular aspects of their lives, but we know less about young women as a social group and the totality of their everyday lives and experiences.

This research aimed to offer a snapshot of the diversity, and perhaps similarity, of experience of young women aged 16-25 throughout Northern Ireland. While the aim was to capture diversity of life we did not wish to do so through generating large sub-samples from which definitive conclusions and generalisations could be drawn, rather to ensure that young women with all different types of life experiences were included. So for example, we aimed to talk to: young women living in rural and urban areas; young women living in predominantly Protestant and predominantly Catholic communities; young women who were in formal education and young women in informal education; young mothers; young women with disabilities; young women from minority ethnic backgrounds; young women in full-time employment; young women still living in the family home and those who were living independently; young women involved in community or youth provision and those with little or no involvement. Obviously, some young women possessed a number of these identified characteristics.

2.3.1 The Focus Group Sample

While aware that we could not adequately represent the views of all of these young women through interviews alone, some were deliberately targeted for inclusion in the focus group stage of the research. The aim of this was two-fold, firstly, to gather information and represent their views as a group and secondly, to better inform ourselves of the issues which were important to them so that we might include these in any interviews which may follow (see section 2.4.1 for a fuller discussion of the aims and rationale of the focus group exercise).

The groups targeted for this stage of the research were those whom we felt we had a particular lack of knowledge about or who have been less-well represented in research more generally (either because of social class and perceived less vulnerable/marginalised, their location or difficult to access). Seven focus groups were set up and run with 48 young women. Two comprised of groups of young women from rural communities (one predominantly Catholic and one predominately Protestant), two from urban/interface areas (one predominantly Protestant and one predominately Catholic), one from Derry/Londonderry, one attending a grammar school and one group of young women from minority ethnic backgrounds.

Once identified, these groups were targeted and accessed in a variety of ways. As YouthAction Northern Ireland is a well-established youth agency with regional bases throughout Northern Ireland we have worked with and have contacts with many statutory, voluntary and community groups. This aided in identifying some key gatekeepers and was the means through which one of the focus groups was successfully accessed. Individual members of the research team either through previous employment, research projects, training courses or personal contacts also had identified possible contacts. While good-will and friendships were an effective means of targeting gatekeepers and possible contact points this was not always a straightforward or successful exercise and back-up plans were always made.

Initial phone calls were made to identified contacts in order to introduce the research. These were followed with a letter and flyer explaining the research in more detail and, within a few days, an additional phone call was made to establish whether the young women were interested in taking part.

Various background characteristics of the focus group sample were collected, some of which are presented in Table 2. As the target age range was 16 to 25 years and we were aware that those aged 16-18 years, for example, may have very different life experiences to those aged 19-21 and 22-25 years, we were keen to equally represent the views of the various age groups of young women. While we requested young women aged between 16 and 25 for the focus groups we had little control over who turned up and in choosing particular age groups. As a result of this, and as can be seen in Table 2, there was an over-representation of young women at the lower age range, with the average age of the focus group sample being 17 years. Additionally, a number of young women fell below the initial sample age but were not excluded from focus groups given that they had taken the time to come along, were eager to take part and had valuable contributions to make. While it was felt that we could more successfully target older young women (i.e. over 19 years) at the interview stage of the research the average age of the focus group sample is an important research finding in itself own. As most of the young women involved in this stage of the research were accessed through youth or community organisations, this is indicative of the age of young women who tend to use organised youth/community facilities.

Table 2: Age and Religion of Focus Group Sample

AGE	Number[1]	Percentage
13-15 yrs	13	31
16-18 yrs	19	45
19-21 yrs	6	14
22-25 yrs	4	10
RELIGIOUS IDENTIFICATION		
Catholic	21	47
Protestant	16	36
Hindu	3	7
None	5	11

In light of previous research experiences which have found higher proportions of those identifying as belonging the Catholic community taking part in research, we deliberately targeted those living in predominantly Protestant areas for inclusion in the research. Despite these efforts, however, we still ended up with a slightly higher proportion of those identifying as belonging to the Catholic community within the focus group sample. If we were, however, to follow many Northern Ireland employment equal opportunity monitoring forms, we would use other identifiers to place participants into categories of belonging to either the Catholic or Protestant community. If we were to do this, this would mean that representation was fairly equal.

2.3.2 The Interview Sample

A purposive sampling technique was adopted for the interview sample in so far as we knew the age groups we wished to target and some further characteristics. For example, guidelines were drawn up in terms of making attempts to have a fairly equal representation of the three age groups and to ensure that the sample was not predominantly Belfast based. While it would have been fairly easy for us to contact young women throughout Northern Ireland given the nature and remit of the work of YouthAction Northern Ireland, we were keen not to merely include those young women whom we knew through the agency's programmes, or through other agencies/organisations. This, it was felt, would limit the findings of the research to only those young women who were involved in organised youth/community activities and not offer an accurate or holistic representation of the diversity of young women's lives throughout Northern Ireland.

As a starting point we did rely on some of our own contacts as potential research participants and to provide the beginnings of a snowballing process. This meant that when we interviewed a young woman we would ask her if she had any friends, of a particular age who might, for example, not be involved in any education, training or employment at the time. This method enabled us to contact more 'hard to reach' young women and ensured that we interviewed young women from all different backgrounds (see section 2.3.1 for overview of how contact was made).

There were a number of occasions when we also made contact with young women through particular agencies as we were keen to ensure that their views were represented. This included young women with disabilities and young women who were or had been involved in informal education programmes. Again, these young women were asked for further possible contacts who might not be involved in any such programmes. While using a snowballing technique can be a lengthy and sometimes fruitless process, its strengths lie in the fact that it can ensure that the views of various young women, particularly those which may be 'hard to reach', are included in research. Through this technique 43 young women took part in one-to-one interviews.

Again a number of background characteristics of the sample were collected and are displayed in Table 3. This reveals that with regards to age a fairly even spread of the three age groups was achieved. As was aimed for, the mean age of interviewees was higher than the focus group sample at 21 years of age. In terms of religious identification, efforts were made to include young women from minority ethnic backgrounds and/or who identified as other than Catholic or Protestant. While numbers are small, this is not wholly unrepresentative of the Northern Ireland population as a whole. Again, despite particularly targeting those who may identify as belonging to the Protestant community, a higher proportion of interviewees identified as Catholic[2].

Table 3: Age and Religion of Interview Sample

AGE	Number	Percentage
16-18 yrs	11	26%
19-21 yrs	15	35%
22-25 yrs	17	39%
RELIGIOUS IDENTIFICATION		
Catholic	23	53%
Protestant	15	35%
Jewish	1	2%
Hindu	1	2%
None	3	7%

In terms of other background characteristics, 36 of the sample self-identified as heterosexual, four identified as lesbian and three identified as being unsure or not knowing. No young women identified as bi-sexual. Eleven young women were living in rural areas and seven were mothers.

Finally, we were eager to ensure that we were not only representing young women who were involved in organised leisure activities such as youth groups/programmes, sports groups, church groups etc. and all were asked about their involvement in such activities – a fairly even mix was achieved in that 49% had involvement while 51% reported no involvement.

2.4 RESEARCH DESIGN AND TECHNIQUES OF DATA COLLECTION

A guiding principle of the research was that the researchers did not wholly define the research and the themes of investigation in their own terms, but that these came from young women themselves – hence implementing the principle that young women are the experts of their own lives (Brayton, 1997). As such the research question was far-reaching and explorative with a view towards young women defining the issues of importance to them and the "subjective aspects of their needs" (Smith et al., 2002: 192). Qualitative research methods were felt to be the most suitable means of data collection as they allow for the exploration of attitudes, experiences, understandings and aspirations and for the research themes to be less pre-determined. Further to this, the variety of methods used in this research project illustrates one of the strengths of feminist research - that is, that it chooses and combines methods that best represent women's situations and experiences (Greaves et al., 1995 cited in Brayton, 1997).

Ninety-one young women took part in the research through focus group discussions (n=48) and one-to-one interviews (n=43). The rationale for the utilisation of these techniques of data collection and the implementation of them is discussed below.

2.4.1 Focus Group Discussions

Focus group discussions acted as the first phase of data collection. While these provided data in their own right[3], the wider aim was that the issues defined and discussed by the young women through this forum would inform those later explored in more depth through one-to-one interviews.

While the research team and a group of young women had identified some themes to be explored in focus groups, the aim was that the young women involved would come up with their own issues and concerns. Before moving into a themed or focused discussion, therefore, a short group exercise which acted as a form of 'stimulus material' was compiled and carried out (Kitzinger & Barbour, 1999). This involved each member of the group considering the good and not so good things about being a young woman and the good and not so good things about being a young man. Each member of the group recorded their thoughts on a sheet provided and reported their points back to the full group. The fact that the young women had written points down and reported them back displayed a willingness to talk about them within a group context.

While each of the seven groups of young women undertook the 'gender exercise' we also designated specific themes for discussion to particular groups in order that we might collect a little information on each. Table 4 provides a breakdown of these.

---

2   Due to the sensitivity of the issue of religion in Northern Ireland we did not feel that it would be conducive to ask young women their religion when making first contact, telling them about the research and trying to engage them in the process.

3   The focus of this report is upon the findings of the individual interviews. A fuller account of the findings from focus group discussions has been discussed elsewhere (McAlister and Neill, in press).

Table 4: Focus Group Discussion Topics

Group	Discussion Topics
Rural area (x2)	Access to information, facilities and services
Urban area	Leisure and community
Interface area	Health
Derry/Londonderry	Education, employment and training
Grammar school	Politics
Minority ethnic	All

While the rationale for the use of focus groups and further details on how these were run is provided elsewhere (McAlister & Neill, In press) the group context provided a supportive environment to discuss views and experiences, particularly when there was commonality and similarity of experience. There were, for example, things which were discussed in this group context which rarely came up in the one-to-one interviews perhaps due to feelings of discomfort talking about them on an individual level with a stranger. The sharing of experience, therefore, could be empowering and consciousness-raising in that it allowed young women to talk about issues that might otherwise be taboo and to see that they may not be alone in their views and experiences (Wilkinson, 1998). Furthermore, the fact that the group talk to each other more than directly to the researcher means that they are more in control of the discussion and interaction. As such there is a clear breaking down of power relationships as the researcher's influence on the group is inevitably reduced. In light of these points, focus groups can be highly suited to feminist research.

2.4.2 Interviews

Interviews are a favoured technique of data collection amongst feminist researchers as it is felt that they provide a forum for allowing women's stories and lives to be conveyed in their own language and terms (Oakley, 1988; Reinharz, 1992). The feminist interview is often viewed as a two-way process, or a 'conversational partnership' (Rubin & Rubin, 2005), where both parties invest part of themselves and where the principles of empathic listening, respect, caring and understanding are paramount.

While we had developed an interview schedule which included a range of topic areas that we hoped to discuss with interviewees (see Appendix 1), the aim was that their responses would guide the order and depth in which these were discussed. It had been pre-agreed, however, that we would never ask about sensitive or personal issues towards the beginning of interviews (unless these were raised by the young women themselves). Interviews opened with a conversation-like question inviting the young woman to tell us a little about herself such as her age, where she lived and what she was doing with her time at the moment. What the young woman revealed here signified what she was willing and comfortable to talk about at this early stage and we would pick-up on something said here and move directly into that theme and a discussion around it. This meant that the young woman was setting the agenda and it put a level of control in her hands. If there was little we could pick-up on from this general introduction we would move into the theme of education as a starting point as this is something that everyone has experience of and is generally a non-threatening topic to begin with.

The adoption of this approach ensured that the young women felt that the research was relevant to them, that they were knowledgeable and had something valuable to contribute (Reinharz, 1992; Rubin & Rubin, 2005). We feel that it also put young women at ease early on and established the interview as non-threatening. Interview participants were also provided with a 'pass cards' at the beginning of the interview and urged to use this at any point if there were issues/questions they did not want to discuss[4]. Again we feel that this assisted in establishing a non-threatening environment early on in which the young woman had some level of power and control while also demonstrating that the researcher respected them as individuals and did not see them merely as research objects.

Further to this, the importance of young women's contribution to the research was reinforced throughout the interview. It was most important to remind young women of this at points in the interview where they offered a "don't know" response to questions. For example, in response to a question regarding knowledge of domestic violence services we often got a "don't know" response. We did not wish young women to feel uninformed or embarrassed about this lack of knowledge and thus potentially disempowered. As such we took this as an opportunity to highlight how this information in itself was valuable as it meant that we could inform organisations such as Women's Aid that their advertising may not be reaching young women and that we and other youth agencies also had work to do on this area in terms of consciousness-raising. This, we believe, helped to validate their responses and input.

Various methods were employed in an attempt to reduce hierarchical relationships and place control in the hands of research participants. This included encouraging young women to choose their own pseudonyms and to ask the researchers questions at any point. This meant that the researcher was willing to 'self-disclose' in terms of investing part of themselves, their identity, their views and their experiences. Not only does self-disclosure aid in establishing rapport and trust but it can initiate true dialogue whereby the interview can become like a fairly natural conversation (Stanley & Wise, 1992). While the degree and timing of self-disclosure is important it is a means of recognising the personal investment research participants put into research. As Rubin & Rubin (2005: 83) remind us - "When interviewees tell you in detail about their experience, they expose themselves to you ... they deposit a part of themselves, an image of who they are, into your safe keeping and in doing so end up feeling vulnerable". Stanley & Wise (1992: 177) suggest that "if they [research participants] are vulnerable, then we [researchers] must be prepared to show ourselves as vulnerable too" by revealing information about ourselves.

While self-disclosure may have facilitated trust, rapport, openness and ensured that the interview was in many ways like a conversation, we feel that it was our gender more than anything which allowed for freeness of conversation around some 'taboo' and highly emotive topics. In many instances women view women researchers as "sympathetic listeners" who have some degree of similarity or at least understanding of experience – "both parties share a subordinate structural position by virtue of their gender. This creates the possibility that a particular kind of identification will develop" (Finch, 1984: 76). We found that interviewees would often open up fairly quickly and invest their trust in us through revealing sometimes very personal and distressing information early on.

There was much to be gained from adopting a feminist approach to interviews, yet with this 'power' comes responsibility. At times when young women were distressed or appeared to find difficulty in talking about issues, they were reminded that they did not have to answer or continue with the interview, were offered a break, glass of water etc. or the tape-recorder was switched off.

Additionally, as a number of the topics discussed were personal and potentially emotive it was important that the interview ended on a more positive note. As such the concluding question of all interviews asked young women if they were Prime Minster for the day and could do anything

---

4   Only one young woman chose to use the pass card (see chapter 7)

what this would be. This took the question out of the personal in some ways and sometimes elicited a humorous response or a desire or wish which more often than not extended beyond the young woman's own life as an individual. Further to this, because in-depth information may have been revealed there was a moral duty on our part to ensure that research participants were informed and empowered by the interview experience. Empowerment can be achieved in many ways, one of which is providing women with the information they need in order to make informed decisions and changes in their lives. At the end of interviews all young women were provided with a leaflet containing various local and national contact points. The researchers took time to talk through these and the services they offered as well as giving their own contact details and encouraging young women to get in touch should they require further information.

Overall, like Janet Finch we found that the young women were almost always enthusiastic to talk to us and that many found "this kind of interview a welcome experience, in contrast with the lack of opportunities to talk about themselves in this way in other circumstances" (1982: 73-74). At the end of interviews (and focus groups) young women would often thank us or tell us that they had enjoyed the experience and/or made realisations about themselves, their lives and/or society.

All interviews, with the consent of the young women were tape-recorded. Most took place in their own homes or other locations arranged and agreed with them. They lasted between 40 minutes and one hour and 20 minutes (with most averaging about an hour). Travel and child care costs where reimbursed were necessary.

2.4.3 The Story Book Method

There are groups in society whose voices are more often silenced than others, and research is often guilty of perpetuating this exclusion. We are of the belief that all young women have the right to be heard and represented in research. As Butler et al. (2003: 25) say of children but which is applicable to all – the "right [to be heard] is not dependent on ... ability to express views, but to form them". Through previous research and practical experience of working with young women with disabilities, (and training in disability awareness during the course of the research), we had an insight into all "communication capabilities" (Detheridge, 2000). This was imperative to the designing of an appropriate technique of data collection and the process of carrying out that data collection.

A story book was designed which worked upon a similar premise to vignettes. It was a resource whereby the young women attached meanings to the story of a fictitious person's life. In other words, they were offered scenarios and invited to respond to these. This method gave the young women room to relay issues from their own starting point, enabling them to define the situation in their own terms. The value of this approach is three-fold, firstly it allows the participant to explore actions or occurrences within a concrete context and consider factors that might impact upon that action. Secondly, it clarifies an individual's judgement on particular issues (for example on gender stereotypes) and finally, it depersonalises sensitive issues hence making them less threatening to explore (Barter & Renold, 1999; Hazel, 1995).

One of the acknowledged problems with this technique of data collection is that it can be difficult to separate belief from experience. Attaching meaning to a character's life and story is not the same as attaching it to your own. This is why we used the story book as one part of an interview. After the young woman had responded to the character's scenario we followed this up with more personal questions. So for example, in the story Sally's favourite subjects in school were PE and Computer Studies and we asked the young women to draw a picture of Sally at school. While they did so we followed this up with questions about their own school experiences. So the story was used in some ways to introduce topics to explore. Asking questions without providing some context or examples to work from may have been too abstract for some of the young women, and the story book provided this context. We feel that the story book engaged the young women in the process and aided in maintaining their interest in a way that an interview alone may not have done.

Four young women with learning disabilities were involved in the research. Two researchers were present at each of these sessions – one to guide the discussion and drawing through the story book and the other to actively listen and pick-up on responses probing questions around the young women's own experiences.

2.5 PARTICIPATORY RESEARCH: THE ROLE OF YOUNG WOMEN

2.5.1 Peer Researcher

A peer researcher was employed on the project for two years with the overall aim of equipping a young woman with the skills to be involved in research with her peers, to be empowered through this experience and for her to empower other young women through research.

It has been noted that empowering a young person to take the lead in research can often yield high quality data. This is because as young people they may be able to communicate more effectively with those of a similar age ('shared language'), especially if they have some understanding and/or insight into the issues which are being researched ('mutual understandings') (Davey et al., 2005; Kirby, 1999; McCartan, 2004; Smith et al., 2002). While involved in many aspects of the research project including research design, data collection and preliminary analysis, one of the primary roles of the peer researcher was to work with groups of young women who would help steer the research and inform the findings and programmes that were to come from it (see section 2.5.2). In light of this role and in order to equip the peer researcher with necessary skills, youth work and research training were both provided.

Despite the various gains that peer researchers can bring to a research project, it would be unwise to assume that they have a clear and informed knowledge of the field of study or an experiential understanding of research skills such as empathy, active listening, an awareness of what issues to probe and when to do so and how to deal with difficult situations (e.g. disclosures, sensitive/emotionally charged issues, child protection concerns etc.) (Smith et al., 2002). Further, although peer researchers may benefit from what Smith et al. (ibid.: 202) refer to as peer researcher's 'insider insights', they caution that this does not necessarily guarantee greater empathy as "external characteristics do not always reflect common subjective realities". Indeed, just because the peer researcher may be of a similar age to research participants and of the same gender does not in itself diminish the inherent imbalance of power in research.

With an awareness of these issues, research training sessions were set up and run which covered all aspects of the research process from deciding upon a research topic; literature searches and reviews; methodologies; techniques of data collection; the practicalities of 'doing research' in the field; ethics; child protection and data protection procedures; analysis and write-up. The obvious difficulties in carrying out research training is that a researcher is essentially attempting to relay a variety of theories, philosophies and practices in a meaningful way in a fairly short space of time. Whilst the topic of research methods can be somewhat 'dry', the task was to ensure that this was delivered and pitched at a level which was relevant, interesting and interactive. The use of tasks and exercises which the whole research team took part in such as information gathering, mock interviews and ethical dilemmas went some way to making the training of more practical value. Along with mock interviews with the research team, the peer researcher were also involved in pilot interviews in which the participants provided feedback to the researchers. This form of 'experiential learning' was of great value for highlighting the realities of 'doing research' and good preparation for the field.

While the peer researcher had input in some of the phases of analysis her primary role after data collection was to organise and run sessions with groups of young women to inform them of some of the issues coming out of the research and to collect their views on these. A further role was the continued recruitment and facilitation of a group of young women who would further steer the research and direct the use of findings (see section 2.5.2).

2.5.2 The Young Women's Working Group

Many of the aims of feminist research can, to a degree, be achieved through collaboration with those who are the focus of the research. This means that young women, particularly those who are research participants, have an input at all levels of the process. As alluded to throughout and illustrated in Table 1, young women, some of whom were research participants, played a key role in this project. This included informing the issues to be explored and the manner in which to explore them, piloting instruments of data collection and suggesting changes, commenting upon initial research findings, deciding upon which aspects of the findings to present to the Research Steering Group (which they did in the form of a DVD), and designing and delivering resources to inform other young women on the issues they had identified as important to them[5].

One of the principles of feminist research is to breakdown the traditional power imbalances associated with research and this close co-operation and work with these young women was one way in which we could keep a check on this power. Through all of these techniques the aim was to reject the notion of 'research on' young women and replace it with 'research with' young women (Stanley & Wise, 1993: 168) and to ensure that 'ownership' of the research and knowledge was not wholly in the hands of the research team (Brayton, 1997). In terms of the work with the Young Women's Working Group, it could be said then that this research represents feminist participatory research in that the voice of the participants was included in all aspects of the research and that it was a collaborative process rather than one where the research team represented "separate, neutral academics theorising about others" (Gatenby & Humphries, 2000: 90).

Although the make-up of this group changed over the duration of the research project it included young women of different backgrounds from all over Northern Ireland. While travel and childcare costs were reimbursed, their time, work and dedication is not something that can be so easily quantified and re-paid. Although it was clear from their evaluations that the young women felt they had gained much from their participation in the Young Women's Working Group (in terms of personal and social development, acquired knowledge and skills and feelings of empowerment), it was felt that their input could be further acknowledged in more concrete terms. As such, they were offered the opportunity and support to have their input and achievements formally recognised and accredited through undertaking a Silver Youth Achievement Award (see Youth Clubs UK & ASDAN, 1997 for full overview of rationale of Youth Achievement Awards).

2.6 RESEARCH PROTOCOL AND ETHICAL PROCEDURES

Various research and ethical guidelines were consulted and utilised. These included the Disability Rights Commission Guidelines for Ethical Research, the National Children's Bureau Guidelines for Research (2006), Statement of Ethical Practice for the British Sociological Association (2002), the University of Ulster's Policy for the Governance of Research Involving Human Subjects (2005) and OFMDFM's Ethical Principles for Researching Vulnerable Groups (Connolly, 2003). At a more general level, feminist ethical principles were adopted throughout and YouthAction Northern Ireland's Child Protection Policy and Procedures (2002) were adhered to.

---

5   The YWWG developed a series of four interactive magazines which could be used individually by young women or act as a programme outline for larger group sessions. These magazines cover the topics of alcohol, sex, relationships and self harm and were identified by the group as being of most concern to them.

2.6.1 Informed Consent

The research team drew up clear guidelines concerning consent procedures and the information to be given to potential research participants. We were of the belief that just because a young woman turned up to an interview or focus group did not mean that her consent was informed. Time was taken at the beginning of interviews and focus groups to provide clear and understandable information about the research project and what young women could expect of the interview/focus group. Such information included: what the research was about, why it was being carried out and what would come of the provided information; the sorts of issues that may be discussed and the potential sensitivity of some; expected time commitment; her right to refuse to discuss anything or withdraw consent at any time, and the ways in which we would endeavour to protect her identity. Further information was provided on how the data would be stored and who would have access to it along with clear guidelines on child protection procedures and our legal obligation to report anything told to us that may make us think that a child was being harmed or at risk of harm.

While this may appear fairly dry and overly informative when written down, the researcher would take as much time as she felt necessary to explain these procedures, intermittently checking that they were understood, answering any questions which arose and providing examples or further information where she felt it was needed. Once this information had been explained the young woman was again asked for her consent and reminded that just because she had previously given it (or it had been given on her behalf by a parent/teacher etc.), did not mean that she had to continue with the interview or focus group. Where appropriate or where there were concerns such as the possible identification of research participants in the writing-up of findings, agreements were made with individuals to, for example, consult them if they were to be talked about/quoted in order that they were happy that they could not be identified.

While consent may be gained at the beginning of an interview/focus group, we felt that it should be a continual process (see Wiles et al., 2004 for a discussion of on-going consent) and as discussed in section 2.4.2 young women were asked at various points in the interview if they wished to continue. Hence offering the option to opt-out and taking the onus off them to state that they wished to do so.

2.6.2 Confidentiality and Child Protection Procedures

The young women were given information on the various ways that we could afford anonymity and confidentiality through for example, removing real names and other identifying characteristics from transcripts (e.g. names of schools, areas etc.) and limiting access of the raw data to the research team and a small team of transcribers. Circumstances where we could not assure such confidentiality and anonymity, however, were clearly outlined particularly around the issue of child protection. It was explained that if anything was revealed that may make us think that a child (someone under the age of 18, including themselves) was being harmed, or at risk of harm, that we were legally obliged to pass this information on. The process of this in accordance with YouthAction Northern Ireland's Child Protection Policy and Procedures was further explained. We agreed, however, that if a disclosure were made that we would (where possible) discuss the process with them and offer information and/or support.

2.6.3 Data Protection and Privacy

In line with the Data Protection Act (1998) all personal information and primary data was stored securely in a lockable filing cabinet in a locked room. In order to maintain the privacy of research participant access to data and other personal information is limited to the research team and transcribers (for the duration of the transcription period), meetings were held with transcribers and the Research Co-ordinator regarding the privacy of personal information and the signing in and out of recordings. Where personal information is kept on computers, these are password protected.

Interview and focus group recordings which contain person details and real names etc. are kept separate to transcripts from which real names have been removed and replaced with pseudonyms. Other identifiers have also been removed.

As a further means of protecting research participant's identity and respecting their privacy, those case studies which are presented in this report have been carefully chosen and some details omitted in order that the young women are not easily identifiable.

2.6.4 Ensuring the Well-Being of Research Participants

As noted in section 2.4.2 research participants were provided with a leaflet containing local and national contact points which may be of value, and time was taken to explain the services these offered. Further, *The Little Book of Stuff* was given to all those who took part in interviews. While the contact points in this tend to be primarily Belfast based it does contain national contact points, useful web sites and information for young people regarding various aspects of their lives and their rights. When interviewees requested further information on for example, YouthAction programmes or contacts not included on our leaflet we endeavoured to send this information on to them. In recognition of the fact that we are not experienced counsellors we did not offer advice if it was sought but steered the young women towards appropriate contact points.

Time was also taken at the end of interviews, particularly when difficult issues had been discussed to wind down and to have a more general discussion with young women before leaving. This sometimes involved the discussion of useful places for information and advice given what they had revealed, but more generally a discussion of something positive they had alluded to in the interview (e.g. plans for the weekend, holidays, previous holidays, areas upon which the researcher also had some knowledge/experience to share) or a discussion of the value of their and other young women's stories.

Young women were also reminded that they would be updated about the research (if they consented to the use of their contact details), invited to the launch of the report and to any programmes that YouthAction were running as a result of the research. A letter was sent to research participants thanking them for taking time to talk with us and for their contribution to the research. This contained our contact details and young women were again encouraged to contact us at any point in the future if they required information about the research or if they felt we could be of any assistance with regards to other issues.

2.6.5 Vulnerable Adults

While similar procedures were followed regarding how the above issues were implemented and explained to all young women, these took a slightly different format for young women with learning disabilities. Disability Awareness Training had been undertaken by the research team and this aided in providing a working knowledge of issues to take into consideration. So, for instance, more time was taken over explaining consent procedures and ensuring that young women understood what the research process was about, parents and/or guardians were informed of the time and location of interviews (although the decision to partake was entirely in the hands of the young women), the concerns of key workers were taken into account when carrying out interviews and all correspondence and information was provided in large print.

Further to this, a number of young women with learning disabilities were actively involved in the research process at all stages through membership of the Young Women's Working Group.

2.7 DATA ANALYSIS

All interviews and focus group discussions were transcribed verbatim. While these were used as the primary source of analysis, original recordings were used for verification purposes. At least two members of the research team took part in all stages of analysis to ensure that data was not being interpreted solely by one person and that the research was strong on internal validity.

The first stage of analysis involved familiarising ourselves with the data through reading the transcripts. Two-thirds of the interview transcripts were read by all team members who made notes on individual transcripts while keeping a record of general feelings, emerging issues and patterns. Two full days were dedicated to a discussion of these transcripts from which a table was formulated noting the main themes within each individual case along with initial views on commonalities and emerging themes.

Based on these discussions and further readings of the transcripts a draft coding frame (or conceptual framework) was developed whereby numerical codes/labels were set up and could be used to identify pieces of text which referred to a particular category of reference. This was an inductive process in that the codes and themes of analysis arose from the data and what the young women had said. In an attempt to reach data saturation a code was allocated to all issues and themes raised (bar those that were completely off-topic) (Rose, 2001). Two members of the research team worked from the draft coding frame in coding a number of transcripts together – this enabled intercoder agreement and additions and amendments to the coding frame.

Once all interviews were coded these were inserted into the assigned categories and an initial analysis of individual categories carried out (vertical reading). An overview of each category was written which provided a descriptive analysis and overview of the data. This was followed by a horizontal reading of the data across all categories whereby cross-cutting and interrelated issues and themes could be identified (explanatory analysis) (Spencer et al., 2006). This deeper level of analysis allowed us to more fully explore the meaning of young women's lives and experiences.

Throughout the process of descriptive analysis, emerging ideas and issues were shared with the full research team and the Young Women's Working Group in order that they could offer thoughts and insight into the higher level of analysis.

2.8 REFLECTIONS ON THE RESEARCH PROCESS

While there is much to be gained from adopting a feminist approach to research, putting the principles into practice is less straight-forward than perhaps appears here. In particular, the research team found the two-month phase of intensive interviews to be a physically and emotionally draining period. With its emphasis on listening, understanding, caring and investing ones self and own emotions, the feminist interview can be an intensive and emotional enterprise. As Reinharz notes and we found in our experiences, "Anyone who reads biographies of women knows that to a large extent they are painful to read" (1994: 47 cited in Gatenby & Humphries, 2000: 98). While we did not deliberately target young women for interview who may have had difficult, painful or traumatic life experiences, we found many instances of this. Although prepared for the types of issues that might emerge, the extent of these and the deeply personal way in which they were shared on a regular basis was something that we could not wholly prepare for.

Many tensions exist in feminist research, often as a result of its very ethos - caring, emotionality and empathy. Despite an awareness of knowing what one should do or how one should act, natural tensions emerge. For example, it can be difficult to allow a young woman to talk freely about painful experiences, to watch her pain unfold as she makes sense of it by sharing it, and ensure that she does not feel uncomfortable doing so when your reaction is to want to shield her from that pain by not talking about it, by moving quickly on. Yet to move on without acknowledging her pain and allowing her to make sense of it may trivialise it. Indeed, it became clear that for a number of young women this was an opportunity to make sense of feelings and the impact of life events in a way that had not be done before (see Gatenby & Humphries, 2000). Further, despite an awareness of child protection procedures and knowing what must be done in cases of disclosure, there is always concern for the research participant – did she fully understand the information she was given at the beginning of the interview concerning this? Had she got so caught up in relaying her story that she had forgotten? How would she be affected by the process that would be triggered by such a disclosure?

There is no easy way to resolve any of these feelings or issues. For us, we found that a strong and supportive research team saw us through the difficult times. Writing field notes after each interview or focus group describing our feelings and experiences could also in some ways be therapeutic. Off-site supervision was also available to those involved in the data collection phase of the research, should they wish to avail of it. It was through these support mechanisms and reflexive practices that we began to see the positives in what might have initially felt like a negative or difficult interview experience. Self-realisation and empowerment had come in many instances and forms. Through relaying her experiences of child abuse and neglect, for example, Susie finally stated and accepted that she perhaps needed to talk to a professional about it. Rachel asked the interviewer to advise someone she could talk to regarding sexual abuse and domestic violence. Erin noted throughout her interview that she had not been able to talk about her experiences of sexual abuse, yet had done so in great depth and without prompting with a woman she did not know and was unlikely to meet again. Ellen came to the realisation that she needed to go to her GP and Carmel requested more information on self-harm and possible contact points for her brother.

Further, for the young women involved in the Young Women's Working Group they saw first hand how their stories and those of other young women could go some way to help and inform others. As their final evaluations revealed, they felt that they had gained much from their involvement:

"Being involved in something that might help someone along the line or be useful to them really makes me feel satisfied and I enjoyed this effect a lot. Watching the idea turn into a tangible magazine was an amazing and exciting experience to be part of"

"I would like to thank YouthAction for the opportunity to be able to participate in something like this. It has really developed my life skills. I am leaving this residential today with knowledge, new friends and the hope that there will be more groups to come."

All of the young women involved in the Young Women's Working Group were offered the opportunity to take part in another programme run through the Gender Equality Unit.

Chapter Three
Home, Family and Relationships

HOME, FAMILY AND RELATIONSHIPS

"I've never had the coming home being asked how my day was, coming home from school and having the dinner on the table, ... treated to family outings, never had any of that and that's something I'd like to experience" (Jo, aged 17).

3.1 INTRODUCTION

The experiences of family life and relationships emerging from this study are varied. In this chapter a range of issues are considered - relationships with families, implications of lack of family support, housing transitions, motherhood and violence and abuse in families. What emerges is a picture of the complexity of family life and the way in which youth transitions are influenced by socio-economic factors, family relationships and the adequacy of state welfare support. Those young women who had a positive relationship with families perceived them as a significant source of support and protection. They provided examples of the help and encouragement given in relation to education, money and emotional support. Those who were or had been in higher education were particularly likely to note the financial help provided by parents. A number of young women described being close to their mother and relying on her as someone to turn to. Michelle (aged 19) talked of how she knew she could rely on her mother and her comment reflects the view of quite a number of young women in the study, including those who were mothers themselves:

"... we get on very well. We're very very close. ...//... if there was something really wrong with me I could turn to her and she wouldn't, she wouldn't judge me. She'd go 'right we'll deal with it' ...//... like we'll get this sorted' ..."

This closeness or connectedness to mothers also came up in discussions about the gendered division of labour in the home (included later in this chapter) with reference being made on several occasions to the fact that their mother was expected to assume responsibility for most work in the home and that they then would have helped with this.

The positive comments about families could be framed in a context of security, of knowing their family were there for them and the feeling of always having a safety net – of being able to venture into independence but also knowing it was possible to turn to the family for help if they encountered problems.

For others though the family was not a source of support and security and young women were forced to make an accelerated transition to independent living. The reasons for this ranged from abuse within the home, parents having problems which resulted in the neglect of children, parents having problems accepting the sexual orientation of their daughter, or difficult relationships with step parents.

3.2 HOUSING TRANSITIONS

When family relationships broke down the result was often a change in housing and /or an early transition to independent living. Housing is accepted as an important factor in the transition to adult life (Catan, 2001; Ford et al., 2002; Jones, 2002; Kemp & Rugg, 2001) and the move to independent housing may be linked to other factors such as going to university, becoming a parent, becoming homeless or coming out of care. Ford et al. (2002) conclude that the type of housing pathways young people follow are a function of differences in the combination and intensity of three main factors: the ability of young people to plan for and control their entry to independent living; the extent and form of constraints that characterise their access to housing and the degree of financial support available to them.

Young women in this study had a variety of housing circumstances. Some had never left the parental home, some had gone to university, lived away from the family home during the week but continued to return home at weekends, some had returned home after longer periods away at university, some lived in independent housing either with partners, or alone or shared with friends, a few had moved into independent housing after becoming mothers, and others had moved from being in state care to independent living.

Most young women envisaged living independently but were very aware of the constraints on their housing choices. Unsurprisingly, cost was a major factor. In Northern Ireland house prices have increased substantially, largely as a result of investment buying. Because for many years the focus in the public sector was on building family homes, there is a lack of social housing for single people. The reduction in Northern Ireland Housing Executive properties has meant that people are increasingly forced to rely on the private rented sector where costs frequently outstrip the level of Housing Benefit and where there is less security of tenure. Evidence submitted to the affordability review commissioned by government (Semple, 2006) has highlighted the difficulty of securing affordable housing. For some young women who had previously lived away from home returning to live with parents was difficult but they felt that housing costs severely limited their options, and they were further constrained by debt accumulated at university. A few young women talked of how they enjoyed living at home, their attachment to families, to mothers and to the area they live in (see also chapter 6). Neimh and Karen's thoughts reflect the views of a number of young women:

"I don't know. I think I would love to move out on my own but I wouldn't go anywhere far away ...//... if I was gonna move out, I think I would just get a flat close to my mummy cus I'm a homebird." (Neimh, aged 17)

"I don't want to leave at the minute ...//... I get on really well with everyone ...//... so I don't really have any plans to move out ...//... Financially I couldn't afford it. Eventually, the way I see it is I'll move out and in with someone like a partner or else I'll not move out." (Karen, aged 19).

A number of young women were forced to make early transitions to independent living because of difficult family circumstances. Rachel (aged 25) left home at 16 because of family difficulties and her housing career could be described as 'chaotic'. She firstly lived with an older boyfriend. When that relationship became problematic she lived for a period with his parents. After getting back together with her boyfriend temporarily she became pregnant but decided to end the relationship. She was categorised as homeless and allocated a house which was in a poor state of physical repair. Rachel now lives alone with her child. Nat (aged 24) was also placed in a position of having to leave home at 18 after 'coming out' to her parents. Her family, and her father and brother in particular, reacted very negatively to finding out she was gay and as a consequence she was physically abused by an older brother. One of the outcomes of this was a very difficult period when she was homeless, experienced serious financial difficulties and lived abroad for a period. She spoke of the practical and emotional hardship relating to moving out of her family home.

Nat's Story

"I cried every night, every single night when I went to sleep. It was really difficult to be on my own, without my parents, and knowing how they felt about me, and knowing how my brothers ...//... they didn't take it well either, so knowing how they felt about me. It was really difficult."

Nat lived in student housing for several months after being asked to leave the parental home. While her rent was paid while she claimed unemployment benefit, on undertaking two part-time casual jobs she found herself in debt and was evicted from her housing a few days before Christmas. As a consequence Nat slept rough for a couple of weeks:

"... I didn't wanna tell anybody ...//... I don't mind telling people now, cus its over with. But at the time I was very proud and very stubborn, and was like ...//... it was really embarrassing."

Nat then went to live for a period abroad and on returning to Northern Ireland lived in the family home. However, the relationship with her family, and particularly her brother remained very difficult (to the point where her brother physically abused her) and, with the help of her mother, she found a house to move in to. It was not until the age of 22 that Nat's housing career reached some level of stability.

Throughout our discussions with Nat, the level of self-blame she apportioned to her situation was extreme and in many ways difficult to listen to. Even today she blames herself for the poor relationship she has with her father and brothers, for not managing her money better and for living on the streets and, to a degree, for the abuse she experienced from her brother.

Nat's story illustrates how the inter-relationship of factors can affect housing. Because she had to make an unplanned housing move from the family home this no doubt contributed to the financial and other difficulties she experienced and her sense of loss and hurt because of the changed relationship with her family furthered her isolation. This feeling of abandonment was picked up on by a number of young women who had disrupted family lives.

Findings from studies of young people in care consistently show that a majority move to independent living between 16 and 18 years old whereas most young people remain in the parental home (albeit many will have periods away at university) until well into their 20s (Wade & Dixon, 2006). An exacerbating factor is the difficulty of finding affordable, appropriate accommodation. Susie spoke of her experience of moving into a hostel at 16. At the time she was doing an NVQ and had a placement at a day nursery starting at 7 am. Yet, she could not leave the hostel until 8 o'clock when the gates were opened.

While those young women who had been in care had faced, and continued to face, difficult housing situations, they also spoke of the positives of independent living seeing it as their first opportunity to have more freedom over their living arrangements and more privacy. There were also examples of successful transitions. Beyoncé, for example, although getting on well with her foster family, decided she wanted to live independently when she was 19. Her foster mother helped her find suitable accommodation nearby and she was able to enjoy the benefits of living in her own home and having the continued support of her foster family. Wade & Dixon (2006) point out that transitions from care are very different as leaving care is a final event. There is often no option to return to family in times of difficultly. This was discussed by Susie who said "I'd love to be able to just phone my mum and go, 'oh can I come down for the weekend or whatever', and I can't ..."

3.3 VIOLENCE AND ABUSE

3.3.1 Child Abuse

While we did not specifically seek to interview those who had had particularly difficult lives the experiences of child abuse and domestic violence recounted by a number of young women presents a worrying picture of the realities of life for many young women in Northern Ireland. Eleven young women (a quarter of the sample) spoke about their experiences of violence and abuse. A number had been removed from or left the family home as a result of parental abuse and continue to be affected by that abuse. Difficult family lives resulted in disrupted education, lack of stability in relation to living arrangements and feelings of stigma and isolation. One young woman spoke of missing out on a 'normal life':

"I've never had the coming home being asked how my day was, coming home from school and having the dinner on the table, ...//... treated to family outings, never had any of that and that's something I'd like to experience." (Jo, aged 17)

For some the trauma of the abuse was exacerbated by feelings of being let down by other adult family members or by professionals who, when the abuse was disclosed to them, did not intervene to stop it or provide appropriate support. Sometimes this was due to the family wishing to keep the abuse hidden; on occasions professionals such as teachers were aware of abuse and did not respond.

A number of young women indicated the long-term consequences of abuse. Erin (aged 19) and her sister, for example, were abused by their stepfather. Social Services became involved when Erin's sister disclosed the abuse in secondary school. Although the stepfather was prosecuted Erin's mother continued to live with him. Erin was clearly still affected and angry because she felt that they were discouraged from talking about the abuse by the rest of the family and that they were abandoned and let down by their mother.

Janine (aged 17) was abused as a child and disclosed the abuse to a school counsellor, but she received no support or counselling at the time the abuse came to light. There were many indications in Janine's interview of how she continues to be affected – such as being scared around men. Like Erin, Janine blamed her mother for knowing about the abuse and not protecting the children and stated that *"...their family with them, they should notice."*

The sense of continuing fear was also relayed by Kimberly (aged 21) who recalled negative memories of places where she had lived because she was being abused while she was there. Poignantly, she notes that one of the most positive things about school was that:

"... when I was at school I didn't get abused so I didn't have to be afraid but in a way I was afraid because there was men at the school ..."

Gráinne's Story

Gráinne (aged 18) lived with her grandmother for the first three years of her life. Her natural father died when she was three and her mother cohabited with a man who adopted her when she was seven. Gráinne's mother and stepfather had other children and she spoke of how she and her siblings were neglected by their mother and how she took on much of the care for them:

"I was left to do everythin', gettin' the kids up for school and tryin' to get out for school maself, doin' the washin' and cleanin' everythin', my ma was sittin' on the computer talkin' to all sorts..."

Gráinne described the violent nature of her family life. She herself reported the violence to social services and the children were removed from the home. Gráinne felt that her mother could have done much more to protect them and feels let down by this. It was also clear from Gráinne's account that her mother experienced domestic violence and that the children witnessed this. Gráinne continues to have a difficult relationship with her mother.

"I can't understand why she didn't leave the first time he hit her. What really gets me is, he hit her, threw her out and she left me in that house, with him."

At the time of interview Gráinne was still obviously concerned about the well-being of her younger siblings and the responsibility she feels towards them. She talked of her concern for her sister who still lives with the stepfather.

"... I do feel sorry for our **** (name of sister) because she's livin' with him, because he's so controllin' and she's not gonna have a life while she's livin' with him, she's not. He buys her all the best of gear but she's not allowed to wear it out, to discos or nothin', so it's wild."

Gráinne's worry about her sisters and the stress this causes was a strong theme emerging from interviews with young women from abusive homes as was the feeling of being let down.

Despite the lack of support emerging in a number of young women's accounts there was at times a very strong attachment to extended family. Some young women maintained very close relationships with wider family members including grandparents, aunts and uncles.

Often, young women who had been through very difficult situations were keen to get across the fact that they were survivors; strong young women who could hold their own and would not be messed around. It was common for them to reflect on the positives and talk about how what had happened to them had made them more independent, made them stand on their own two feet, made them able to stand up for themselves "because all the bad stuff that's happened made me a stronger person". Yet it was clear that a number of these young women were still very vulnerable and in many respects were still not getting the support they needed.

One of the positives which tended to be cited was how, because of their responsibilities and having to cope they were more mature than peers:

"... it kinda made me grow up a lot quicker, because I was having to look after the kids and stuff, and be thinking ...//... I have to get home and make their dinner, have to do this and that. Whereas when you go from school [meaning other people her age] you do your homework and you go out and play with your friends ...//... I met one of them [her friend] in the shopping centre a few months ago and she was all ...//... 'you always saw you with a trail of children behind you' ...//... its never just me on my own ..." (Susie, aged 20)

Their own difficult experiences led to a view that their own children would be more protected:

"... my children are gonna be loved, my children are gonna be part of a family." (Jo, aged 17)

In a similar vein, Janine (aged 17) was adamant that she would not make:

"... them same mistakes that them certain people made in my life, I'll not make with my kids. I'll not do that on themins and I'll not let anybody hurt themins the way that they hurt us.

The need to look at how children and young people can be helped and supported through traumatic events at home is clear. Britton et al. found in their 2002 study that events were often not responded to or even known about in schools so young people in need of a lifeline were not offered one. Although this is a small sample and therefore caution should be adopted in terms of generalisations, the discussions around lack of support when abuse was disclosed are striking. This is an issue which also comes up in discussions about domestic violence and self harm. To have their trauma ignored or swept under the carpet can only reinforce feelings of stigma.

3.3.2 Domestic Violence

Young women's views were obtained on the extent, causes and response to domestic violence and it emerged that a number had lived in homes where domestic violence occurred or had been victims of domestic violence themselves. When presented with a statistic from a recent survey suggesting that one in five young women had experienced domestic violence, very few expressed surprise. The number of young women who knew of friends/ family being abused goes some way to explaining this. Through relaying their own experience or the experiences of friends they showed an awareness of different forms of abuse and of the impact of domestic violence.

"... I've seen one of my friends in an abusive relationship but she can't really see it for herself ...//... and she won't leave him. It was going on before they moved in and she still moved in with him ...//... he doesn't let her go anywhere, do anything ...//... he actually left her ...//... she said she would never have left him – she would have stayed with him because she thought it was her duty, cos they were married to stay married." (Louise, aged 23)

A number of comments made by young women seem to indicate a level of acceptance of domestic violence and that in some circumstances domestic violence is almost inevitable. These ranged from a comment by one young woman that "I attract them as my mum says" to the suggestion that stress and pressure led to men drinking and that there was an inevitability about men being violent when they had been drinking.

Explanations for women staying in violent relationships included a range of factors such as being too afraid of the partner to leave, fear of loneliness, fear of not being believed, lack of self worth and stigma around domestic violence. Some comments reflected an understanding of the complexities of leaving a violent partner:

"They just think that's what happens ...//... and you're like, cus I, like my dad like, was violent towards my mum and all the whole time they were married and then me and stuff as well, so I know, like no matter how many times they say they'll stop it they never do, and like my mum went through it for twenty years, and I'm saying to them 'you need to get out now' ...//... cus I know what happens, like they'll end up dead or something." (Susie, aged 20)

There was also some suggestion that this was something that happened to 'other' women who could have/should have behaved differently. This was sometimes accompanied by a rationalization of violence as something which other people put up with but which the young woman herself would not. A few espoused the view that women had to stand up for themselves and fight back. This was presented by the young women as a kind of equality which would make women seem less like victims, however, instead it appeared to mask the presence of violence in a relationship. For example, Jo suggests that what she was experiencing was not domestic violence because she had *"just been pushed"*:

"... no he's pushed me , but he's never actually hit me. But with him being twenty years old, in a bad mood, more often than not drunk, pushing me about – because when you push me and I fall over, but when I get up, I hit you and I hit you hard, you know what I mean... //... I've hit him a couple of times, busted his lip a couple of times, but he pushes me and he scares me." (Jo, aged 17)

Jo sees the fact that she hits her boyfriend back as not being prepared to tolerate violence. She noted that she was:

" ... a very big exception to the rule of submissiveness, a lot more girls basically wouldn't have the balls to turn around and say 'get away from me' ...//... there's far too many people thinking right well this is the norm ...//... and a lot more girls need to realise he hits you, you hit him back."

However, tellingly, earlier in the interview Jo talked of the misconceptions about what constitutes domestic violence, "... domestic violence is [perceived as] this big, bad, mad, beating you around the house but ...//... it can be about someone shouting in your face."

The experience and consequences of living in violent relationships were described by Carmel (aged 23) who was abused by two partners, latterly by a boyfriend and father of her child, for a year and a half. She provided a graphic account of how it had begun as emotional and verbal abuse and then how she was subjected to physical abuse as well.

Carmel's Story

Carmel spoke of how the abuse she experienced was:

" ... very much emotionally at the start... //... I was battered around the house I don't know how many times when I was pregnant. More than when I wasn't...//... And then it got really bad. I was afraid for my life so I had to leave him."

Carmel, like a number of the young women, spoke of how her boyfriend had tried to control her and how her dependence on him had contributed to her staying in a violent relationship, including being encouraged to feel that it was something in her that led to the violence:

"Well that is what would happen just after a series, no just after an incident of him using violence against me. He would sit down, make a big joint, pour the coffee out lovely and perfect. Now sit me down an' I'd be shakin' there, blood everywhere, 'now Carmel do you realise what you've done?' ...//... all my friends be like 'why didn't you open your mouth and say'. You just don't. Too scared. An' you're that dependent on them at that stage you don't think there's anyway out."

Carmel did get support from her family and also sought support from Women's Aid who are assisting and supporting her in terms of a pending court case. She had also confided in a midwife during an antenatal appointment after the midwife asked about her injuries. This, she feels, "... *was a good thing to do*".

Generally responses suggested limited knowledge of services for victims of domestic violence. Although a number of young women mentioned Women's Aid and other organisations including Rape Crisis and CAB, most felt there was insufficient information and/or had a lack of knowledge about where to obtain information – especially for young people. The fact that domestic violence was not generally recognised as a problem in same-sex relationships and the lack of information and knowledge of support services regarding this was also identified as a problem.

While Carmel's experience of disclosing her abuse to a health professional was a positive one there were also examples of other professionals not responding to signs of abuse or to the impact of domestic violence on children and young people. This included teachers not responding to obvious signs of abuse or distress.

The fact that so few young women were shocked or surprised by the statistic on domestic violence warrants further attention. It suggests attitudes of, if not acceptance, inevitability and is likely to be, at least to some extent, a reflection on the pervasiveness of domestic violence. Some of the young women identified a need for more education about relationships and domestic violence in schools. Research evidence in Britain suggests that anti-violence work in schools may play a role in setting out guidelines for healthy relationships (Mullender, 2001; Hester and Westmarland, 2005). To date, there would appear to have been little specific emphasis on these issues in Northern Ireland schools. The lack of prescription and uniformity with regard to the curriculum for Relationships and Sex Education in Northern Ireland (see chapter 7) means that schools have significant autonomy in this area. However, the role of education in the prevention of domestic violence is being increasingly highlighted. In the Northern Ireland strategy for addressing domestic violence (NIO, 2005), the Secretary of State for Northern Ireland stresses the importance of changing attitudes among young people. Hester and Westmarland (2005) conclude that the most effective strategy for violence prevention is a school-wide effort, rather than a stand-alone class-based curriculum programme. They report on the positive findings from three pilot projects which adopted this approach, but caution that the long-term impact is likely to depend on the extent to which issues are embedded within wider school activities.

A number of issues have arisen with regard to the way in which professionals respond to suspicions of or disclosures about abuse. The extent to which professionals such as teachers and health service professionals feel equipped to be proactive in dealing with abuse and violence or dealing with disclosures has been raised in other studies. Within the health service for example, while the value of screening for domestic violence has been acknowledged, sufficient training is often not provided.

3.4 CARING RESPONSIBILITIES

Some young women assumed major caring responsibilities early in life, for the care of a parent, siblings, or other relatives. Six young women had significant caring responsibilities for adults who were family members. As noted previously, it was very apparent that where young women had experienced difficult family circumstances, particularly relating to abuse and neglect, they had major feelings of responsibility towards siblings and considerable concern for them to the point of suffering worry and stress. Susie (aged 20) had taken on major caring responsibilities for siblings. She was forced into independent living at age 16 as a result of her mother taking her siblings and moving away without Susie. However, she continued to attempt to care for her siblings–to the extent that she could given the geographical distance–and her concern and worry for them was a dominant theme in her interview. There was evidence of this worry continuing even where siblings were older. Neimh (aged 17) talked of how worried she was about her brother taking drugs:

"My brother, I was worried about him there. He got a claim last year and went on drugs and it was terrible ...//... he'd a girlfriend and them two had broke up ...//... and she was stopping him from seeing the baby and he hit the drugs, drink and then ended up it came to a point where he was trying to hang himself...//... I found that stressful. Couldn't go to work or nothing ...//... And I missed loads of work in college ...//... it was all worry, worry, worry that I'd fallen so far behind. But I caught up. I brought home piles and piles of work ..."

One young woman had looked after her mother who had a serious illness for over a year. In addition to the personal care of her mother, she had looked after her mother's business and continued with her schooling (Jill, aged 17). For those young women caring for adults, the amount of work involved was onerous. One young woman, Tara, who was 19 at the time of interview, talked about helping to care for her uncle who had severe physical disabilities over a 3-4 year period. Those young women who did have caring responsibilities talked of how it had made them more mature, more adult, and how they had had to grow up more quickly.

Research on young carers (Dearden and Becker, 2000; 2004) has drawn attention to the implications arising from children and young people assuming caring responsibilities. These include increased vulnerability to poverty, adverse effects on education and future employment and friendship difficulties. The data from our study also provides evidence of the way in which caring erodes opportunity for social and leisure pursuits. The third national survey of young carers in Britain (Dearden and Becker, 2004) noted that the proportion of young carers experiencing educational problems remained more marked in the 11-15 age group – a time when young people are making significant educational decisions. In our study there was evidence of a very negative impact on school work with time missed from school and no time or energy to do homework. Susie talked of most of her homework being done at break time or being copied from someone else. Jo (aged 17) talked of how she was:

" ... looking after him, my wee brother, trying to do all my school work, cooking, cleaning, you name it I was doing it. See by the time I came to sit down and do my homework I was shattered."

While provision exists for young carers to receive an assessment of need this often does not happen. Caring may be hidden as a result of embarrassment on the part of adults receiving care or the young carer. Fear about the response of Social Services may reduce likelihood of seeking help. And, of course, the very concept of young people who should be dependants, but are carers, raises moral and ethical issues for society and for social policy.

3.5 EXPERIENCES OF BEING IN CARE

Five young women had experience of being in care. For three of these young women this was the result of abuse within the family home. The poorer outcomes for children and young people in care have been well documented and recent policy developments have acknowledged the continuing challenges facing care leavers.

A number of issues raised by these young women provide an insight into the reality of being in care for many young people. These young women felt they had had little involvement in decisions about their life and had had limited support while in care or on leaving care (see also NICCY, 2006). For most, being in care was associated with disruptive moves between children's homes and relatives and/or foster parents which had a detrimental impact on education and being forced into independent living considerably earlier than other young people. The housing outcomes with regard to young people leaving care have been discussed in the earlier section on housing. The detrimental effect on education summed up here by Beyoncé was a common feature of life in care:

"If I did get settled somewhere then you know it wasn't long before I was moving on again. I think that's why in Belfast whenever I went to school ...//... I just couldn't settle at all. Cos I was only there for a year so I just thought why should I settle here when I'm going to be moved again probably anyway." (Beyoncé, aged 25)

However, Beyoncé's experience also points to the difference that can be made by the right kind of support. She had lived with her mother until the age of three when she was taken into care as a result of physical abuse. As with a number of young women in the study her experience was one of moving between children homes and foster homes and then facing the prospect of being forced to live independently at 16 in an area she did not know or feel comfortable in. However, at the age of 16 Beyoncé had the opportunity to live with a 'foster family' and to develop a strong relationship with them. She recounted Social Services agreeing that she could live with her foster mother as the first time that she "ever said what she wanted and got it".

The factors which appear to facilitate smoother transitions from care have been discussed by Sinclair et al. (2005). These include strong attachment to a family member, partner or partner's family or a good relationship with a foster carer. What is apparent from a range of research is that there is a need for a more comprehensive set of responses across the life course (see for example Mullen et al., 2007).

In Northern Ireland the Leaving Care Order 2002 came into operation in 2005 and creates a new legal framework for leaving and aftercare services. The key objectives are to improve life prospects, prevent premature discharge from care and improve preparation and planning. However, a review of children and young people's participation in the care planning process, commissioned by the Northern Ireland Commissioner for Children and Young People (NICCY, 2006: 38), concludes that the current review process is "neither appropriate, nor effective, for many young people".

3.6 MOTHERHOOD

Six of the young women who took part in interviews were mothers. All of the pregnancies were unplanned. While they were all very happy and positive with their children, two of the young women had difficulties because of abusive partners. Even where the pregnancy had added to already very difficult lives the young women reflected that their lives had been affected in a positive way. For instance, Carmel was physically and mentally abused prior to and during her pregnancy. On finding she was pregnant she said that she reflected on what she did not have – she was in an abusive relationship, she did not love her partner and she had no job. She added, *"What else did I have to look forward to?" "I wanted to have him. I knew it would turn my life around and it did"*.

The value of family support emerged as a key theme in the accounts of these young women. Some spoke of how their mothers had been upset and disappointed initially but had gone on to provide high levels of support. There were several examples of grandmothers adapting their own working and social lives to help care for grandchildren.

There has been much attention focused on the way in which early pregnancy and motherhood impacts negatively on education. Although none of these young mothers were in education at the time of their pregnancy, in terms of future plans and aspirations, pregnancy could be said to have had a positive impact. They had strong educational and career aspirations and were determined to provide opportunities for their children. There was a clear sense that it was necessary to get qualifications and skills to access better paid employment. Reflecting on her own life and plans for work Rachel (aged 25) said:

"I just didn't want to be another statistic collecting the bru you know ...//... I always wanted better for myself and for ***** (daughter)."

However, they did perceive significant challenges to entering and remaining in paid work. In terms of accessing training and employment, reference was made to the limitations of government training and employment programmes such as New Deal. These included that in most cases New Deal will only support courses up to NVQ Level 2 but in order to get a job which pays sufficient wages it is necessary to access more than a minimum wage job. These are very pertinent concerns which reflect the limitations of social policy. This is particularly important when the impact of earnings on other benefits such as Housing Benefit is considered. Other concerns centred on the difficulty of accessing accurate information and advice about benefits, tax credits and childcare costs.

In discussions about mothering and working outside the home, there was evidence of dilemmas and contradictions. All wanted to be in paid employment and could see the benefits, not just in terms of income but also self-confidence and esteem. Yet, there was also concern from some young women that being a good mother meant being with the child. Comments made in relation to combining a job and parenting reinforces views expressed elsewhere in interviews that it is a mother's responsibility to take the primary role of caring for children and looking after the house. On asked if she thought you could be a good mother and work at the same time Erin (aged 19), who was planning to go back to work when her child was in primary two or three, said:

" ... well you could but you'd be fittin' it in around his school hours an stuff an I don't think you, well I don't think you can say that nobody can't be a good mother but I think you can only be a good mother if you're gonna be there for the wean [child] when the wean's there ...//... it'd be different when they're in secondary school like, you could have that job."

While Erin did have aspirations relating to the kind of job she wanted to do, she kept reinforcing that she did not want her child to be neglected. She did not see the solution as more childcare provision, but rather that fathers would take 50% responsibility for the care of children. This, she argued, would have a two fold benefit; mothers would have more opportunity to work and fathers could work shorter hours and spend more time with children.   Kim (aged 21) felt that you could not be a good mum and have a full time job:

"... that's cruel ...//... I love staying at home like ...//... but as soon as he goes to school I'm getting a job."

Some young women had experience of government programmes such as SureStart, others had participated in community education programmes, including a project specifically for young mothers, and some were involved in voluntary work. The benefits of involvement in courses/programmes were discussed. These included the peer support provided by other young mothers and the opportunity for social interaction as well as any educational value. The positive impact on confidence and self-esteem was very evident:

"It's like meeting everybody ...//... it's like something to get up for in the morning instead of sitting watching daytime TV ...//... A feeling of well-being and a sense of achievement is unbelievable. An' I come out of it feeling so happy."
(Carmel, aged 23).

As with other young women who had caring responsibilities, there was a real squeeze on leisure time. A number were doing courses, working in full or part-time jobs, perhaps doing voluntary work and looking after homes and children. Descriptions of daily lives gave an impression of how little time there was for leisure pursuits or relaxation. For some, the value of being able to rely on their own or partner's families cannot be over-estimated. However, analysis of their accounts provides less evidence of support being provided by welfare authorities.

Graham and McDermott (2006) argue that resilience is not an intrinsic capacity residing in the young person but one that develops and is sustained through the active interaction of the individual and their environment. Three protective factors are central to positive outcomes in the face of adversity. These are - attributes of the young person, those of their families and of the wider context. In their analysis of qualitative research on young mothers they identify the important individual attributes as a sense of moral worth, belief in one's maternal capacity and priority setting and idealism. Families contributed to resilience through the provision of material resources and practical help. The wider context was predominantly one of barriers including difficulty in accessing help from welfare agencies and hostility or disapproval. The value the young mothers in this study attached to programmes—particularly in relation to personal and emotional support and confidence building, and to the help some had received from key professionals such as health visitors—points to their importance. The role which needs to be played by welfare agencies and professionals is even more important if one of the factors contributing to resilience – such as family support - is absent. One of the young mothers in this study had found a Social Security Adviser to be a good source of advice about benefits and returning to work, though, as noted earlier in this section, it was clear from many other comments that there were often problems in accessing such information.

The positive aspects of becoming mothers permeated much of these young women's discussions. They considered their roles as mothers to be valuable roles. The fact that social policy focuses almost exclusively on paid work as a route out of poverty and the means of promoting social inclusion is likely to contribute to the marginalisation of those young mothers who choose to focus on motherhood. At the same time, policy discussions are themselves contradictory as they stress the importance of families spending time with children and, at times, the tone of such discussions is in danger of blaming a range of social ills on mothers working (Duncan & Edwards, 1999).

3.7 GENDER ROLES IN FAMILIES

Given the emphasis young women in the study placed on education (chapter 4) and their view that much had been achieved in terms of gender equality, it might have been expected that this would be linked to views that tasks in the home need to be equally shared. This, however, was not the case. Rather, there was substantial evidence of very distinct gender roles within families, starting in childhood with very strong divisions of responsibilities between male and female children in relation to small household tasks, and often conservative attitudes about gender roles. Fenton, Bradley and West (2003) in their study of young people's employment trajectories found that half of the young women in their sample saw the ideal family situation as one where mothers either work part-time or not at all. The Northern Ireland Life and Times Survey found that only 8% of people felt that a woman should work outside the home when there was a child under school age. Although the majority of respondents believed that a working mother can establish just as warm and secure a relationship with her children than a mother who does not work, 23% disagreed or strongly disagreed with this (Gray and Robinson, 2004).

In relation to tasks in the home, a number of young women made reference to brothers being asked to do more "manly jobs" (e.g. washing the car, brushing, cutting the grass) and referred to an assumption that women "do the stuff in the house" (e.g. cooking, cleaning, ironing etc.). Many young women envisaged that even if they were in full-time work this would be the case for them. Only a few young women cited examples of seeing their father make a significant contribution to housework and take primary responsibility for children.

Although it was perceived as inevitable that women do and would continue to bear the brunt of domestic responsibilities, there was a sense of the unfairness of this:

"... I always crack up with my mummy that the girls get made to do more than the boys ...//... and my mummy has always done everything for all of us and I just went along with it until I realized actually this isn't fair on her. Partly because when it was me getting to do it too ...//... she would like wash, iron, everything and she's stopped it now under my influence ..." (Karen, aged 19)

Participants living with male partners generally felt that their partners did less in the house, illustrating a continuance of what they had observed and experienced when children:

*"He does nothing, he does nothing, I had an argument with him last night about it. All he does is do dishes and walk that dog ...//... he's out working every day apart from Saturday and Sunday and I do the whole lot but he was going "all I ever ******* do is dishes, dishes, dishes ...//... He does nothing and I don't know how many arguments I've had with him about it ..."* (Gráinne, aged 18)

What emerges is a complex and somewhat contradictory picture about attitudes to gender equality. If views across a range of areas such as education, equality, employment and childcare are considered, the picture is one of young women seeing themselves as better off in equality terms than their mother's generation, especially in relation to educational and career opportunities. Yet, their accounts invariably suggest they expect to bear the brunt of child rearing and household responsibilities. While only a small minority of the young women stated explicitly that they do not think that women should work when children are young, there is a strong sense of paid work being accommodated around other responsibilities with references to part-time work when they have families (this is discussed further in chapter 4).

The young women also gave examples of being treated differently from brothers, by parents, in terms of the degree of independence and freedom they were allowed when growing up. It was felt that parents and older brothers were protective of them, which the young women generally put down to their gender. Instances of the different expectations parents had of young women related to very different views about the behaviours of daughters and sons in relation to activities such as sex, drinking alcohol in public or hanging around the street:

"My dad found out that *** [brother] was having sex, 'just don't get her pregnant'. My dad found out I was having sex and world war three began. I don't think it's the same with fellas, for the simple reason a fella can't come home ...//... pregnant." (Jo, aged 17).

One young woman told how she was expected to go to church on Sunday when her brothers were allowed to stay in bed and of being made to feel guilty if she did not go as it would be a worse reflection on the family if the girl didn't go.

3.8 FAMILY LIFE AND THE CONFLICT

The conflict in Northern Ireland has affected children and young people in many ways. Despite research, however, the impact on family life is not fully understood (Kilkelly et al., 2004). Within our research, the conflict could be said to have impacted directly upon the family life of young women in three main ways. Firstly, through the imprisonment of a parent, secondly through the death of a parent or member of the extended family as a result of a paramilitary killing and thirdly, through a paramilitary attack on the family. While the number of young women with any of these experiences was small (n=5), it is important to reiterate here, that the sample was in some respects opportunistic and young women with such life experiences were not sought out for inclusion in the research. Further to this, more indirect ways in which the conflict impacted upon family life were sectarian/prejudicial attitudes of parents and the concern of mothers in the sample for the safety and well-being of their children. Others were affected in more individual ways. Sue (aged 25), for example, did not see one side of her extended family as they would not accept her parents 'mixed marriage' and Jemima felt under constant threat while growing up as her father was in the security forces.

There was a general view among many of the young women that parental upbringing was an important factor in their own (and others) attitudes towards 'the other community'. A number noted, for example, that they had been "brought up to accept both sides" (Pauline, aged 23), while a smaller number pointed to the sectarian attitudes of their family and extended family. Kim (aged 21) explained her parents attitudes and the possible reasoning behind them:

"...both my parents were very republican an' ye know they'd drill into ya, my ma still doesn't understand why I speak to Protestants ...//... the likes of my parents and stuff like had people who were killed an' stuff like that maybe hold a grudge an' I think that they just pass a grudge on ...//... if everyone just let go we'd be fine ..."

What is clear from this example, and in most others, was a rejection by these young women of parental attitudes, yet these young women were now older and had, through time, been exposed to different religions. When younger, they noted that they were encouraged "not to mix". Other research has found that negative attitudes towards 'the other community' continue to be passed down from one generation to the next at a young age (Connolly, 2004).

With regards to the more direct impact of the conflict, Gráinne (aged 18) told us:

"... my Daddy was shot by the UVF, my uncle was shot by the UVF and then a couple of my friends ..."

Gráinne noted how these experiences continued to impact heavily upon her life—she was living in a high conflict area at the time of interview and she carefully regulated her movements and had constant fears for her boyfriend's safety. Gráinne also talked of her fear that her uncle who was now her father figure would be killed. The impact of these experiences upon Gráinne's emotional well-being were evident:

*"...that's my worst fears. Fears, that really, if anything happened, see if my uncle **** (name) was to be shot dead that would be it I would just have to go myself. I couldn't, I couldn't live without my uncle **** (name) being there."*

Oscar (aged 17) also lost an uncle in 'the troubles' and reported that another had a death threat out on him. Susie (aged 20) also experienced the conflict directly when she was aged 10 and her family were held hostage by a paramilitary group.

Finally, for those young women whose fathers had been prisoners, they talked about missing out on having a father for most of their childhood, the difficulty of prison visits, confusing and difficult emotions upon their father's release and mother's and other members of the family not talking to them about it as they wished to protect them.

The legacy of the conflict continues to impact upon young women in Northern Ireland and permeates into all areas of their lives, including their family life. It has been noted here that the impact can be obvious and direct, but that it can also take on more subtle forms. The family and the community, Smyth (1998) notes, are the main means through which cultural attitudes are passed on. As displayed here, this can take a very worrying form in a Northern Ireland context. While the true impact of the conflict (and post-conflict) on the lives of young people in Northern Ireland is not fully understood, the forthcoming chapters will note the ways in which it impacted upon other areas of these young women's lives.

3.9 CONCLUSION

The family is a major factor influencing youth transitions. Positive family relationship can provide a cushion against risk and facilitate a freedom to venture into independent living knowing that there is a safety net if necessary. Yet, as illustrated by a number of young women, families themselves are places of risk and danger. The inadequacy or inappropriateness of support available to young people in need has been highlighted. Social policy changes over the past two decades – intended to increase young people's dependence on families rather than the state – have resulted in increasing difficulties for those young people who cannot, for whatever reason, rely on family (Coles, 1995; Jones, 2002; Jones & Bell, 2000; Morrow & Richards, 1996).

Across many of the sections contained in this chapter there is an idea of adopted gender conventions. For example, the nature of domestic life that young women envisage for themselves is very characteristic of established norms as discussed in Gershon (2003) on changes in work and family life and the new moral dilemmas created for women whereby women seek and are encouraged to seek economic self-sufficiency while continuing to bear responsibility for the care of others. It is clear that young women perceived a number of areas as being resistant to gender equality - sex stereotyping in domestic roles and double standards relating to sexual practices.

3.10 RECOMMENDATIONS

- There needs to be a safety net for those who lack family support in their transition to independent living. This is particularly important when it is a 'forced' move and requires a co-ordinated approach by housing agencies, social services and relevant NGOs.

- The negative experiences of a number of young women in this study as a result of their sexual orientation highlights the need for awareness raising. Negative societal, family and often professional attitudes (in school for example) resulted in exclusion, isolation and low self-esteem. There needs to be a pro-active approach on the part of education and youth agencies in promoting and valuing diversity in relationships.

- Findings point to a failure to recognise and understand the continuing impact of abuse. There is a clear need for greater access to appropriate services/counselling. Services were often not offered to the young women in this research who had been abused, or not until some time afterwards. Their experiences highlighted the need for appropriate timely intervention. It is important that teachers in particular are well informed and supported in terms of responding to disclosures of, or suspicions about abuse and know where to refer young people for specialist support.

- Domestic violence should be explored within the school setting. Research appears to suggest this works best as part of a school-wide effort rather than being isolated to RSE or PSE. This should provide a greater understanding of what constitutes abuse and explore, with young women, responses to it.

- There should be an advertising campaign about domestic violence services, which is targeted at informing young women/people.

- There is a continuing need for relevant agencies, including schools, to have a greater awareness of the caring responsibilities carried out by young women and the way in which this affects many aspects of their lives and to ensure that appropriate and adequate support is available for them.

- We endorse recommendations emerging from research on young people in care and the concerns voiced by NICCY about the need to include the young person's voice in care planning, the need for stable placements and good quality aftercare.

- There is a need for more funding for programmes for young mothers which aim to enhance their social inclusion and value their role as parents. These need to be in the areas of (though these are not mutually exclusive): personal and social development and education/accreditation. It is also important that models of good practice which have been developed in the NGO sector be mainstreamed.

- The New Deal for Lone Parents needs to offer and support a greater range of education and employment routes for those who want it and these should not be restricted to or capped at NVQ Level 2.

- There is a need to challenge stereotypical gender attitudes in relation to roles in the home and paid work. One aspect of this could be school based, but there is a need for a range of agencies including the youth service to focus specifically on addressing gender issues.

Chapter Four
Education, Training and Employment

EDUCATION, TRAINING AND EMPLOYMENT

"I'd this teacher, she was amazing ...//... she made me really want to go in the direction that I'm goin' in" (Anna, aged 18)

"... but like there is the whole kinda like stereotyping ...//... like for example a man cant be a nurse ...//... like no way would a man be a nurse kinda thing, even though there is men's nurses but they are not that popular and ...//... you couldn't imagine a woman being a mechanic like it's more a man's job." (Michelle, aged 19)

4.1 INTRODUCTION

Much has been made of the advances for girls and young women in education over the past three decades. Young women are outperforming young men in GCSEs, A-levels [6] and are more likely to enter higher education (Furlong and Cartmel, 1997; McCarthy, 2004). However, we aim to show the realities behind the soundbytes. Furlong and Cartmel (1997: 11) argue that 'the illusion of choice created by the martketisation of education masks the continued retrenchment of traditional forms of inequality'- that although more young people are staying on in education, especially those from working class backgrounds, that the choice of routes taken and levels of attainment achieved, remain divided along lines of class and gender (among other things). In general, young people from middle class backgrounds continue to take the traditional academic routes of A-levels and university degrees, while those from working class backgrounds are more likely to take NVQs and other forms of vocational qualifications. In Northern Ireland, where the existence of the 11+ results in a strong secondary/grammar school divide in post primary education, the results of this exam largely determines the future educational prospects of young people.

Therefore the advances made by women in education do not apply uniformly to all women. Additionally, the 'gendered curriculum' and the gendered nature of careers advice, which tends to associate certain subjects, skills and professions with females more than males (Leach, 2000; Livesey, 2005) means that women continue to be under-represented in some subject areas, such as maths, science and technology. As will be illustrated, these trends in education have to varying degrees, impacted upon the occupational routes open to young women and their position in the labour market.

Despite the advances made by women in education, these have not been replicated in the labour market, despite the movement of some women into traditionally male occupied professions. The report of the Women and Work Commission (2006) notes that women continue to be crowded into a narrow range of low paying occupations, make up the majority people in low skilled jobs, are more likely to work part-time and are very under-represented in senior positions in both the public and private sector (McCarthy, 2004; Belfast Telegraph, 2005). This unequal position in the labour market is further reflected in women's earnings. In 2006 the median gross weekly earnings (full-time and part-time work combined) were £391.50 for men and £261.80 for women (DETI, 2006). If full-time earnings only are considered the gap is narrower. The continuing inequality in hourly pay for part-time work has important implications for women who often move to part-time hours in an attempt

---

6   In 2003/04, 68% of girls compared to 54% of boys achieved at least 5 A-C grades at GCSE; 50% of girls compared to 35% of boys left school with 2 or more A Levels; and 60% of all students enrolled in N.I universities were women (DENI, 2006).

to balance family and paid work commitments. Also, while at an overall level the gender pay gap is reducing it continues to be very marked in various occupational and industry groupings.

There has been much academic research exploring the causes of women's inequality in paid work (Rake et al, 2000; EOC, 2005). Certainly there is evidence from a range of studies, and from this research, to suggest that the gendering of paid and unpaid work takes root very early in life through the role models children have, traditional social attitudes, the gendered curriculum in schools and colleges and the strong gender division in the earliest experiences of paid work. For example, Leonard (1999a; 1999b) found that the most popular jobs undertaken by school aged young men in Belfast included delivery work and manual labour and the most popular for young women included shop work and work in hotels and catering.

A significant factor which relates to women's ability to undertake paid work and impacts negatively on their position in the labour market is unequal division of labour in the home where women mostly bear the brunt of child and domestic responsibilities (Gray and Robinson, 2004). This is an important factor accounting for the large proportion of women working part-time. In fact much of the increase in women's employment has been in the service sector where employers seek 'flexible' part-time workers. The lack of affordable childcare places greater pressure on women to take work which they can attempt to fit around children's school hours (Gray and Carragher, 2006).

Discussions of women's unequal position in the labour market have often provoked the response that women 'choose' to opt out of full-time employment etc. This suggests that women have genuine choices about how they wish to live their lives, the amount they earn; that they have unfettered access to education and training. However, this chapter draws attention to the constraints facing many young women, including the range of demands that can be placed on women, even at a young age. It examines a range of issues relating to education, training and work. It provides information on the educational aspirations of young women and analysis of the factors impacting on their experiences of the school system. The findings demonstrate the difficulties faced by some young women, many of which are external to school and looks at the support provided by the formal and informal education sectors. Data on training shows that young women have a limited range of 'choices' in relation to vocational training and that these choices are heavily gendered. Finally, the chapter sets out young women's views on employment and on reconciling work and family.

4.2 SCHOOLING: SCHOOL EXPERIENCES AND SCHOOL SUPPORT

Most young women were able to recount at least one positive aspect of school. The most frequently cited 'good things' about school were[7]:

1. Friends/the social aspects of school (n=23)
2. Subjects, sports, activities (n=8)
3. Good relationships with teachers (n=4)
4. School as a safe haven (n=3)

Irrespective of school type (i.e. Catholic, Protestant, Integrated, Independent, Irish Medium, Special School, Grammar, Secondary, Co-educational or Single-sex)[8], most young women cited friendship and the social aspects of school as the most positive aspect of their school experience. For a small number, friendships were the only good things about school.

---

7   Young women may have cited more than one 'good thing' about school

8   Northern Ireland operates on a tiered post-primary education system) i.e secondary schools and grammar schools), and schools are often split on the basis of religious background and thus maintained by different bodies (e.g. Roman Catholic Maintained, State Controlled-Protestant, Voluntary – often grammar schools, Grant Maintained Integrated and Other Maintained – e.g. independent schools or Irish Medium schools. Furthermore, some schools are co-educational while others are single sex.

Friendships made through school were of particular importance for some, who for example, because of where they lived, had few social outlets outside of school:

"I only really seen my friends in school cus I didn't really have friends where I lived. So that's what made school for me, cus it was like socialisin' for me."
(Ellen, aged 22 – Grammar, RCM, single-sex)

Further, it provided a new set of friends often from different areas, backgrounds, religions and/or cultural backgrounds for some. This was most evident for Kativa (a 17 year old asylum seeker):

> **SM:** What would you say were the best things about school for you?
> **Kativa:** Just mixing with other people ...//... where I come from there are very limited young people ...//... just because [of the] troubles going on around our area ...//... we couldn't really go out, I only have limited friends, close friends, so when I come here there were twenty people in my class, mixed classes so I know more people. (Secondary, controlled, co-ed)

Young women were asked what they disliked most about school. While some mentioned a number of issues, others focused upon one and discussed this in some depth. The most frequently cited dislikes of school or difficulties associated with it were:

1. School environment/routines (n=13)
2. Bullying (n=9)
3. Teachers/no support (n=8)
3. Moving schools (n=8)
3. Personal difficulties outside school (n=8)
4. Studying/homework/exams (n=3)
5. Lack of subject choice (n=2)
5. Lack of resources/activities (n=2)

A number of young women noted their main dislike of school as the actual structure, routine, environment or culture of school. Some simply felt unsuited to the formal school environment and found it difficult and not conducive to learning, sometimes leading to a general disinterest which manifested itself in truanting, 'dropping out' or not paying attention. For others, however, it was a mere annoyance which they put up with throughout their school lives and accepted as just the way it was. The main contention related to a lack of control and choice over their own studies and identity within schools.

Nine young women cited bullying as their main reason for disliking school. Data from the Northern Ireland Young Life and Times Survey (2005) showed that same-sex attracted people are particularly vulnerable in terms of school bullying. In our research, three of the four young women who had attended Special Schools (or SEN Units within mainstream schools) reported having experienced bullying. Bullying had been dealt with to varying degrees of success by young women themselves, parents and teachers. As with other reports of young women and bullying (Collins et al., 2004), bullying was mainly indirect in nature and included verbal abuse (e.g. name-calling, bitchiness and ridicule) and isolating and exclusionary behaviour. Shirley (aged 24) summed up the form bullying took among boys and girls in her school in the following way:

"... if you're looking at bullying ...//... if a fella had an issue with another fella it would just been bump, bump you know and then they woulda been besta friends straight afterwards whereas I woulda found girls more malicious and devious."
(Secondary & Secondary, RCM, co-ed & single-sex)

Bullying can have a very debilitating effect on young women and impact on educational, physical and emotional wellbeing (YWCA, 2002). In our research, the impact of bullying could be seen upon young women's self-esteem in a number of cases. Kativa (aged 17), for instance, would not speak in class for fear of saying something wrong and being laughed at due to her accent and having been made fun of before in school. Additionally, even now at the age of 25, Nicole felt that the constant bullying she experienced in primary and secondary school had a lasting impact:

"It knocked my whole self-confidence ...//... [I'd] be very, very conscious of meeting new people and I suppose in some ways I would still kinda be like that, that you're always conscious of what people think of you ...//... it took me a long time to trust people ...//... If people were laughing you'd almost feel they were laughing at me even though they probably weren't like. Or like talking, and you're conscious sitting over there 'are they talking about me?' So it knocked my whole confidence to no end." (Secondary, RCM, co-ed)

There was also evidence of the way in which confidence could be negatively affected by major educational changes, such as moving school. The move from one post-primary school to another was discussed by eight young women as having been particularly difficult. Moving schools tended to be a result of doing well at GCSEs and moving to another secondary or grammar school which offered more subjects and/or the opportunity to undertake A-Levels. In two cases, however, moving schools was directly related to care experiences and moving foster and/or residential care homes.

Almost all of those who made the transition (often around the age 16) talked about the difficulty of it and few reported positive experiences in their second post-primary school experience. Some not only made the move from secondary to grammar school but from co-ed to single-sex or from small local rural school to a larger urban school. Difficulties for some, therefore, were multiple and the transition was made more difficult by a number of these factors. In the main, however, settling in and making new friends was the biggest issue. Further, a number reported feeling that they never fitted in or belonged and that they felt like second class citizens:

"They were nice but ye just kinda felt a bit like they were kinda lookin' down their noses (giggles) at ye ...//... causea the fact that you came in from secondary school an' these girls had been here the whole five years ...//... it wasn't my cuppa tea so I left (laughs)." (Michelle, aged 19 – Secondary-Grammar, single-sex)

While Michelle's experience is fairly illustrative of others in terms of feeling that she was not accepted, she was one of the few who actually decided to leave and return to her previous school. Others noted that they felt out of place and that clear class differences (elitist attitudes) existed and they struggled along not really enjoying the experience for their two years there.

These comments highlight the barriers facing young women (who may be perceived as working class) as they attempt to benefit from a grammar school education. Such difficulties may effectively put young women off making the transition to grammar schools or those schools which offer a greater choice of subjects. These barriers (both real and perceptual) are a consequence of an education system in Northern Ireland which offers hierarchical and differential learning. In light of these young women's experiences we must ask – do school realise the nature of these problems and take steps to deal with them? Are they open in their attempts to welcome and integrate young women into their schools? Is the impact of this transition – at a crucial stage in young women's developmental and educational life – fully understood and explored?

Those who had some of the most difficult school experiences in terms of either not being able to get on/cope within the formal school setting, or who found it a struggle and highly stressful, were those young women who were experiencing difficulties/pressures outside school (generally in the home). This included: dealing with sexual abuse, physical abuse, neglect, domestic violence, parental illness, caring and bereavement. These strains sometimes made it impossible for young women to cope within the school environment and appeared to act as a catalyst for some to move to Alternative Education Provision where they reporting receiving more support and one-to-one attention. In reality, for a number of young women, there were more pressing issues for them during their school years rather than education and exams. Below is a breakdown of some of the personal difficulties young women experienced while at school and some of the consequences of these (see Table 1).

Table 1: Experiences, Support and Outcomes

Young Woman	Age	Difficulties Experienced	Support received	Outcome
Oscar	17	Bereavement + mother took overdose. As a result attended school only rarely	Support from teachers + School Counsellor	Took GCSE's and did better than expected
Jo	17	Bereavement; abuse; caring responsibilities; working part-time	No school support	Highly stressed
Mia	17	Home life seriously affected by domestic violence and unable to focus on school work	Alternative Education Programme	Positive experience of programme
Jill	17	Mother had serious illness; caring and employment responsibilities during GCSEs; stressed and exhausted.	No support from School	Did well in exams despite difficulties
Janine	17	Sexually abused; major impact on school work	School support and school counsellor	Few exam passes
Susie	20	Home life affected by domestic violence and child abuse; caring responsibilities for siblings; rarely at school despite desire to attend	No support	Few exam passes
Tara	19	Intimated out of family home; lived in variety of hostels; physically abused by father	No support	Dropped out of school
Beyoncé	25	In the care system; multiple care placements; disruption to education resulting In poor attendance	Lack of support	No formal qualifications

With regards to many of the problems these young women experienced while at school, it is clear that school support was imperative. Furthermore, school could act as a safe haven from the home for some but as an additional pressure for others.

Exam pressure emerged as a key cause of stress for many young women. While this related particularly to GCSEs and A-Levels, it was applied to the general workload in schools and universities.

Considering the issues related to schools here, the young women noted that because of exam pressure they experienced nightmares, a severe lack of sleep and/or were often 'emotional wrecks' at exam times. While this was true for young women attending all types of schools, discussions with young women who had/were attending grammar schools tended to involve much more detail about the nature of pressure put on them by schools, teachers and, consequently, themselves.

At a general level, Karen (aged 19) explained why exams were important and where some of the stress came from:

"... it's all you, I mean you are responsible for your future ...//... like I felt it more at GCSEs more than A-Levels because suddenly at like age 16 you're supposed to get all these exams and this is going to be the basis of your future career ...//... when I look back now I'm like GCSEs weren't even that bad but at the time exams are just so much on you, it's like you're all alone" [her emphasis] (Grammar, RCM, single sex)

The pressure young women may feel at GCSE time due to a realisation of the future importance of these exams, coupled with other issues they may be dealing with at the time (for Shirley it was her weight and body image, for Nat it was her sexual orientation, for others it was caring responsibilities or various personal issues), can compound the stress/pressure they deal with on a daily basis.

The point Karen makes about being on your own and in charge of your own future/destiny ("you get annoyed at yourself because who else can you blame? ...//... it all falls on you"), is interesting in light of recent sociological debates regarding young people and risk society (Beck, 1992). That is, that although there are less certainties for young people today as they make the transition from youth to adulthood that there are more opportunities as traditional class and gender barriers are less influential. All young people, therefore, must negotiate a similar set of risks but identities, choices and life chances have become more individualised. Thus, in Karen's assessment of the situation, the opportunities have been presented to her and it is how she individually manages these which will shape her future. This is a clear example, of how Karen, among others, has begun to individualise her own failure/or possible failure. This process, some argue (e.g. Furlong & Cartel, 1997), is based upon the epistemological fallacy that options and choices are free and open and that traditional class and gender divisions are less pertinent.

The manner in which other young women discussed the competition between peers in schools further demonstrates the pressures upon young women and how it is not only about getting good grades but about getting A stars and further certificates which are open to all to achieve:

"They [the teachers] all tell us after our marks we were the lowest score class in five years, so that puts pressure on us to beat, improve. Afterwards they always tell ya 97% got As and all that. So that's quite a lot of pressure ...//... It is competitive, cus you get awards for how many like GCSEs, how many A stars and As you get throughout the whole year. And you get improvement awards as well."
(Ruth, aged 17 – Grammar, controlled, co-ed)

In Ruth's school, as in other grammar schools, a system which stressed achievement and competition among pupils appeared to be at work, a system that could be seen to reflect the economic system in the world outside the school environment. The mentality, therefore, was not only to do well for yourself, but to do better than others:

"... the teachers were always pushing ...//... and there were all high expectations, like among students as well, there was always smart people in your class and there was always pressure to keep up with them from the teachers" (Louise, aged 23 – Grammar, controlled, co-ed)

The meritocratic principle of hard work equals just rewards (e.g. in terms of grades and outside school in terms of jobs) was evident within the ethos of many of these young women's schools – and many young women believed and adhered to this principle. As will be displayed later, however, young women were finding that despite the message passed on to them in school - that they could achieve anything with hard work (e.g. good jobs), traditional barriers continued to exist.

Young people can therefore individualise their own failure and often fail to recognise that traditional class and gender inequalities which they have little control over, continue to impact upon their lives. Thus, it was that they didn't work hard enough at school, choose the wrong career path etc. which was the reason for their current position rather than the larger structures of an unequal education system, labour market and patriarchal society. While these issues will be returned to, here it can be seen that pressure and stress within schools particularly related to exams impacted negatively upon young women's well-being (physically and emotionally) at key developmental/transitional points in their lives, and even more so when they were experiencing further stresses outside school.

A number of young women discussed relationships with teachers and/or their view of them. Summing up the factors which made relationships between pupils and teachers positive or negative, the following themes emerged:

Positive	Negative
Open, approachable	Hierarchy between pupil and teacher
Supportive	Singled out/treated unfairly/favouritism
Good role model	Lack of respect
Treated like an adult	Not listened to
Mutual respect	Lack of care
Listened to	Treated as a child/patronised
Judgemental	Pressurising

The potential value of good relationships could be seen in cases, for example, where a particular teacher had acted as a role-model or been supportive when a young women was experiencing personal problems:

"I'd this teacher, she was amazing ...//... she made me really want to go in the direction that I'm goin' in." (Anna, aged 18 – Independent, other maintained, co-ed)

"The teachers, two of them were there from the start of 4th year right up, they were a real big support ...//... I'm sure it was hard for them teaching too at the same time, but they were always there if I needed to talk. And they got me help, they got help in the school for me". (Janine, aged 17 – Secondary, controlled, single-sex)

Conversely, poor relationships with teachers or a negative view of them could taint the school/education experience. Gráinne (aged 18), for example, left school to take part in Alternative Education Provision, one of the motivating factors being her difficulty with teachers and how she felt she had been treated by them:

"I enjoyed school but I just didn't like the way the teachers got on towards ya ...//... the teachers treated you like you were crap on the ground ...//... they didn't have no time for ya". (Secondary, RCM, single-sex)

These issues of lack of respect, understanding and care by teachers were recurrent themes in the accounts of those who had negative views of teachers. For Nat (aged 24), who was experiencing difficulties outside school, she felt that the teachers did not notice because they did not look and they did not look because they did not care:

"I don't think they care, I don't think they really care ...//... I just don't think they care enough, I don't think teachers care enough."

And later

"I don't think teachers look enough, I don't think people recognise these things [self harm] enough ...//... tons of girls do it in the school like and if you're constantly walking in the hot weather with their sleeves down, teachers don't pick up on these things." (Grammar, controlled, co-ed)

Given the educational pressure and the nature of the difficulties facing some young women it was important to explore with them the nature of support provided by schools and their views on provision. Young women were asked about support in school, if and how they felt supported and if they felt there was anyone they could talk to should they have a problem. The following section provides an overview of their views.

Aside from friends, 11 young women noted that there was someone within the school they could talk to. This included teachers, chaplains, counsellor, and/or peers (through buddying/mentoring schemes). On the other hand, 15 young women felt that there was no support available to them within their schools.

With regards to school counsellors, of the 26 young women who were asked specifically about their schools, 18 said that there had been none while the remaining 8 noted that a school counsellor was/had been present in their school. Perhaps unsurprisingly, most of those who had school counsellors within their schools were in the younger age group (average age 19 years). Also of interest, of the 26 young women who responded to this question, 16 attended secondary school, 8 attended grammar schools and two attended special schools. 56% (n=9) of those attending secondary schools had school counsellors as opposed to 13% of those attending grammar schools and none of those attending special schools.

While the issue of school counsellors and examples of the potential positive value of them will be discussed in more detail shortly, it is important to note factors which for the young women made, or would make, counsellors good. The main point raised here was that in order to be of value and facilitate trust, these should be external to the school, not teachers and not related to pupils in anyway. Tara (aged 19), for example, talked of why she would not talk openly to her school counsellor of the difficulties she was experiencing at home:

" ... she was like the Vice Principal an' she was more for the values of the school rather than the pupils ...//... so ye couldn't really talk about domestic violence cus they had like a convent school teachin' on them typa issues, so it was quite difficult". (Grammar, voluntary, single-sex)

Ruth's (aged 17) school was currently considering employing a school counsellor, while agreeing with the idea in principle, it was how this was to be implemented that caused her some concern:

"...they're talking about getting somebody in. One of the parents is a trained counsellor, so they're talking about getting her in, but I don't know how I would feel about going to someone's parent who I know". (Grammar, controlled, co-ed)

Rather than going into detail of the young women's examples of good and poor support in school it is perhaps more useful to make a few general points and to use two contrasting examples to highlight good practice.

At a general level, those who felt they had little support in school felt that schools did not understand the pressures young women might be facing in school or outside it. For those who had the most pressing problems, they felt that their school had turned a blind eye or did not care. Susie (aged 20) felt that her school had not picked up on many warning signs – she was rarely in school, was distracted and distant when she was there, and often went in with bruises. She was either not asked about this or when asked her explanations were accepted without question or further investigation:

"...sometimes I would like be really nervous and quiet an' stuff in school, people just thought I was strange, but if the school hada actually took time to think there's something goin' on there, but they never did. So I kinda dandered along gettin' on with it. And goin' into school with bruises an' all, 'Oh, I was fightin' with the kids'." (Grammar, voluntary, single-sex)

This was not an isolated case and there were other instances where warning signs were not picked up and acted upon. While not wishing to apportion blame, the aim here is to highlight that teachers may require further training in issues of Child Protection and that teachers should also be supported when such issues do arise. While we can expect teachers to pick up on warning signs, we cannot expect them to be experts and to deal with these (and other issues) facing pupils, it is for this reason, that school counsellors are so important.

Highlighting good practice and the value of support to young women within schools is perhaps one of the best ways that lessons can be provided to others. Here we use the experiences of Carmel (aged 23) and Janine (aged 17) to illustrate how two fairly similar incidents were dealt with by two different schools, and the impact on the young women involved:

"... I got into a bit of bother one day taking tablets at schools an' I fell down all the stairs an' had to go into hospital. An' there was a whole big uproar about where the tablets were from and who got them, but that was it. Ya know there was no support network after." (Carmel, aged 23 - Grammar, voluntary, single-sex)

Janine: ... there was times when I had diazepam at school ...//... you're meant to be expelled for that cus it's like a drug, cus they looked into it and realised I was going through a real rough time and they didn't, they supported me instead of shouting at me.
...//...

SM: ... you yourself were saying that it wasn't 'til a certain time at school when there was a teacher or counsellor that you could talk to, if that hadn't been there for you –

Janine: I wouldn't be here! I said that to my mummy, cus I used to cut myself really badly ...//... And I just knew it was time to talk, I didn't wanna kill myself. I wanted to fight it and prove to the people that hurt me that I'm a survivor and that I'm bigger and stronger than what they are. (Secondary, controlled, single-sex)

Janine's experiences provide a good example of good practice at work. Teachers picked up on warning signs and were able to provide expert help, which according to Janine, was the difference between life and death. While teachers cannot be expected to deal with difficult issues like these alone, appropriate training can equip them with the skills to pick up upon warning signs and a counsellor attached to the school means that the young women can be provided with expert help within the school setting.

Good Practice Example: Michelle's Experience

Michelle (aged 19) talked about the programmes of pupil support within her school, these are worth noting here as a further example of good practice due to the holistic nature of them. Within Michelle's school, there was an independent counsellor, teacher awareness and peer support structures, all of which worked together:

"...they got a school counsellor in an' she came an' she talked to us an' then we actually got roles in playin' kind of counsellors as well, we were mentors ...//... it was called the 'Buddying Programme' an' we were introduced to wee first years an' we had like a wee buddy an' she could come to us then if she'd any problems." (Secondary, single-sex)

4.3 GENDER AND SCHOOLING

4.3.1 Subject Choice

While most young women noted that there were a range of subjects open to them in schools and there was only one case where a young woman stated that a subject within her school was restricted to boys only ("I wasn't allowed to do technology an' design or motor vehicle studies cus I was a girl" – Kim, aged 21), many young women were clear that some subjects were more popular among young women than young men (and vice-versa) or that some subjects were perceived as mainly male or female. In addition to this, the subjects that young women tended to choose at GCSE, A-Level, and in terms of college and university courses, were those typically associated with females and the gender divisions in their classes were prominent.

Concentrating upon school, when the young women were asked if there were subjects which were more often associated with boys than girls, and vice versa, those most often cited included:

Boy's subjects	Girl's subjects
CDT	Home Economics
Motor Vehicles	Art
Science	English
P.E/Sports Studies	Health and Social Care
Woodwork	Child Development
Computer Studies	Word Processing
Technology	

Those subjects which young women deemed as 'girls or boys subjects' were based on their perceptions and/or experiences of predominantly female/male classes within co-educational schools. While seven young women felt that fairly equal numbers of boys and girls undertook all subjects or that 'traditionally male' subjects were offered in single-sex school, the remainder felt that there were some differences in the subjects undertaken/chosen by boys and girls. The clearest and most often cited examples were in terms of Home Economics and CDT. While each was compulsory in many schools until third year, many noted that when choices were offered after this that "typically the boys would do CDT and the girls do Home Economics" (Rachel, aged 25). The other main subjects where differences were noted in terms of the gender make-up of classes were Child Development, Health and Social Care and P.E. Typical responses to the gender make-up of classes included:

"...technology was one of the things that boys mainly did and I only know one girl who did Technology in my school. ...//... Child Development, that's only girls."
(Kativa, aged 17)

"I also did Child Development as well, that was a real girls' subject and no guys in the class. I even picked Home Economics and there was two boys in the class ...//... You woulda found that the boys were taking on technology and things like that ...//... the guys woulda went for more male dominated subjects ...".
(Adrienne, aged 23)

"... we'd the option between Word Processing and Computer Studies. Where the fellas woulda picked Computer Studies the girls woulda picked Word Processing ...".
(Nicole, aged 25)

These accounts are illustrative of many of those given by the young women we spoke to irrespective of their age or the type of school they attended (e.g. grammar/secondary). There are a number of interesting points to consider from here, the first of which concerns choice. The young women were clear that this was a choice, but we want to examine the nature of these choices in terms of how they are made, structured and acted on. Second, we want to consider the young women's acceptance of these differences/divisions as somewhat natural or as just the ways things are.

Young women offered varying explanations regarding the gendered nature of subject choice by young men and women, these included: school, teacher and societal expectations of what each sex would choose; certain subjects being more closely related to women or men's jobs, roles and natural interests and peer pressure:

"I think girls may be more interested, in that maybe boys wouldn't that was all, health promotion an' eh social care an' all that there I don't know too many boys that would be interested in it, but then they'd probably be turned off it if was all girls too even if they were interested, boys would mostly go for the manly jobs."
(Kim, aged 21 - her emphasis)

Kim's explanation is illustrative of others and it takes in all of the above factors - that women and men naturally have different interests, that subject areas are related to jobs which may be perceived as being female or male orientated and that societal assumptions and beliefs may act as barriers to young women or young men crossing these traditional divides.

The view that women and men are naturally more adept to different areas of work or types of study ("Home Economics was cooking and girls like to cook...the physics class, the boys were all better at the subject"), appeared to be accepted by many young women as simply the way things were. Few challenged or had an awareness of how young women and men are socialised into these roles, disciplines etc. and of how the school was part of that socialising process. To say that there was a 'false consciousness' at work may be going a little too far, but perhaps the fact that choice was portrayed as free and open and that individuals personally chose these traditional routes appeared to make the young women feel that agency and choice was unrestricted.

A further issue concerns expectations, with a number of young women noting that subjects might not be taken for fear of the signals they may give out – it is for this reason that we do not suggest a 'false consciousness':

"I know some boys in my class, they kinda considered doing it [Home Economics] but then they were like 'no it's a girl's subject, can't do that', and I think they would be thought of as being sissies ..." (Louise, aged 23)

Thus, while choice may have been free to an extent, there were factors that impacted these choices and traditional stereotypes and expectations continue to impact upon the nature of subjects chosen by young men and women. This was not restricted to school, if we examine the nature of courses undertaken by young women in further and higher education and young women's educational aspirations, we also find a gendered pattern. The courses which featured most prominently were those related to business, administration, health, social/child care and beauty. Two young women had undertaken (but not necessarily completed) courses traditionally associated with young men - Service and Replacement (i.e. motor vehicle repair) and Engineering. Likewise, those courses most cited as being undertaken, having been or desired in higher education were in the social sciences (e.g. sociology, social policy), youth work, business and teacher training. The 'choices' young women continue to make in post-16 education, therefore, illustrate the continued existence of gendered paths in education and routes into gendered employment (this will be returned to later). Interestingly, all of those in higher education saw the gendered division of their courses when asked directly about this. While their explanations for this differed, in that similarly to school subjects, some young women felt that women and men were simply interested in different things:

"...the fact that it's talking about like lone parents and poverty an' a lot of males mightn't be interested in that while females might be more interested ...//... females wouldn't be interested in cars maybe (laughs) but like men might be ... "
(Michelle, aged 19 – studying at university)

Two young women in particular recognised the irony of this, given the respective position of men and women in their professions. Of her degree in Community Youth Work, Adrienne (aged 23) noted that within her year, only five of the twenty students were male:

"...there was definitely more girls than fellas. I didn't know why like, when you think of all the youth workers and senior positions, there's definitely more men."

Finally, the difficultly for young women of undertaking subjects and courses often associated with young men and/or where classes are male dominated was experienced by a small number of young women. Tara (aged 19), for instance, had started an AVC in Engineering but due to the treatment of females on the course by her tutor, had decided to leave:

"I lasted four weeks or somethin' cus there was eight girls in the class an' seven boys ...//... the tutor kept chuckin' girls outta the class which was nasty ..." [her emphasis]

Oscar (aged 17), on the other hand experienced less direct discrimination by staff when undertaking a BTEC Diploma in Sports Studies in an institute of further education. While she was initially one of three young women on the course, the other two dropped out. Oscar noted that while tutors took various steps to accommodate her, a number of aspects of her identity and being the only female on the course made her feel uncomfortable and led to her eventual drop-out:

"...I was left there, like I was the only girl in the class, like I got a whole lot of attention like an' em the lads all got on well with me but it was weird, especially me being gay an' stuff an' they were always being flirty an' stuff it was just weird, I think that's partly why I left ...//... it was just kinda the atmosphere you're in, it's just like bein' the only girls it's jus like, it is uncomfortable ..." [her emphasis]

In conclusion, while there may be more options available to young women today and less physical restrictions on their choices of subjects, perceptual barriers remain, as does the gendered and hidden curriculum within schools (Leach, 2000; Livesey, 2005a). Although most of those we spoke to talked of not choosing some subjects because they were not interested in them or they were too difficult, Sharpe (1976: 148) encourages us to step back and consider where these beliefs might come from. She suggests that it is of little surprise that young women have little interest in or understanding of scientific/technical subjects as they have little experience of these in the home, the first point of the socialisation process. That is, they are not called upon to aid in repairing things at home (this is usually the father and sons job) and hence their analytical skills (among others) are not developed, technical toys are given to boys and rarely girls and they witness the non-scientific nature of the adult woman's role in the home. In terms of their future roles in the home and indeed the workplace (again in that certain jobs appear from an early age to be associated with men and others with women), therefore, technical or scientific subjects may appear irrelevant.

While we have of course witnessed changes since the time of Sharpe's writing in terms of increasing numbers of young women undertaking and succeeding in science/technical subjects (particularly noticeable in compulsory education with the introduction of the National Curriculum in 1988), inequalities still exist in post-compulsory education with fewer females than males undertaking A-Level and degree courses in the sciences (Breitenbach & Galligan, 2004; Francis, 2000; Leach, 2000). Sharpe (1976: 149) explains why these trends may be continuing despite the changes to the curriculum:

Making it possible for girls and boys to study all subjects is of no use unless the jobs that the subjects relate to are seen to be accessible, suitable and acceptable for either sex. If this condition is not fulfilled the exclusion and inequalities will continue but with curriculum restrictions removed, and the reasons for boys' and girls' continuing rejection of the other sex's more exclusive subjects will provide even more justification for the assumption of 'natural' aptitudes and abilities.

4.4 SPORTS AND PHYSICAL EDUCATION

Most of the young women enjoyed PE and other sports at school with only four explicitly stating that they hated or disliked it. The potential positive value of sports and encouragement of young women is clearly seen in the case of Oscar (aged17) who regularly truanted from school, but who would attend all her sports training:

"The things that probably kept me at it [school] was ma sports ...//... I woulda went in late to school jus' so that I could go till like the football an' stuff ...//... I think that there kinda encourage me to go a bit as well."
(Secondary, controlled, single-sex)

Those who disliked sports at school tended to have very particular reasons. Sue (aged 25) and Melissa (aged 16) felt that the competitive nature of spots in their schools put too much pressure on young people, took the enjoyment out of it and could impact negatively upon the self-esteem of those not as proficient as others:

"I think activities are good, but sports activities isn't always about running from A to B as fast as you can and getting between the two goals ...//... I believe that can actually make your self-esteem decrease or worsen ...//... I felt intimidated at times because I wasn't the most sporty ...//... I wasn't good at those things and I would have felt embarrassed." (Grammar, voluntary, co-ed)

The theme of embarrassment was also evident within the other two accounts of young women who did not enjoy sports at school. While not being 'good' at sports was part of the issue, the larger issue for Kativa (aged 17) and Nat (aged 24) was around body image, feeling embarrassed and shy changing in front of friends and wearing the school PE outfit:

"...girls woulda had to wear those bloody wee knickers things, I hated them, absolutely really embarrassed ...//... I hated it cus I was overweight ...//... If you can't do it, then everybody else will laugh at you ...//... it's just embarrassing, you don't wanna put yourself through it, especially in school like when any tiny wee bit of gossip is great gossip." (Nat, Grammar, controlled, co-ed)

A further related issue was mentioned by only one young woman, but is noteworthy. This concerns the issue of sexual orientation and PE within school. Susie (aged 20) discussed how her (perceived) sexual orientation had led her to be put out of the changing room by the PE teacher as her classmates had complained that they did not want her 'watching them' while they were changing. Rather than challenge the attitudes of the young women, Susie was singled out which may have led to a reinforcement of her classmate's prejudices.

On a more positive note, it was encouraging to find that most young women reported fairly good sports facilities in their schools and/or a wide range of sports on offer. While there were few schools where sports appeared highly limited or restricted, gender differences in the sports offered to young women and young men continued to be evident. Those sports most often offered to young women included netball, hockey, gymnastics and camogie while those offered to young men included basketball, football, rugby, hockey, hurling and Gaelic football. Most (but not all) who reported the continuation of gender differences in sports within co-educational schools were in their early to mid-20s (average age 21 years), and things may well have changed in these schools since they had left. That said, Ruth (aged 17) who was still at school reported differences in her current school experiences:

"...there's not much activities in school, a lack of them that's one of the bad things in school ...//... but the guys have more activities, they have football, hockey and rugby. They get more on the sport side." (Grammar, controlled, co-ed)

One of the big issues for young women regarding sports in school was football – there being no female football team or females not being allowed to join the male football team. Of those who spoke explicitly of football in school, 8 reported having a girl's football team within their schools, while 15 reported not being afforded the opportunity to play football within a female only team or as part of the school team. The average age of those with the opportunity to play football in school was 21 years, while the average age of those without any such opportunity was 20 years. This may suggest that girl's football teams are not particularly new or that there are still relatively few opportunities for girls to play football at school. This may, of course, be due to a lack of interest among young women, but in light of the interest among our sample, we feel this is unlikely to be the case. Given the difficulties experienced by some of the young women here in setting up their own teams or playing for the school team, it is more likely to be a result of lack of school support.

Furthermore, the view that young women were fragile and thus unsuited to playing football was evident in a number of young women's accounts, particularly Susie's:

"... they wouldn't let us have a football team cus it was an all girls school and they were like 'oh no, you have to do hockey, you have to do netball' ...//... that annoyed me too, because it was all 'oh it's a girl's school, we can't have girls playin' football, it's so rough' ..." (Grammar, voluntary, single-sex)

While traditional stereotypes in terms of sports within schools appear to be addressed in some schools, it is clear to see that these still remain in others. Further, young women often noted that while a range of sports may be open to both boys and girls within their schools that young women often choose not to partake in those traditionally associated with young men. This appeared to be because teachers would steer them towards other sports or young women themselves were not interested. Thus, while opportunities may be open to more young women today, perceptual barriers still remain.

4.5 EQUAL TREATMENT?

Sixteen young women who had experience of co-education were asked or talked specifically about the differential treatment of boys and girls within their schools. While five felt that there was no difference, the remaining eleven noted some differences. These differences may have related to the treatment and/or expectations of a single teacher, or to the general school experience. The main issues raised and discussed included: preferential treatment given to boys (e.g. male teachers favouring boys); differential expectation in terms of behaviour and differential expectation in terms of educational success.

Within a number of the young women's accounts of their experiences we could see evidence of how the 'hidden curriculum' works within schools. This refers to the non-formal, subtle and powerful messages implicitly passed on and learned on a daily basis. These, in many ways, shape the education experience and impact upon the outcomes (Leach, 2000; Livesey, 2005a). They are messages which tend to encompass an approach to living and behaving, and an attitude to learning. Generally and implicitly, they are messages about authority, control, order and power (Livesey, 2005a; Sharpe, 1976). As such, schools are said to play a key formative role in the socialisation process, communicating messages about the 'acceptable' behaviours and roles of different groups, preparing young people for taking their place in the adult world (Kilpatrick et al., 1997).

Some examples of the differential treatment of boys and girls were obvious in terms of clear favouritism, discrimination or sexism. While important, these were few in number, and it is the more subtle messages as part of the hidden curriculum which we are interested in here. This is particularly in light of the fact that although often recognised by young women, they appeared to be accepted and internalised by them. So for instance, a number of young women noted that boy's disruptive or 'boyish' behaviour was accepted and indeed expected within their schools:

"...I think that boys get away with more in school ...//...I suppose that's cos they're boys but, you know, sure what does it matter?" (Jill, aged 17)

"Maybe just with the behaviour and that ...//... they knew the boys would probably mess about more, and you know, normal teenage fellas carrying on." (Donna, aged 21)

Within both of these accounts we see that the young women are also accepting of this behaviour, that it matters little to them and represents 'normal' behaviour for young men. The implication then, is that if young women were involved in such behaviour it would matter as it was not viewed as 'normal' behaviour for them. The expectations of girls, then, were different. They were expected to be more passive/quiet, hard working and high achieving:

"In our class it probably woulda been more expected for the boys to be the messers ...//... one of the classes, [it] was expected for the girls to be better than the boys. It was more acceptable for a fella to fail or not do as well, but you know the girls, it was more acceptable for them to succeed ..." (Shirley, aged 24)

This was not only expected of them but was viewed in some respects as 'the natural order of things'. To the detriment of some young men, there was the belief of some young women that teachers simply stopped teaching them due to their behaviour and expectations regarding their attitudes and aspirations towards education.

In all of these cases we see that the education experience particularly at the 'person formation' stage of early adolescence, can act to further reinforce, perpetuate or perhaps 'normalise' existing gender roles and inequalities (Leach, 2000; Leonard, 1999; Sharpe, 1976) as evidenced through the experiences of a number of the young women we spoke to. If the experience in the classroom, in relation to subject choice and perceptions of teachers, is influenced by stereotypical ideas this may impact on the 'choices' young women make in relation to further education and occupations.

4.6 CAREERS ADVICE

Influences on the post-16 'choices' made by young women discussed in the previous section will feature in a subsequent section on employment and work. While the routes taken by young women are influenced by a variety of factors, the advice and guidance they received about education and careers, or the lack of it is a significant factor which emerged from the interviews.

The importance of careers education and guidance has been recognised in a range of government reports and policies. In Northern Ireland, the Department of Employment and Learning (2001:2) has acknowledged that "Careers education and guidance are recognised as key factors in both individual and economic success ...". Recently, the report of the Women and Work Commission (2006) concluded that the nature of careers advice and guidance provided to girls and young women contributed to the persistence of gender inequalities in the workplace. It recommended that young women needed to be provided with work experience opportunities and guidance and advice free from gender stereotyping.

The majority of young women (all but 2 out of 38) did receive some careers advice in school and/or college. Of the two who reported receiving no career advice, one said that there was a careers day once a year at her school. The other young women said she did not receive careers advice because she had a 'mild learning disability'. While the majority of young women in the study had encountered some careers provision, important issues were raised relating to the nature and quality of provision. Only four out of 38 young women referred to the careers advice they had received as 'good' with many comments pointing to the limitations of provision.

Despite the increasing policy emphasis on careers guidance over the past decade, there was little difference in the experience of careers classes and nature of advice provided across the different age groups in the research. Only one young woman suggested improvement over time when she compared the careers advice provided to her brother with her own experience. Carmel (aged 23) spoke of how her careers advice had been:

"Very limited. I look back now at the amount of careers stuff my brothers doing ... gosh we didn't have that in school, an its only a few years in the difference. And, ah, we would ask, ya know, ah, we're interested in this. An ah no I don't think you'd be that qualified, you won't get that. They'd tell ya, you look you're not gonna do this and you're not gonna do that. But in other ways they'd make you fill out all the UCAS forms and you would have it all done."

Points raised by the young women on this topic suggest that while many of them found careers advice useful up to a point there were many things that it did not cover.   Comments about the lack of usefulness of careers advice tended to refer to the lack of individuality in approach, the use of 'tests' to determine interests and aptitude and the general lack of information about study options and future careers. Louise (aged 23) relayed her experience:

"Not very useful...We did something in third year, when you were 14 to decide what career you'd be good at and it was just basically asking you what kind of stuff you like, what subjects you like, what your hobbies were and they compiled it and – it was a load of rubbish. It didn't help at all. And then they just gave you leaflets about different careers and you got one chat with a careers person I think in fifth form but again like it doesn't stick in my mind going to it or anything so ..."

Neither does there appear to be a common experience of careers education with substantial diversity between secondary and grammar schools, but also within the various categories of schools in the post-primary sector. There is clear evidence of an expectation on the part of grammar schools that young people will take the more traditional academic route – A Levels and university. This therefore tends to be the focus of careers advice in grammar schools. In many cases this was limited to discussion of and advice on subject choices at GCSE level–but particularly at A Level–with little consideration of options such as more vocational courses or labour market opportunities.

This was considered insufficient by many young women. Ruth (aged 17) said:

"I think it needs more cus there's not enough, like am, it's basically, we're told you're better to go on to uni and everything than try to get a job and careers has been about going to uni, not about finding a job or trying to go back to tech or anything".

Often the advice about going to university was limited to a discussion of what subjects should be taken at A level and the number of points required for university entry rather than a discussion of careers options associated with particular courses or employability issues.

Many of the young women would have preferred a more individual, personal approach. Karen (aged 19) suggested that:

"Maybe if they took you individually it would have been better, a bit better. But it was very general, they go around and 'what do you wanna do' and 'why do you wanna do that' and 'what's the reasons' and I didn't know what I wanted to do ..."

Donna (aged 21) put forward a similar argument:

"... their was someone I think from [training programme] came in and we'd to do like a questionnaire with them and he, you told him what you'd like to do. He went back to his office and copied you a like a form of what like you would need to get into do that. That was it, there was nothing, it wasn't like you could go to one of the teachers and say 'look I would really like to do this'. What do I do?, how do I get from here to there?, there was nothing."

Molly (aged 20) on the other hand, illustrated the benefits of being able to access individual advice at the FE college she attended:

"The woman you went down to her, she was in the wee office, she was always there. You could go anytime, she always helped you. I found tech very helpful, I loved it like."

Young women who were involved in informal education through Alternative Education Programmes found great value in the personal guidance and support they were given with regard to future steps and careers. Neimh (aged 17) told of her experience:

*"They [AEP] got me into the Hair Academy, College and then they were getting me into job interviews for hairdressing and I got into a few good ones. Like I was in **** [hairdressers] and all, but it just wasn't my atmosphere, and then I got into **** [hairdressers] it's a five star salon. And its really, really good. They're just opened and you have a good craic and all and you're allowed to talk to your clients. ****[first hairdressers] didn't let you talk to anybody, just cleaned and cleaned and that was it. But if it wasn't for ****[AEP] I wouldn't have got to where I am today, really."*

Findings from this research suggest that careers advice continues to be heavily influenced by traditional assumptions about gender. There were many examples of young women being encouraged to conform to gender stereotypes:

"I remember we used to have to do these a, I remember having to do these questions or forms, the career classes and sort of saying do you like doing such and such, do you like doing such and such and all this here and I remember all the sheets saying a secretary, and I was sorta going I want to be more than a secretary. And then I was sort of thinking God now is that all I can do." (Shirley, aged 24)

"... one of my friends wanted to be an engineer, and the careers teacher was like no and now she is. The careers teacher was just goin' no, we think you should do this and she was adamant and they just weren't supporting her in it at all..." (Susie, aged 20)

The existence of careers provision in terms of resources did not necessarily mean that those resources were utilized effectively. Nat (aged, 23) said of her school:

"We had a careers room, and we had different books and stuff, and then we had a careers teacher, I can't remember seeing her about ... //...our careers teacher was ...//...our French teacher. I don't remember seeing her in ...//... that respect."

There were examples of the consequences of undertaking the wrong education or training path. A number of young women spoke of pursuing a particular route because they did not know what else to do or because it was what was expected by teachers and parents and perhaps peers.

"When you think about it, from primary school...//...they tell you about going for a career, what do you want to be when you grow up? That's all you hear...//...and you have to be like the doctor, the nurse, you know...//... And I ended up saying an accountant, cus all my family has a background in accountancy." (Sue, aged 25)

Sue had changed courses, ending up with a degree in Business and Computing. She looked for full-time employment but to her frustration ended up working in a call centre. After leaving this job she worked in a number of voluntary posts in order to build up experience to re-train as a youth worker. Upon reflection she felt that if the value of the vocational routes had been open to her she may not have jumped into a degree she knew little about.

A number of young women who took part in the study who had gone through higher education found themselves 'in limbo'. In retrospect they realised they had received poor advice, still lacked direction or accepted that they had to gain better qualifications or to retrain. The consequences of inadequate and inappropriate guidance included dropping out of courses, moving in and out of different courses in an attempt to find one that was suitable or being 'forced' into insecure low paid work.

The generally negative view of careers advice expressed by the young women in this research may in part be a reflection of the age and experience of a number of young women who took part in the research, in that they may have been more likely to feel that school had not prepared them well for the educational and employment experiences they have had to face.

Other research in Northern Ireland has also found young people to be critical of the careers advice they received in schools expressing the view that teachers are not always equipped to deliver this (Kilkelly et al., 2004) and that they received limited advice about future careers and subject choices (Save the Children Fund and the Children's Law Centre, 2002).

4.7 ALTERNATIVE EDUCATION

One thing that became abundantly clear through the research was the polarity of experience in terms of education. While some young women 'loved school' others 'hated it' and found that they could not achieve in the school environment. The reasons for this often related to difficult personal and family circumstances. What is also evident is the school system does not cater to the needs of all young women, be this because of structure or routine or the complexities of the issues faced by the young women. For a number of young women, informal education provided the opportunity to re-engage with learning. Sometimes this was through Alternative Education Programmes or the opportunity to take courses at local community venues.

Beyoncé (aged 25) had a disrupted school life as a result of moving in and out of foster and residential care. She left school with no qualifications and said that she "... had to build herself up after school". After starting an NVQ and a work experience placement which she enjoyed she was motivated to improve her job prospects by obtaining more qualifications and did a number of GCSEs and computer courses at a local community centre. She then learned about another project which led to her getting a permanent job:

"And then they said to me about health learning works project and it was like two months training and the last lot of months was on a work placement and there was a chance you'd get a job at the end of it so that was how I got my job."

For some young women alternative education projects provided a positive environment and experience. Neimh (aged17) persistently truanted from school but after getting into an AEP found that:

"It was dead on, I went everyday. I loved it. Cus they were fair with yee, you weared your own clothes, didn't have to wear a uniform and they weren't strict about lunches and all, it was just far better than school and I learn't far more. I actually sat and listened."

Gráinne (aged 18) attended an alternative education programme in the final year of her compulsory education and said "that out of my five years of schoolin' it was the best year of my life". Her comments are reflective of the experiences of other young women who had experience of alternative education programmes:

"They were more one-to-one with ya, they were able to help ya with your problems and give ya advice and all, where teachers in school wouldn't do something like that ...//... at the end of the day they had time for ya, you were treated as an adult and respected as an adult."

Education, Training and Employment

4.8 TRAINING, FURTHER AND HIGHER EDUCATION EXPERIENCES

4.8.1 Training

While it was by no means always the case, the trend was for young women attending grammar schools to remain at the school with a view to entering higher education and for young women attending secondary schools to enter colleges of further education and/or undertake vocational courses. There is a noticeable lack of published material on training schemes in Northern Ireland, and the UK in general. Information available shows that young women tend to be under-represented in training schemes. Those schemes that do enrol higher numbers of young women are highly gendered.

Department of Education for Northern Ireland statistics show that of those 16 and 17 year olds participating in Jobskills courses in 2004/2005, 88% were male and 12% were female (DENI, 2005). This pattern was identified by Leonard (1999) in her research with post-primary school young people in that only 2% of young women intended to undertake training compared to one-fifth (20%) of young men. Further, Kilpatrick et al. (1997), in their review of 59 training units throughout Belfast, found that only five reported having more female than male trainees. Only six of the training organisations had crèches, which could present a problem to young women wishing to engage in training.

Research suggests that those involved in training schemes are typically those who are low achievers in schools (Armstrong and McVicar, 2000), making it imperative that the training available meets their needs and caters to their interests. Yet, it is clear that this is not happening. In 2005, the House of Commons Public Accounts Committee found the Northern Ireland Jobskills programme (one of Northern Ireland's biggest training programmes) to be "one of the worst-run programmes that this committee has examined in recent years" (House of Commons Committee of Public Accounts, 2005: 3).

Few young women in our sample reported having been given details of training opportunities whilst at school. Where information was given it tended to be piecemeal and related to gender specific subjects and traditional female occupational areas. Courses taken in further education and vocational courses taken generally fell into the following sectors: hospitality/catering; health and social care; child care; beauty; hairdressing and business/administration.

Twelve of the young women interviewed had at least one training experience. This ranged from placements through New Deal (for Young People/Lone Parents), local training and employment programmes, for example for those with leaning disabilities, and training through local community/voluntary groups.

The vocational nature of the courses and the fact that they were employment-linked was seen as a positive aspect. Training was also of value in terms of increasing social skills and for providing qualifications and experience they had been unable to attain through school:

*"...I enjoyed it more as I was off on work placement 4 days a week. And ***(name of work placement) was good, everyone was nice... //... realised that I did want to go back to work again ...//... they [the courses she had been on] gave me loads of confidence cos after leaving **** (her previous place of employment) you know I thought I was never going to get a job again, but then working in the wee advice centre was good."* (Beyoncé, aged 25).

Furthermore, the training that a small number of young women were taking or had undertaken had led them to a clear realisation of their future career desires. One young women training as a hairdresser was determined to undertake further courses with a view to opening her own salon and a further two young women who had undertaken courses in youth work were considering entering higher education to become professionally trained youth workers.

The value of the social aspects of training and employment programmes was most evident in the accounts of young women with learning disabilities, who regardless of the nature of the programme and their enjoyment of it, often pointed to the social aspects of it as positive – "it got me out, got me doin' stuff, helping people" (Kimberly, aged 21 – courses included catering and child care). It is also interesting to note that these young women tended to have a number of training experiences and that those who were now working were not necessarily working in the areas for which they had trained. Vanessa (aged 21), for example, had spent two years undertaking an NVQ Level 1 in catering, a further two years undertaking an NVQ Level 1 in Child Care (which she did not complete) and was currently considering undertaking training in retail. At the time of interview, she attended a job club through a local charity and was undertaking a work placement in a supermarket. Likewise, Avril (aged 21) had attended a training college where she undertook training in upholstery, catering and horticulture and was working in a local grocery store at the time of interview. Although the sample of those with learning disabilities is small, given the patterns of their training and employment placements and experiences, it might not be unreasonable to suggest that it remains at a fairly low/basic level (preparing them for poor positions in the labour market) and that their subsequent positions in the labour market are not necessarily reflective of their training backgrounds.

The ways in which a variety of young women benefited from training programmes have been discussed. While not aiming to distract from this it is important to note why experiences have not always been so positive, as it is from these experiences that important lessons for the future may be learned. While only one young woman noted wholly negative training experiences, certain aspects of other young women's training were negative or difficult. A number of young women had tried various courses but had dropped out due to not enjoying them. The main factors which made training experiences difficult or somewhat negative included:

• Travel to training locations (particularly for those living outside Belfast and/or in rural areas);

Erin, a young mother, had to travel a number of miles to her training location – "its just a bit of an extra rush cos I've to get him ready that bit quicker before the bus leaves".

• The nature of placements;

*"The ***** (placement hairdressers) didn't let you talk to anybody, just cleaned and cleaned and cleaned and that was it"* (Neimh, aged 17)

The lack of courses on offer, leading to taking up options which were undesired and for which the participant had little enthusiasm. Of the list of training options she was provided with, Gráinne (aged 18) stated:

*"There's nothing much on this, so I might as well, I went to Child Care in **** (name of college) and I wasn't getting into it...//... I came outta that and so that was really the only thing there and hairdressin', I wouldn't be into hairdressin', just standin' on your feet all day, washin hair? Brushin' floors? No, I wouldn't be into that."*

Most of the twelve young women discussed in this section had more than one training experience, often starting courses and dropping out or completing one period of training and moving into a different area. Training experiences most often cited as having been undertaken/started included:

- Catering (n=4)
- Business Administration (n=3)
- Hairdressing (n=3)
- Child Care (n=3)
- Youth Work (n=3)
- Retail (n=2)
- Other care (n=2)

While only three young women talked specifically about the gendered nature of training options, it is clear from the experiences of these young women that their training experiences are heavily gendered. Going back to the example of Gráinne (aged 18) who talked of the lack of options available to her, she clearly felt that young men had more options than young women:

GN: ...What kind of training programmes did they offer?
Gráinne: Em child care and youth work or play work or somethin' or paintin' and decoratin', y'know all that gear but there's not really enough stuff for wee girls.
GN: Is that right?
Gráinne: Yeah, its all to me it seems like its all for fellas, like buildin', brickwork' joinery, weldin', paintin, an decoratin' and electrics, car maintenance, it all just seemed more for fellas like.

While Gráinne did acknowledge that she probably could have done such courses, she noted that the fact that the classes would be all male would dissuade her from doing so. Likewise, Beyoncé (aged 25) noted that her Business Administration class was made up primarily of women and that there tended to be different courses available to men. She told us:

Beyoncé: Emmm, there is programmes for men, yeah cos I know a friend of mine who is a fella who had to do the same as I had to do as well [ie: a training course]
GN: And where are their placements?
Beyoncé: Probably chefs and catering and stuff I would think and joinery and all that kinda stuff...//... its probably cos I was doin' admin. And not many men are in admin. If you know what I mean.

There are two issues of importance here. Firstly, training courses remain typically gendered and expectations, stereotypes and difficulties in moving across gender divides remain difficult. And secondly, as was pointed out by a number of young women, the types of courses open to young men are those which provide skills in trades which are more highly paid, and hold a higher degree of status than those open to young women. Indeed, the Women's Tech report that 30 years after the first employment equality legislation was introduced only 1% of women are going into trades such as building, carpentry, plumbing etc (Broghan, 2006).

4.9 FURTHER AND HIGHER EDUCATION

It has been government policy since the 1980s to encourage, through compulsion if necessary, young people to be in education, training or employment. The emphasis on continuing education has largely been justified by the anticipated outcomes for individuals and society in terms of greater economic success and because the over 16 participation rate in the UK was poor in relation to many other OECD countries. Many studies have shown that a person's income is related to their level of education. In relation to Northern Ireland, Harmon et al. (2000) have demonstrated that an extra year of education on average adds 8% to male earnings and 12% to female earnings.

In recent years participation rates in post-compulsory education have risen steadily in Northern Ireland and a higher proportion of females aged 16 and 17 years (85%) are involved in full-time education than males in the same age group (78%) Participation rates are higher among this age group in Northern Ireland (72%) than in England (67%) (DENI, 2005). Young women are also much more likely to stay in school and enter mainstream college courses than undertake Jobskills courses.

Because of the link between vocational training and the FE sector many of the points made in relation to training relate to the class based component of qualifications like NVQs. A small number of young women in the sample went to FE college after school to do BTEC, GNVQ or HND courses.

There were examples of very positive experiences and success in achieving qualifications and reference was made to FE not being as 'pressured as school.' Nat (age 23) identified some of the positive aspects of her move from school to college:

"...a lot more grown up, you had to do a lot more on your own ...//... it wasn't as competitive...//... in tech you were literally on your own...//... I think I found I took in a lot more, rather than just messing about with your mates..."

The benefits of having to take more personal responsibility were also cited by Victoria (aged 22):

"I loved my course, sports studies, I loved it like...//... if you weren't prepared to do your work you weren't going to get anywhere like ...//... I think that was good that you were kinda set on your own...//... there were a group of us done the work and we got further..."

Molly (aged 20) also felt that more responsibility placed on students in FE prepared them better for university study by allowing them time and space to adjust to the freedom associated with college but also learning to appreciate the requirements of independent study, something which she said she witnessed school leavers starting university having difficulty with.

While there were clearly good experiences, it is also clear that the problem of lack of appropriate careers guidance continued to be a problem. Kim (aged 21) felt that she lost track on leaving school:

> **GN:** Whenever you look back are you happy enough the way things panned out for you or would you, in terms of education, or would you change any of that?
> **Kim:** Well in high school I wouldn't change anythin' but then after I left there I went to the Tec to do eh a health and social care course but eh I dropped outta that for a, I can't remember why, because it was, it was gettin' too much into social work an stuff like that there an I wasn't that interested so then I went an done an art course then I dropped outta it, an went to America.

Sue felt as though she had been channelled into university because it was expected of her:

*"Our school was very much geared up for that. I went to **** (school), which was a grammar school. So they were pushing you from a very young age that the natural progression after doing your A'Levels was to go into university. So I did go to **** (university) and ended up going to the university of (university), which wasn't the place I wanted to go. But I had to go to university, it was a must, em, and I stayed there for two years. And then says enough was enough and came home."*

The transition from a very structured school environment to college or university where there is considerably less surveillance and the emphasis is more on independent learning is potentially a difficult one. It is clear from our findings that while some young women relished the independence and greater autonomy and responsibility that came with further and higher education courses, others had more difficulty adjusting to a less structured learning environment. Louise (aged 23) found the experience daunting at first but said that:

"I loved my first year over there – it was one of the best, best years ever. It was just so much fun, like moving in with all your friends and just having all your friends there – being able to do what you want, when you want and not having like your parents there to say oh you can't do this or you can't come home at 4 or 5 in the morning – you can just go mad – and I loved it."

Michelle (aged 19) also spoke of the difficulty of adjusting initially:

"It was a <u>very</u> <u>very</u> big change now at first I didn't like it here at all I hated it I just couldn't wait to get home ...//... it took about six months to get me settled here an then once I did get settled I'm happy like I don't don't mind bein' here like I love getting' home but I don't mind bein' here it doesn't bother me." [her emphasis]

For other young women the experience was more problematic. The lack of structure at college added to Kim's difficulties as she explained:

"Em well you were too laid back, you were let away with everythin' so you weren't, whereas in high school ye were made do this that an' the other in Tech ye could have got away with, if you didn't do your work nobody cared an' ye weren't kinda set rules to, so then people just steered off course an like em like I did an I gave up, quit it."

Rachel (aged 25) expressed a similar view:

"...so I left and did A'Levels at tech. So I started in September and left in October, no structure no nothing, you didn't have to go you could just dander about town and then after that I just left home and moved thirty miles away."

Rachel had initially left home when she was 16 and had a difficult personal relationship with a partner but following the birth of her daughter she returned to college, obtained a HND and got a job.

CARMEL'S STORY

Carmel experienced severe problems during her period at university:

"It was just maybe my own eh freedom (laughs lightly) and I eh I would never go into college at all and ended up hitting drink and takin' drugs and I got into bother with that then, that's how I had to leave ...//... but that's ya know that's part of my life, what made me who I am now. Eh whenever I went to college I just never clicked really and I ended up getting into the wrong crowd of people and I've eh got an addictive personality to begin with anyway and em I ended up in rehab, so, that's what happened. But I was there for a while then I had to go back and forth and back and forth and I've been in and out since. And eh it was good for me ya know I thought, but it just keeps on getting a hold of me (Laughs)...//... But I'm stronger now that I was before, I was very vulnerable at that stage when I was on my own, in Belfast."

Carmel then found that it was difficult to get the support she required and recounted a negative experience of the university counselling support service:

"Yeah I went to see someone an' eh I had ta tell ya it was awful. She said 'there's nothing I can do Carmel'. And I really was in a bad way cos that day I was very shook up. I can't really remember, I don't want to tell you like. I was em. I can remember bein' in this wee room waitin' for to speak to her an' it was like all the other shrinks I went into see before, the big couch and lovely wallpaper an' all. And I explained to her, an' I told her. An' she goes 'I think it would be best for you just to go home'. And I was like em 'I don't want to hmm I'm afraid'. And I couldn't really say that to her either cos I was tryin' to be strong but I couldn't (voice raises slightly) I was a mess. And I really needed someone to say to me to do this to do that, take this route. And she was not helpful. I came out feelin' worse that when I went in."

Carmel did however talk about the good support she had received from her tutor at college:

"I could come in and speak to her and she would be like 'look at all this you're missin an' all'. ...//... Ya know I could relate to her."

Rachel and Carmel's very difficult personal circumstances highlight the need for accessible, individual support. A number of points have been raised by those young women with experience of the further and higher education sector which raise issues relating to pastoral care and availability of advice and guidance. While we would not attempt to make generalisations from such a small sample, other studies such as Hope et al. (2005) and Kracen (2003) have drawn attention to the concerns about health and wellbeing of students in higher education suggesting that there needs to be attention given to the nature of pastoral care and the extent of support services and the way in which they can be accessed.

4.10 FINANCES

For young women in higher education, finances and the debts incurred were a concern. Kelly (aged, 21) recounted the major expenses:

"It is because the tuition fees have gone up now and you get, you get some of your tuition fees paid for you and you have to pay the rest of them and then you have to pay your accommodation, like you have to put down a big deposit to get the house and then some houses are looking you to pay three months in advance and then you have your text books, text books are really expensive to buy. So you have to really stretch your money out, that's why most students look for jobs. So it's, it is a push like, but it can be done."

Families were frequently cited as an important source of financial support in terms of contributions towards fees and living expenses, but it is clear from data collected in the course of the interviews that a substantial proportion of young women take on part-time jobs while studying.

Throughout the discussion on education and training, time and again, young women have spoken of concerns about not having a clear career path or not being able to get employment related to their area of study or graduate level employment. Louise (aged 23) had graduated with a degree in Business and Computing and said that her inability to get a graduate job (she was working in a bank) was putting her off doing a post-graduate course:

"Well that's just what I'm trying to figure out now actually, em I'd always thought I'd maybe go on to do some more studying after I'd finished, maybe, y'know do a PHD or a Masters em subjects like Physiotherapy or something like that but you see after studying in my last, my final year, it has just totally put me off doing it so I'm not really sure what it's gonna lead me to now; I mean I'm just working in the bank and I don't know ultimately what I want to do."

What is interesting is that even where young women were experiencing or had experienced major difficulties in relation to their education, this did not result in them rejecting education. Most spoke of the value of education and had a positive view of it. A number of young women who had dropped out of education for a variety of reasons indicated a desire to return to education or training with a much clearer knowledge of what they wanted to do and were clear about the outcomes they wanted.

4.11 ATTITUDES/ASPIRATIONS TO EDUCATION

With regards to the educational background[9] of the sample, at the time of interview:

- Five young women were still in school
- Two were in further education
- Six were in higher education
- Four were undertaking various local/community courses

9   This list refers to the young women's highest level of education

Previously:

- Six had undertaken courses in further education colleges (2 incomplete)
- Seven had studied at university (3 incomplete)
- Many had undertaken various local/community courses

Desire for, further education, or a return to education was also high among the sample with five young women desiring to return to further education at some point in the future to undertake various courses. In the main, these were young women who had left school with few or no formal qualifications. A further ten young women expressed a desire to go to or return to higher education. While a number of these were at school at the time of interview, others were in paid employment and wished to return to education to retrain, qualify and/or undertake post-graduate qualifications. Overall, therefore, we can say that the general educational background of the sample was fairly high as were aspirations towards education.

Unexpectedly then, most of the sample had a positive attitude towards education in terms of viewing it as important. This was irrespective of whether their own education experience/s in the past had been positive or not. Most of those who had left school with few formal qualifications, for instance, regretted this and stated that they wished they had worked harder (despite the varying personal issues and barriers standing in their way at the time). In fact, there were only three young women who were unsure of the real value of education (these will be returned to shortly). By far the most frequently given reason for the importance of education was in terms of employment prospects:

"I don't want to finish at A-Level and be a dosser and do nothing and get crap pay" (Ruth, aged 17 - School)

"... you need exams. You even need GCSEs to be a bin man! ...//... You're not gonna get anywhere in this life with no exams, no education – you don't get anywhere." (Gráinne, aged 18 - NEET)

"If you want to do well like, if you want a good, a half decent job you need to have an education" (Molly, aged 20 – University)

"Like it's your GCSEs if you don't get them when you leave school, where do you go (pause), the bru?" (Fiona, aged 22 – P/T employment, P/T F.E)

While many were of this belief, it was particularly true of those holding few qualifications and in low-paid employment and those still in education (school, further or higher). Some of those who had finished higher education, as will be discussed shortly, were finding the promise that education equates to good money and a good job was not quite so straightforward.

Some went further than seeing education as merely a ticket to employment, perceiving it as opening a world of possibilities with few limitations:

"If you've a good education you can go anywhere and get a job anywhere" (Pauline, aged 23 – F/T employment)

There were, however, contradictions in Pauline's and others accounts. She noted, for example, that there remained more opportunities for men in terms of going directly into trades and that education may not, therefore, be as important or necessary to them. Young men were perceived as having opportunities that did not necessitate prolonged education and the 'boundless opportunities' open to women with a good education, still did not open these opportunities to them. Despite openly stating this, Pauline still clung to the idea that education provided a world of opportunities and she did not foresee any barriers to further education for herself or other young women.

The view that education may be more important to women than men was held by a number of other young women. Karen (aged 19), for example, stated an awareness of the wage gap between men and women and was of the belief that although this had decreased that an education (particularly) a degree would enable women to earn similar wages to men. Molly, who had stated that you cannot get a decent job, felt, like Pauline, that this was not necessarily the case for young men, citing young men she knew who had successfully entered trades and family businesses with few qualifications. And Nicola (aged 20) openly stated that education was of more importance and benefit to women:

> **Nicola:** I think it's more beneficial for women, education
> **KM:** Just for to get a job or ...
> **Nicola:** To get a job makin' the same money equivalent to their partner.

While some young women recognised inequalities such as these, they appeared to accept them as just the way things were and put great faith in the value of education and the meritocratic system of hard work in education equals just reward in employment.

Even those who were less sure of the value of education, their attitudes could in no way be viewed as negative. Again, there were many inconsistencies in their views in that they appeared to see the value of education although it may not necessarily have yielded them much reward to date. Sue (aged 25) as noted earlier, had completed a degree in Business and Computing and since then had worked in a call centre and a clothes shop. She was currently re-training as a youth worker and working in this field part-time:

"I didn't have blinkers on that you could go straight into a management job, I knew that you had to work your way up. But it became very frustrating when you found out that you know, I could have entered into some of the jobs that was available to me without a degree, never mind having the degree. ...//... you know a degree didn't get you into step two of a job. But you still had to start at step one, I knew that, but I think I kinda had tried to fool myself into thinking that it might help me."

While Sue had begun to realise that her belief that a good education equated with a good job did not necessarily play itself out in reality, she blamed herself, her naivety and her choice of career route rather than the messages enforced throughout her school and university life (hence she was individualising her 'failure'). As such, she continued to put faith in education and was undertaking vocational courses in youth work with a view to returning to university to undertake another degree.

Louise's case is also interesting to look at from a similar viewpoint, because again despite seeing inequalities in the opportunities open to young women and young men and seeing that not all young people need a good education to get a good job, she still very much believed it. Despite the fact that she is currently under-employed and working in a bank, which she states, is poorly paid, she still feels that there are lots of options open to her due to having a good education:

"I don't think it's [education] like the be all and end all of getting a good job, I mean, my two cousins, they left school with about two GCSEs each and eh, they're both working now. They got apprenticeships doing like, one's a plumber and one's an electrician and they, like my cousin – he's 19 and he's bought his own house and all now with his money. Whereas the rest of us, we've been scrimping our way through university not able to afford anything and he's sitting there with his big house and car and everything, so he's done really really well ...//... but I think it helps ...//... I mean if I hadn't gone to university or that, I would probably just end up working in the bank and it doesn't really pay that great money, whereas now I have all these options of other things I can do. I just need to think about what I want to do and y'know they're all gonna be a lot better for me". (aged 23)

Again, Louise appears to be individualising her 'failure' to get a well-paid job by stating that she hasn't made up her mind what direction to go in yet – although she does indicate that her lack of success in finding a job equivalent to her qualifications has made her hesitant about doing a post-graduate course. There is still the firm belief in the meritocratic principles espoused and fed to young women throughout their education careers that a good education is bound to lead to a good job with good pay and that if it doesn't, that the individual is in some way to blame.

Related to these points are the barriers, or lack thereof, that young women foresaw to education. Few young women perceived any barriers to young women prolonging their stay in education or returning to education with Jill (aged 17 and in full-time education) stating:

"I don't think there is any [barriers]. I think it'll bring more opening than like barriers really."

Those that did note potential barriers, however, tended to have a knowledge or awareness of these based on their own experiences or those of people they knew. The barriers they discussed were financial, spatial (e.g. travelling to education institutions) or familial (e.g. child care – time and expense). Jemima (aged 20), for example, although feeling that she needed to go to university to become a qualified Youth Worker was not overly keen on the prospect, especially in light of the level of debt her brother had left university with:

"... how is any young person meant to go to university, come out, be £13, 000 in debt then expected to get a job straight away and pay it off ...//... it's bound to be disheartening cus I know if I went to university an' then couldn't get a job, I'd be disheartened ..."

Overall, the young women in this sample had fairly good educational achievements with many aspiring to further and higher education. Their attitudes towards education were, in the main, positive with many seeing it as essential to getting a good job and equating a good education to open choices, a job and good pay. Few perceived the barriers to education for young women (or particular groups of them). Furthermore, those who were highly educated and unemployed tended to blame their unrealistic expectations, lack of knowledge of what to do next and choosing the wrong course/career path rather than looking to the education structure, the nature of courses and jobs women undertake and are routed into. While young women today may achieve better educationally than young men, the data here would suggest that they feel that they have to do so in order to access opportunities and wages equivalent to men. Further, despite the fact that women may be over-represented in higher education, their success here does not appear to transfer to their position in the labour market. While young women may believe that opportunities are in some ways boundless and many traditional barriers removed, class and gender divisions still clearly exist. These can be seen in the types of education young women undertake (e.g. NVQs vs. degrees), the nature of the subjects they study and the career paths open to them as a result of these (often low-paid or low-level) along with the traditional barriers of childcare and expectations regarding the position of women in the family.

4.12 EMPLOYMENT AND WORK

4.12.1 Experience of the Labour Market

Seventeen young women over 16 years old were in full-time or regular part-time employment at the time of interview (this does not include those young women combining work and full-time study). They were predominantly employed in the care and service sectors. For these young women there had been a variety of routes into employment. Some had gone into employment directly from education, others had completed training schemes/programmes. There were a few examples of employment opportunities arising from work experience linked to training or of a training experience creating a motivation to obtain further qualifications. Beyoncé (aged 25) had left secondary school with no qualifications. After completing a training programme and having a work placement which she enjoyed, she was keen to improve her chances of employment and started to do as many courses as she could which resulted in her gaining a secure job she very much enjoyed.

Many young women had started working part-time when they were still at school, predominantly in the retail and catering sectors, and a number had quite lengthy work histories. It is noteworthy that while the majority of young women did work while studying, these jobs tended to be in female dominated employment sectors, most commonly working as sales assistants in retail outlets or working in restaurants and bars, cleaning and working as care assistants. It was also very apparent that work can add to the stress of young women's lives. The following quotation illustrates the juggle of studying and working for one young woman:

"The one thing I find really hard is whenever I go to work, right, I come home from school on a Monday and I don't get down to [hometown] until 6 o'clock in the evening. By that time I'm shattered because I've been up since 6 o'clock in the morning ...//... Wednesdays, Thursdays and Fridays I go straight to work, don't get back [to home town] until 11 o'clock and the last thing I want to do is school work so I go straight to bed. I work on a Saturday..." (Jo, aged 17)

While this particular young woman worked very long hours, there were many examples of young women leading very busy lives and juggling a range of activities and responsibilities.

Young women in employment (but not studying full-time) tended to have obtained a variety of employment experience since leaving school. Hannah, a single mother with two children, was doing two jobs – working as a care assistant (often up to 25 hours a week) and working part-time from home doing hair and beauty. She had previously worked for the civil service on a number of 51-week contracts and had worked as a child minder. Máiréad (aged 22) was working as a classroom assistant but had worked as a waitress for five years before that and altogether had had six jobs. She had also initially started to train as a mechanic. A number of young women talked of staying in jobs for relatively short periods of time and moving between jobs – these tended to be in the retail and hospitality sectors.

The majority of young women had positive views about the value of being employed in a job they liked and having a decent wage. There was a strong desire to be financially independent. Some young women spoke of how it was rather degrading having to depend on social security. The difficulties caused by trying to move from benefits to employment were illustrated. This was particularly the case for young women with dependants who could financially lose out by going into low wage jobs. For these young women the need to maintain a regular source of income, albeit a minimum one from the state, was a more secure option than temporary low wage employment. Carmel (aged 23) had been keen to get back to work but discovered that she would be no better off by entering a minimum wage job. She felt that she needed to gain better qualifications so she could get higher pay. There are also difficulties for young women receiving some payments such as Care Allowance if they want to apply for a training programme like New Deal. Prospective participants need to be in receipt of Job Seekers Allowance and this can create problems relating to benefit delay and subsequent financial hardship – a point well documented on research on lone mothers and employment (Miller, 2005; Gray 2005).

There were a variety of perceptions about current work situations. For those young women who were enjoying their work, benefits cited were: financial independence; the respect the job brought with it; interesting work, enjoying the challenge and the social benefits of having a job. Pauline, a 23 year old Project Manager in the NHS talked of how she loved her job and the satisfaction she got from it. There were also examples of the negative impact of having a job that was disliked or where working conditions were difficult. Fiona (aged 22) had made the decision to leave an office job which she had held for three years because the job had a detrimental impact on her well-being. She believes that because she found it so boring she became introverted and lost her confidence. She talked about people's perception that she had gone backwards after taking on a job as a cleaner in a hostel but she herself did not agree this was the case. In terms of negative views about jobs, boredom was the most often expressed feeling.

A number of the young women's observations point to lack of knowledge and careers advice, a topic covered earlier in the report. A number of young women were considering re-training or moving job and would clearly benefit from information and advice on options. Máiréad, for example, was working as a classroom assistant but was also doing an NVQ and was concerned about what would happen if she was not kept on in her job which was insecure because of funding difficulties. There were also examples of misperceptions, e.g. Máiréad was also under the impression that mature students could get a university grant which they did not have to pay back.

For many of the young women the main aspiration was to have a job they enjoyed and a decent income. Some had little clear idea about what they wanted to/could do. For others the experience of employment had motivated them to look at other educational/training opportunities – either because they enjoyed the kind of work they were doing and wanted to progress or because they were clearer about what they did not want to do but perceived better qualifications to be a route out of it.

Fiona (aged 22) talked about liking her job as a cleaner at the moment but doesn't see her future there

"definitely not like, but I still don't know what I wanna do so …//… until I get further educated then I'll move on".

Donna (aged 21) was working as a Community Health Worker. She had started a nursing course in England when she was 19 but had left, a decision she feels she made because at the time she had not been ready to move away from home. While she loves her job she now thinks it is time for a change and has applied to study nursing again.

When asked about local job opportunities, reference was made to growth in retail sector and to seasonal work. Frequent reference was made to people they knew who had good qualifications but could not get jobs locally. For many (coming out across other areas of the research) there was a strong attachment to area. Louise (aged 23) said she was concerned about not getting a job in the future:

"Because I'm finding at the minute whenever I've been looking y'know on job pages and stuff ...//... and there's not really very much about. And I've kinda been thinking if I do want to go and have a good career I may have to move to England...//... but I don't know. I don't want too. I want to stay here but in my field like science there doesn't seem to be a terrible lot here, that'll be my biggest fear, not getting a job, stuck at home forever."

Shirley (aged 24) also talked about a number of her peers having moved away. The perception was that apart from retail jobs, in local areas outside of Belfast there are not many job opportunities. For a number of young women there was a difficulty in attempting to reconcile their desire for a career in a chosen area with an attachment to local area and family.

4.12.2 Equality and Gender Divisions in the Workplace

As noted earlier, many of the young women worked in workplaces where many/majority of employees were female. A number of participants, while feeling that their workplaces were mixed, pointed to the starker differences at senior levels and showed an awareness of gender inequalities in the workplace. Some young women put forward explanations as to why they felt this was the case; others struggled to understand it. Hannah (aged 23) perceived that one difficulty for women may be the need to retain entitlement to a level of Tax Credits. If they earned over the eligibility level they would lose the credits (such as Housing Benefit) and she felt this was one of the factors inhibiting women from applying for senior posts. She also commented however that " ... a lot of people then because they have kids, you know like women I mean, because they have kids can't do the longer hours..." suggesting that she felt there had to be a trade off between focusing on work or family.

Shirley (aged 24) recalled having read an article in a newsletter at work about the small number of men working in the whole health care area – but that they took up the majority of top posts:

"... Like there was loads and loads of women doing the grafting and they [the men] ended up having the top high earning jobs and you sort of think why?"

A number of young women posed questions about why there were such inequalities in higher positions. A factor mentioned by many was the implications of women requiring maternity leave. There was also some discussion of the small number of men working in what were perceived to be traditional female positions – such as child care work and nursing and how gender stereotyping acted to keep them out of those areas. Reference was made to the dominance of men in senior positions in the youth service and in teaching, areas where there are large numbers of female workers. Adrienne (aged 23), in response to a question about why this might be the case in the youth service, said:

"I don't know, hopefully its nothing to do with the fact that they get more respect or anything like that maybe they are more career driven ...//...maybe it's to do with because women have family and stuff. Like you wouldn't like to think that that would be an obstacle to progressing like, but who knows?"

Nat felt that women had to try harder and do better to be recognised:

"I feel its easier for men to climb the ladders in certain jobs ...//... women have to work harder for their jobs to be noticed...//... if I don't work as hard as I do then I wouldn't get any recognition for what I do, whereas the boys would." (Nat, aged 24)

Nat works in a very male dominated environment (door work at bar) and talked of having to be a different person at work:

" ... it can be quite difficult sometimes because you have to be a different person like in work ...//... I would be all quite macho and get on quite blokey because I'm surrounded by guys and you have to be in that or you'll be seen as quite weak."

The view was also expressed that sometimes women 'got on' particularly in managerial positions by behaving like men. Nat did not feel this was a good approach arguing that: "... I don't think anything's going to change if they are continually gonna go that way ..."

The young women who tended to have most to say on the above issues were at the upper end of the age band, perhaps because they had more experience of working full time and were observing visible inequalities. However, young women across the age range provided a range of examples of stereotyping in employment and perceptions of what are 'appropriate' jobs for women and men. Some young women indicated that they felt men were more suited than women to particular jobs. Examples given tended to be trades or jobs requiring physical strength. For example, Rachel talked about how if she required a plumber she would feel happier with it being a man. Michelle (aged 19), while responding that there are not jobs that women can't do, went to say:

"...but like there is the whole kinda like stereotyping ...//... like for example a man can't be a nurse ...//... like no way would a man be a nurse kinda thing even though there is men's nurses but they are not that popular and ye couldn't imagine a woman being a mechanic like, its more a man's job."

Youth work was provided as an example of being perceived more as a woman's job because it was perceived to be part of the 'caring professions'. A few young women mentioned the lack of women in trades – which were seen as 'good jobs' that women didn't have the opportunity to do.

Molly, a 20 year old university student, was very adamant that while she thought joinery was a very good job she wouldn't go into it, adding that

"Maybe if things were different you know. If say women ... did go into that sort of thing".

Avril, a 21 year old woman with a disability noted that: "girls can do nursing and boys can do doctoring ... boys can't do like dancing, like a dance teacher. Boys can't do that". A strong idea of division of jobs along gender lines was a feature of the interviews with young women with disabilities (see McAllister and Neill, 2005 for further discussion).

There was a fairly strong sense of injustice from many of the young women about the unequal treatment of women and men, especially in relation to the labour market. And yet, as will be seen in the subsequent section on home and family, there was often an assumption that women would take on the bulk of household responsibilities.

"...I don't think its fair the fact that men get promoted quicker than females do an I don't think its fair that they get a better wage because even though they're doing the same job just because he's a man an she's a woman like its not fair ...//... a woman works ten times harder I would feel cause she's goes home and she raises the family too ..." (Michelle, aged 19)

"They say its more equal but I still think that there's inequality still in the workplace ...//... that the majority of managers and things like that there are still male... so okay like the woman can work here, yes that's ok, ...//...but once you go up the tiers of the workplace ...//...generally more male orientated." (Nicola, aged 20)

"First of all people keep saying about equal opportunities in the workplace. Now first of all, maternity leave, a fella will not employ a woman if she's married. I don't care what the law says, he'll think up a reason to turn round and tell her she hasn't got the job because she's likely to have a child. Women do not get into places of power..." (Jo, aged 17)

Kativa (aged 17), a young women from an ethnic minority background, portrayed a picture of a very gendered home environment and talked of how traditional perceptions in her culture would be that women should be mostly housewives and should not go into higher education. But she noted that some things were changing and gave the example of women becoming pilots and bus drivers.

The thoughts of one young woman rather depressingly portrayed a view of gender stereotyping which subscribes to the idea that women gain advantages over men by virtue of their sex and sexuality. Women, she said, can progress by using the fact that they are women:

"No I think its harder for men, for like getting jobs, cos women have, as people would mostly say, they have their assets basically...they do use that as an advantage."

She linked this to ability to get a job and to get into clubs she pointed out that although she herself would not do this that all girls have to do "is show a bit of skin". (Melissa, aged 16)

One young woman found that the reality of doing a job generally perceived as 'man's work' was that she could do it differently (ironically often because of male perceptions about women in that role) and therefore more effectively. Working as a door person in a club she observed that the response from customers was very different when they realised she was a woman. This diffused difficult situations because men would not want to be seen hitting a woman. Interestingly, she had initially perceived her job as one that a woman couldn't do but now she realised that doing it well did not require physical strength but the ability to talk and reason with people.

Generally, while there were some strong views about the lack of equality in the workplace and the injustice and unfairness of this, these views have to be understood in the context of views on the division of labour within the home and the assumption of many that being with a partner and/or having children would mean focusing less on a career.

4.12.3 Employment, career and family

There is no doubt that women's lives have changed significantly over the last century, but to what extent are traditional gender roles being challenged? A review of social attitudes in Northern Ireland between 1994 and 2002 (Gray and Robinson, 2004) suggests that attitudes towards gender roles did not differ greatly over these years and the 2002 findings show little significant difference by age of respondent. Responses to a number of questions in the 2002 survey suggest a conservative view of gender roles in Northern Ireland. Particularly strong views emerged when people were asked about when women should or should not work outside the home with only 8% of respondents agreeing that a woman should work outside the home when there was a child under school age. What then were the views of the young woman in this research?

Erin (aged 19), when asked if it was possible for a woman to be a good mother and a have a job at the same time, said:

"you could fit it in ...//...but you'd be fitting it in round his school hours and stuff...//...I think you can only be a good mother if you're gonna be there for the wean...//... when they're in secondary school like you could have that job cos they're gonna be coming in from school at 4 o'clock...//...you're gonna have your full days work done."

The idea that employment as something which should be fitted in around the needs of children was very common:

"What they can do is stay at home until the baby is about 3, and then when the child goes into play group then they can go back to work." (Vanessa, aged 21)

Although a significant number of young women in this study had mothers who worked, a number of references were made to mothers fitting work around family commitments by taking on part-time work. There were a number of references to mothers having a 'wee part-time job', or in one case making a decision to leave work because she could not manage to undertake all the household responsibilities and work full-time. There was an implicit assumption that this juggling on the parts of mothers was 'normal' and something that women just had to do. It is also noteworthy that several young women referred to grandmothers taking a key role in terms of housework and childcare when mothers worked.

"She didn't work for a while, for a long time, just because she was raising us. Then she got a part-time job..." (Nat, aged 24)

"... My mum didn't, or if she did it was kinda like part-time jobs, like during the day if we were at school or whatever..." (Susie, aged 20)

Interestingly, a number of young women talked about mothers seeking different employment or gaining qualifications when children were older. Again, this was seen as 'natural' and ok, although one respondent noted that her mother's studying had resulted in other people in the house having to do more.

A number of young women were emphatic that you could have a career and be a good mother. Those young women who expressed this view frequently cited their own mothers as examples. A number linked the ability to have a career to being well enough paid to afford good child care. One young woman pointed to the success of her mother in working and having a family and said that she herself would like to continue to work when she had a family but raised the issue of social perceptions:

"I just think they are under more pressure [women] as well like in the home as well... they say that roles are starting to reverse slightly but still the pressures on the woman or if they have children does the women go back to work, does the woman stay at home, is she expected to look after the children and work and clean the house?" (Nicola, aged 20)

The ability of women to be able to juggle their various commitments, the need for mothers to spend time with children and the implications of doing all this were raised by some of the young women. Kativa (aged 17) expressed the view that it would be very difficult and might depend on the job. She was concerned about how she would manage and about how her mother managed to do so much. A number of the young women who were mothers spoke of the difficulties of juggling housework, a job and possibly education as well.

One young woman felt pessimist about the ability to do it all, saying, "its trying to balance the impossible" and concluded that she wouldn't want to see herself in that position (Karen, aged 19).

Nicole, a 25 year old youth worker suggested that if she met someone and had children she would give up her career

"... I also think if I ever met someone and please God I will, I mean got married, I think I would give up my career".

Her views linked to her feeling that she would "love the 'housewife role" pointing out that she wouldn't leave her children with a child minder. She would consider the option of working part-time. Her rationale is based on a number of things: she begins by saying she would love to be a housewife and bring up her own children and then goes on to say that she feels it would be "too emotionally draining to be working with young people" and then going home to look after her own children.

The sometimes conflicting feelings young women have about family and about work are hardly surprising. They are subject to the strong messages that have been emanating from governments extolling the virtues of paid work (particularly stressed in relation to lone parents and other welfare claimants). Carole Pateman (1992) has argued that employment is the key to citizenship pointing to the problems this creates for a number of groups in society. The emphasis on paid work as the only route to inclusion has been challenged for the way in which it relegates and demotes the important and demanding nature of other forms of work that many women in society are involved in (McAlister, 2007; Lister, 1997; Witz, 1997). On a practical level, this 'other' work (including the caring work carried out by a number of young women in this study) impacts on the ability of women to take up employment and results in part-time employment being seen as the best way to juggle domestic and family responsibilities (McKie, 2001). There are pressures to conform to traditional expectations about gender roles set down by society – by parental practices in the home and expectations of children and young people regarding domestic labour (as can be seen in chapter 3). Leonard (1999: 626) argues that "young people are not just observers of a sexual division of labour within the household but are the direct participants in such a segregated system".

4.13 EDUCATION, TRAINING AND THE CONFLICT

One of the most distinctive features of the Northern Ireland schools system is segregation. The system is segregated by ability (and some would suggest class) into grammar and secondary schools, many schools are segregated by gender[10] and around 95% of school children attend Catholic or predominantly Protestant primary and secondary schools. While only about 5% of all school pupils in Northern Ireland attend integrated schools, it is estimated that due to a shortage of places that around 1,000 pupils each year are turned away (McGlynn, 2004). Furthermore, despite plans to expand the provision of integrated schools this has been slow and met with a number of stumbling blocks (Smith, 1999). As a result, some areas still have no integrated school provision and access for others is limited (Kilkelly et al., 2004).

While there is a lack of agreement about the impact of the religious segregation of schools, research since the 1970s has indicated the potential harmful affects in terms of perpetuating negative inter-group attitudes and ultimately the conflict (Neins & Cairns, 2004: 337). As Kilkelly et al. (2004: xvii) note in their analysis of children's rights in Northern Ireland:

> Far from being 'havens of peace' in an otherwise 'conflict affected society' the heavily segregated education system ... is considered by many to exacerbate the legacy of sectarianism and division.

In recognition of this, a number of initiatives have been devised over the past 30 years or so in an attempt to minimise the impact of institutional segregation. This has included initiatives to increase contact between Catholic and Protestant schools and the incorporation of community relations into all areas of teaching through the integration of Education for Mutual Understand (EMU)[11] and Cultural Heritage as cross cutting themes in the statutory curriculum.

Evidence of the impact and value of each of these initiatives, however, remains disappointing. It is suggested that there is still no direct form of co-operation between controlled and maintained schools (Kilkelly et al., 2004) and evidence of the long-term success of contact programmes on sectarian attitudes is far from clear-cut (Neins & Cairns, 2004). Furthermore, over a decade after the inclusion of EMU and Cultural Heritage into the statutory curriculum, research suggests that its impact has been limited (Leitch & Kilpatrick, 1999). It is the view of some that the very nature of these programmes in terms of their content, their implementation as a peripheral rather than focused aspect of the school curriculum and the lack of adequate training for teachers in dealing with sensitive issues has been a major reason for their perceived lack of success (see Neins & Cairns, 2004: 339; Smith, 1990: 6). Indeed in relation to the various initiatives undertaken it has been suggested that "some of these may merely represent morphological change at a relatively superficial level which does little to challenge the existing power relationships within the society" (Lemish, 1993 cited in Smith, 1999: 10).

These issues are important to this research in terms of setting the context in which young women experience compulsory education but also in relation to what they did, or did not, talk about in relation to their education experiences. On first analysis of our data, for example, we found that when explicitly discussing the conflict that few young women made reference to schools and education. Further, that when discussing education that there was no great discussion of the impact of religious segregation (this was not true of all and will be returned to shortly). Yet, an absence of this discussion is revealing because all of the young women who took part in the

---

10 Smith (1999: 3) notes that a quarter of secondary schools and almost one half of grammar schools in Northern Ireland are single-sex.

11 "Education for Mutual Understanding is about self-respect, and respect for others, and the improvement of relationships between people of differing cultural traditions" (cited in Smith, 1999: 5).

research were asked about their experiences of PSE, pastoral care and related subjects in schools (e.g. form class, Home Economics and Religious Education). While to varying degrees they discussed covering issues such as drugs and alcohol, bullying and peer relations, sex education, road safety, healthy eating and emotional health, little reference was made of any discussion of community relations and the exploration of cultural difference. Indeed, in light of her life experiences after school, Nat (aged 24) reflected of her school experience that:

"There's nothing to prepare you, for you know how do you balance your money properly and teaching you about money and different cultures, and respect for people, it's nothing to do with that ..." (Grammar, controlled, co-ed.)

While Nat was one of the older young women in the sample, she was still at school when EMU was introduced into the statutory school curriculum (1992). Furthermore, across all school types and ages there was little discussion of work being undertaken in schools around cultural diversity (bar two young women who had attended integrated schools) - this is despite the relatively recent introduction of Citizenship Education in schools. Interestingly, Kativa (aged 17) told us that as part of a community group that she had been involved in the production of a school resource with a voluntary agency aimed at informing school pupils about different cultures. Kativa felt that this was an important resource yet had no knowledge of it ever being used[12]. Furthermore, there was no discussion of cross-community contact programmes as part of formal education but some young women had experience of these as part of youth and community groups (informal education) that had input on culture and diversity.

Despite the lack of discussion of the impact of the religious segregation of schools, many young women, (as illustrated throughout this report), were aware of the passing down of sectarian and divisive attitudes through parents and communities and Ellen (aged 22), felt strongly that schools were the place where children could be exposed to different attitudes and educated about difference:

" ... like no matter what it is, people bein' afraid of gay people, black, coloured people, people being afraid of Catholic, Protestant people. I think it's just their parents mindset and they just pass it onto their children, so I don't think it's got you know, I think it's just through generation and generation, and I think it just needs to be brought into children in school so that they're parents can't just go duh, duh, duh ..." (Grammar, RCM, single-sex).

Jemima (aged 20) also noted that in her community that those attending the local Catholic and Protestant schools which were positioned close to each other, would even walk up different sides of the street. This example further highlights the difficulty schools face in setting up and ensuring the long-term impact of school contact programmes.

The informal and hidden curriculum in schools has also been implicated in playing a part in the perpetuation and passing down of sectarian and/or divisive attitudes. Within our research, ten young women (all of whom attended Catholic Maintained or Irish Medium Schools) noted that sports within their schools included Gaelic Football, Camogie and/or Hurling. These sports, clearly associated with Irish culture, were not offered in any other type of school and in Catholic schools

---

12 While Kativa knew that the resource was not being used in her own school or any of the schools her friends attended, this does not necessarily mean that it was not being used in other schools. Yet her view and experience highlight the importance of those carrying out research and consultation with young people feeding back to them and informing them of what comes of the information they provide.

were often offered instead of the likes of Rugby. In research carried out regarding values in education in Northern Ireland, teachers noted the persisting political, religious and sectarian badges still associated with these sports (Smith & Montgomery, 1997: 2). Furthermore, competing with other schools through team sports means that some, because of the sports they offer (and do not offer), are limited to meeting with schools from their own religious community.

Additionally, while the young women noted that there was no direct discussion of segregation that there were implicit messages about 'the other community' from teachers and peers in school. Kim (aged 21), for example, noted that while it was not always explicit, that the message was clear:

"... it wasn't drilled into ye but it was just like 'don't hang round with Protestants' an' stuff like that there but ye were always told not to hang round with Protestants but I always did. ...//... in the Tech I hung around with Protestants an' even somea my friends were like "ah she's Protestant" an "do you know she's a Protestant?" an' I'm like "I don't care" like it's nothin to me it's the person it's not their religion or their colour or anythin' like that I really don't understand people like that." (Secondary, CMS, co-ed)

As seen here, these attitudes and views often extended beyond compulsory education and into further education. While children and young people may have little choice in the schools they attend, more choice is often available in post-compulsory education. Yet Donna (aged 21) told us how religious background could continue to limit or impact upon choices. She told us, for example, that young people in her community would decide upon which college of further education to attend based on their location and thus perceived religious background. She noted that those in her community would travel to a particularly college despite the added cost and the fact that the one located closer to their community offered much the same courses. Of the nearest college, Donna told us:

*" ... because it was mainly Protestant young people going, I think there's the fear ...//... a lot of the young fellas who wanted to go on and do a trade wouldn't go to **** (area). I think it was more fear."*

Furthermore, Oscar (aged 17) gave a vivid example of how religion continues to impact upon education decisions and the education experience beyond compulsory education. As well as the gender imbalance in her course, the religious imbalance also caused her discomfort:

"... the class was mixed as well so it was Catholic and Protestant an' it was a majority of Catholic and I'm Protestant and there was only two Protestants in the class as well so it was a bit uncomfortable cos they were all comin' in with their like Celtic [football] tops an' stuff on ..."

The religious segregation of communities not only impacts on decisions about where to study can also impact upon decisions of where to undertake training and jobs (see also chapter 6). A small number of young women told us of experiences or knowledge of religious discrimination in their places of employment, others noted that trades people would not enter certain areas to carry out work and Gráinne told us of how she would not attend a training programme in a particular area despite knowing that there were more young women on it because:

*"... if I was in **** [area] I wouldn't feel comfortable cos you don't know who's watchin' ye, you don't know who's wathcin' ye here either [her own community], but you feel more comfortable so you do."*

The religious segregation of schools and communities appear in many respects to complement each other and it remains difficult to see how full integration of either can be achieved without the other. Despite movement forward in terms of the increasing numbers of integrated schools, programmes for cross-community school contact and recognition and inclusion of issues regarding cultural diversity into the curriculum, there is clearly much work still to be done. Within this context it should be noted that schools face a difficult task and ever expanding roles in that "they have to deal with the impact on their pupils of the wider divisions in society while at the same time are expected to improve community relations through the education process" (Kilkelly et al., 2004: 195). While schools are receiving increased support in relation to the emotional development of young people, support and recognition in dealing with issues relating to the conflict appear in some respects to have lost political momentum.

4.14 RECOMMENDATIONS

- For many young women school, and pressure to succeed, is a major source of stress. For some this impacts negatively on general health and well-being. Schools need to ensure a balanced approach to study. This could be done by promoting positive physical and mental health as an integrated aspect of the school ethos.

- Examples of good practice emerging from the research include the value of appropriate counselling support in schools. The recent announcement of £1.7 million for counselling services in post-primary schools in Northern Ireland is to be welcomed. Monitoring and evaluation of this should consider the extent to which needs are being met and how timely access can be ensured.

- Given policy concerns about obesity and the physical and emotional well- being of young women and the health targets government has set for improvement in these areas, it is important that negative perceptions of sports and PE in schools are understood and addressed. This means that the issues should be examined from a gender perspective and include the psychology of young women's non-participation.

- The findings from the NICCY commissioned research on bullying (Schubotz and Sinclair, 2006) showed that individual schools vary greatly in the way in which they develop and implement anti-bullying policies. Much of the research in this area points to the need for more stringent requirements to be placed on schools (taking account of good practice recommendations emanating from research) to ensure effective policies are developed, implemented, standardised and monitored.

- The findings from this research point to teachers requiring additional information and support in a number of areas. These include:

  - Child protection and abuse: there were examples of teachers not acknowledging abuse or intervening appropriately. Teachers need to be supported to feel confident to react positively;

  - Traditional and sexist gender roles and stereotypes: these were being reinforced in school. Understanding of gender roles and diversity needs to be integrated across the curriculum for teacher training;

  - Subject choice: this has been shown to often be gendered, and ideas about 'suitable' subjects and careers appear to be very entrenched. Addressing this requires schools and teachers to understand the subtleties regarding gender stereotyping in careers and work proactively to widen opportunities and choices for young women.

- In the Northern Ireland context there could be a tendency for citizenship education in schools to focus largely on religious difference. It is important that the potential for using this part of the curriculum to address gender, race and class issues is maximised.

- It would appear from the findings of a number of research studies that the core components of effective careers education and guidance are not fully implemented. A number of recommendations were made in the report of the Women and Work Commission (2006) regarding careers guidance. The Department for Communities and Local Government in England (DCLG, 2006) has published an action plan setting out its planned actions with regard to the Commission's recommendations. The Department for Education and Skills in England is developing National Standards to ensure that young people receive careers information, advice and guidance that is free from gender stereotyping. This is due to be published in 2007. Clearly this issue also requires policy attention and action and subsequent implementation in Northern Ireland by DE and DEL. This should include provision for more individually tailored and holistic advice. It is worth considering if this is something that can best be provided by teachers in light of the weight of their other commitments or whether young people would benefit from more structured, on-going contact with independent careers advisers in formal partnerships with schools.

- Gender stereotyping and discrimination also needs to be addressed in relation to work experience. This means ensuring that not only are limitations, overt or more subtle, removed but that girls and young women are actively encouraged to choose non-traditional placements.

- We endorse the recommendation of research conducted on behalf of the Northern Ireland Commissioner for Children and Young People that "there should be a concerted strategy to address issues relating to the impact of the conflict and religious segregation in schools" (Kilkelly et al., 2004: 195).

Education, Training and Employment

Chapter Five

Place, Space and Time:
Young Women
and Leisure

PLACE, SPACE AND TIME: YOUNG WOMEN AND LEISURE

"Work, go to school, do my homework ...//... I don't really have much time for anything else." (Jill, aged 17)

5.1 INTRODUCTION

With the introduction of the Welfare State (1945) and the 1944 Youth Welfare Act (NI) one could say that we saw the full establishment of a Youth Service in Northern Ireland. That is, one based within the policy of government rather than churches and communities with an expectation of greater regulation and accountability. Further to this, a key priority outlined by the Youth Welfare Act (1944) was that work with girls (sic) should be regarded with equal importance as work with boys (sic). That said, the Act also suggested that the new positions of full-time Youth Workers might be best filled by ex-military. From its establishment, therefore, there was a dominance of male staff with a focus on physical pursuits most often associated with young men.

The main change to this approach came in the Northern Ireland 1961 White Paper Development of the Youth Service which emphasised a move away from youth work focusing merely on physical sport and recreation to a more general focus on the role of youth work as informal education. Although this signalled a clear opportunity for a more inclusive Youth Service which could work more holistically with and for young women as well as young men, by the 1970s the Youth Service in Northern Ireland was making a distinct break from that of the rest of the UK. At a time of heightened civil unrest in Northern Ireland and fears about the levels of violence among young men who spent much of their free time on 'the streets', attention once again turned to them. In an attempt to occupy the free time of young men, it is arguable that the needs of young women became invisible. Indeed, although a 1978 report outlined the lack of provision for young women in the Youth Service and young women's 'drop-out' from youth clubs at a fairly young age, by the late 1980s little was being done to address the under-representation of young women in the Youth Service in Northern Ireland.

It could be argued that this trend continued into the 1990s and is still evident in many respects today. In the 1990s YouthAction Northern Ireland carried out research assessing Youth Service provision for young women which again highlighted many inadequacies (Trimble, 1991). The findings of this research revealed that young women were continuing to disengage with Youth Service provision at a young age, that they were not actively encouraged to attend youth provision and that programmes continued to be aimed at boys and young men and were, therefore, unattractive to girls and young women. This report was pivotal in informing policy and practice and many providers took the recommendation onboard that single-sex youth work was of value. That said, research continues to suggest that young people are dropping out of youth provision between the ages of 14 and 16 (Geraghty et al., 1997; Hall et al., 1999).

Further to this, while not disaggregated by gender, Northern Ireland based research provides us with some information about young people's use of youth provision and their views of it. Research commissioned by the Youth Council for Northern Ireland in 2004, for example, revealed that 65% of those aged 16-25 did not feel that there was sufficient provision for teenagers and young adults in the areas in which they lived. Having said this, 77% of this age group reported that they had, at some point, attended youth service organisations. The reasons most often put forward for stopping attendance at youth provision were that young people had simply grown out of it (68%), while significant proportions also noted 'having other things to do' (38%) and a 'poor range of activities' (27%) (YCNI, 2004: 95-97). The majority of young people who attend youth services in Northern Ireland are under 16 years of age, and in 2004 only a quarter of all 16-18 year olds attended such provision (cited in Kilkelly et al., 2004: 205). Further research in Northern Ireland with school children up to the age of 16 found that 66% of those who discussed play and leisure complained about being unable to access appropriate play, leisure or youth provision within their local areas. This research reports that "pupils aged 14-16 were particularly likely to criticise the recreational amenities available to teenagers ..." (Davey et al., 2004: 32). Our research allows for a greater qualitative examination of some of the issues raised in previous research with direct reference to young women's views and experiences.

A pivotal moment for the development of work with young women lay with the implementation of the 1987 *Policy for the Youth Service in Northern Ireland* (DENI), which defined a curriculum for youth work. The policy included nine core requirements which should be taken into account in the design and delivery of youth work programmes; one of which referred specifically to the "encouragement and preparation for participation on an equal basis by young men and young women" (DENI, 1987a). This policy gained further momentum through the publication of *Into the Mainstream* (YCNI, 1994) which provided curriculum guidelines to promote the participation of young women in youth service provision. These policy guidelines raised awareness of gendered programming and the under-representation of young women in the youth service. However, the full potential of *Into the Mainstream* was lost through the ensuing Policy and Curriculum Review process, which lasted from 1996 to 1999. The *Into the Mainstream* document did not sufficiently imbed into youth work practice in the integral way that the Curriculum Core Requirements did. As such, an opportunity for the comprehensive participation of girls and young women advocated through the *Into the Mainstream* document was lost. As a consequence, provision for girls and young women very much depended on how each individual youth worker interpreted the core requirement from the Youth Service Curriculum: provision of hairdressing and powder rooms through to young women's health projects, could equally fulfil this core requirement.

Despite clear advances in the youth service in Northern Ireland in terms of its focus and the breadth of work it encompasses, even by the late 1990s the specific gender focus within youth service policy had been sidelined. *Youth Work: A Model for Effective Practice* (1997), the revised youth curriculum 10 years on, set out the three key principles of youth work as preparation for participation, testing values and beliefs, and acceptance and understanding of others. Perhaps then, there is the assumption that issues relating to gender and youth provision have been reconciled and that 'equality of opportunity' has been achieved.

This chapter examines young women's use of youth provision within their own communities and beyond and their views and experiences of it. Particular attention will be paid to the barriers they face in relation to accessing and using youth provision and conversely the value of it for young women in their early years through to young adulthood. More generally, it will offer an examination of young women's leisure or free time, the factors which influence and impact upon it and the challenges this poses for the Youth Service. Further to this, in light of the prevalence of young women's involvement in 'street-based' leisure and the under-researched nature of this issue, we will pay particular attention to this from a female viewpoint.

While much research has examined the experiences of young people in rural areas in relation to accessing youth provision and other services (e.g. Geraghty et al., 1997; Shucksmith, 2004; Storey & Brannen, 2000), this research–through including sub-samples of young women from urban, rural and suburban areas–provides a more holistic picture of their experiences of youth provision. It will be shown here, that much the same issues affect all young women regardless of geographical setting. Indeed, the issues of age, gender and place/locality are pertinent in all of the young women's accounts and it will be illustrated that despite the assumption that gender no longer needs to be explicit on the youth work agenda, in light of these young women's experiences this is certainly not the case.

5.2 AGE, GENDER AND LOCALITY: BARRIERS TO PARTICIPATION IN YOUTH PROVISION

Thirty-one of the forty-three young women interviewed (72%) reported having, at some stage, been involved in youth provision. This ranged from local youth clubs, faith-based youth provision (e.g. Youth Fellowship), uniformed organisations (e.g. Girl's Brigade) and youth programmes (e.g. structured programmes). Those who reported no involvement noted that this was because there was no provision within their local area, that provision was not accessible or appropriate to their needs or that they were involved in other forms of leisure such as sports clubs. While some young women had more than one experience, 18 had been involved in youth clubs at some point, 14 were involved in youth programmes (seven on more than one occasion), seven were involved in uniformed youth groups and three were involved in faith-based youth groups. Indeed six young women noted that their main (and sometimes only) leisure activity at the time of interview was involvement in youth groups. Such groups included: youth clubs, youth drama groups, youth fellowship (church-based groups) and programmes specific to their needs (e.g. groups for young women/people with disabilities, young mothers, LGBT youth). Of further interest, one young woman with learning disabilities noted that involvement in a youth group was her only social activity as she had limited social networks and opportunities for socialising.

5.2.1 Local Provision and Transport Disadvantage

Thirty-six young women discussed the facilities within their local areas available to young people and the vast majority (83%) felt that these were insufficient. While there was little difference in the views of those from urban and rural areas (82% of the former and 83% of the latter felt there were insufficient facilities), all of those living in suburban areas (n=5) felt that there was a lack of facilities within their area for young people. Indeed, those young women who reported that most of their leisure time when younger was spent in friend's housing or visiting the cinema etc., noted that this was often because there were no accessible youth facilities in their local areas.

While a number of young women reported no local youth clubs (often because of losing funding), others noted that they had to travel some distance to the nearest youth club, that youth clubs were based in churches which put them off attending or that they were not age appropriate. Thus, while there may well have been some youth provision, its value for young women is questionable given that they felt there was little for young people in their local area. There was also a sense of frustration among a number of young women who had attempted to set things up themselves, seen their local provision close due to lack of funding or felt they had been promised something and been let down. Kelly told us of a local rural development initiative in her area, which despite promises, had set up nothing specific for children and young people. As a result, children were attending adult events with parents just for something to do:

"They're not really putting stuff on for them [young people], there was talk em, like at Christmas time there was talk that they were going to do a summer scheme on for the kids, like me and my sister were asked to do it, then there was nothing else came of it. So, the kids are coming maybe, cus they're only about six or seven, like seven year olds, they're coming cus their parents are coming, but there's

nothing really, nothing really for them. But they enjoy coming just to see everybody else." (Kelly aged, 21 – rural area)

Funding was an issue of concern raised by young women in urban and rural areas alike, a number of whom stated that their local youth clubs had closed due to a lack of funding. Of their local youth club and annual sports day and festival Victoria told us:

"A lot of things lookin' back has fell through now, like we used to have a sports day and a festival every year and there used to be youth clubs and everything but ...//... there was a committee but I think it's all to do with insurance now that they can't get it up and runnin'." (Victoria, aged 22 - rural area)

Furthermore, the drop-in centre in Nicola's local area (also rural) had closed due to a lack of funding leaving only a club for children and nothing for young people in the area, and Janine had seen her local youth club close and was now worried that detached youth workers within the area (who had previously helped her) were also going to loose their funding:

"... all their funding's running out soon and they don't know if they'll get their jobs back, which is wrong because a lot of kids do need youth workers to be able to show them their way." (Janine, aged 17 - urban area)

Young women in all areas made a link between a lack of appropriate youth provision, young people 'hanging about the streets' and anti-social behaviour. Indeed, most of those who said that they spent most of their free-time involved in underage drinking (in homes, parks or the street), related this to a lack of other activities within their local areas, or the inaccessibility of youth provision. When asked what she used to do when a teenager, Carmel (aged, 23 – urban area) answered similarly to other young women:

> **Carmel:** Nothin', drunk and smoked joints
> **SM:** Just hang out?
> **Carmel:** Hang out yeah in fields or building sites or up at the shop. Ya know there was nowhere else really to go ...//... There was places to go maybe eh in ya know like the council estate. They had big places. Community Centres that's what you call them (laughs) ...//... We weren't in [them], we used to drink outside them cos we came from the other end of town ya know.

Carmel, by her own definition, lived in a middle class area and it is interesting to note that she felt that there was more available for young people in working class areas. That said, her experiences, among others, perhaps highlights the fact that service deprivation or inaccessibility of services can be a feature of all areas and impacts upon all young people, irrespective of socio-economic status.

Also related to the issue of youth provision and locality, all but one of those who discussed the difficulties of accessing services due to a lack of good quality and affordable transport were young women living in rural areas. These discussed how where they lived, the isolation of areas, limited local facilities and services, a poor bus service and/or a reliance on lifts, meant that they would often spend much of their free-time in their own area. Indeed these young women often noted how they and their friends were eager to learn to drive and often did so at the earliest opportunity and talked about the 'freedom' this had brought.

Living in an isolated area, often with poor public transport impacted upon the young women in different ways. All noted that they often had to rely on lifts from parents or the expense of taxis and that this limited their social opportunities/activities. Pauline (aged 23), for example, talked of how her friends lived too far away for her to visit them often which resulted in her hanging about 'the streets' with a group of older young men when she was younger. Shirley (aged 24), on the other hand, felt that the greatest impact was upon her opportunities to be involved in after school activities:

"I loved football, but it started after school, and that was a disaster cus there was only one bus home from *** [area where school was] and mummy was working so she couldn't collect us you know afterwards. So I sorta had to give that there up cus there was no way I could get home …//… [I] just remember it being a pain in the ass if you wanted to stay behind afterwards it was always a disaster trying to get home."

Reliance upon parents for lifts, as Shirley says, is not always possible. Jill (aged 17) also noted that until recently when she passed her driving test that she had curbed her social life as she did not want to continually ask for lifts:

"Mummy always had to take me everywhere and that wasn't really fair I didn't think, and I got to the point where I didn't ask her to take me places."

Storey & Brannen (2000: 2) note that reliance on lifts "underlines young people's dependence on their parents and limits their autonomy".

While all of these young women lived in different rural areas, buses were typically limited. In one area there were only two buses to the closest town everyday, in others the service stopped around 7.00-8.00 every night meaning that there was no way home from friend's houses or the cinema. Furthermore, it was noted that buses were not particularly cheap and that the journey was often long or they would have to get up very early in order to ensure that they got the bus to be in time for college. Related to this, a number of young women noted that actually getting to the nearest bus stop could be difficult. Nicole (aged 25) explained:

"For me like I would have to walk about I suppose two or three mile to kinda get the local [bus]. The Ulsterbus went on the main road and whenever you lived four or five side roads away from that like it was never just a casea getting the bus. Never had access to anything."

A lack of accessible public transport, reliance on lifts and the added expense of accessing facilities and services meant that many young women from rural areas spent much of their younger years in their own local areas (where facilities were also limited). While many now drove and had access to their own car, this may not be particularly reflective of young women in general as this is an expense that all may not be able to afford (see Hine & Grieco, 2003). Furthermore, while the focus here is upon transport disadvantage and the impact upon young women's access to leisure and social activities/opportunities, it is illustrated in chapter 7 that this can also impact upon access to other services, particularly those relating to young women's sexual health.

Research suggests that for those living in rural areas, isolation, access to transport, facilities and services and the visibility of living in a small community can compound feelings and experiences of exclusion and add to the usual list of factors (e.g. class, gender, sexuality, disability etc.) that can affect young people's lives and life chances (Pavis et al., 2001; Shucksmith, 2004). While not detracting from this, it is important to reiterate the point that within this research, young women from all areas discussed a lack of appropriate youth provision within their local areas. This, in fact, appeared to be the case particularly for those living in suburban, and what might be perceived as middle class areas.

5.2.2 Perceptions and Experiences of Youth Clubs

Many young women had experience of local youth clubs, from their descriptions it became clear that these almost all involved unstructured activities and were predominantly focused upon sports and physical activities. While many described their experiences of youth clubs when younger in a positive way, it became clear that this was often because of a lack of alternatives, and that if nothing else these provided a place to meet. The following accounts are typical of the young women's experiences of youth clubs:

"We just went and chatted and watched TV and played the Playstation and had movie nights and stuff." (Jill, aged 17 – rural area)

> **Jemima:** I've went to youth clubs an' stuff whenever I was growin' up an' things like that but ye jus' never had a big range of activities, it was either football or pool. An' like I jus' wasn't one for playin' football so.
> **KM:** An' was, it was mostly the boys that were interested in -
> **Jemima:** It was boys an' football.
> **KM:** An' what did the girls do when -
> **Jemima:** The girls usually jus' sat an' played a board game or somethin' an' hang about, ye know, 'I wanna go an' play board games on a Friday night' it doesn't quite work does it? (aged 20 – rural area)

For young women not interested or confident in sports, in many cases the only other option was watching TV or listening to music. In short, their needs were often not being assessed or met. The activities on offer acted as a disincentive for some young women to attend youth clubs and impacted others' decisions to cease attending:

"I just couldn't be bothered goin' to these clubs cus there's nothin' else to do just playin' pool and tennis and football." (Avril, aged 21 – rural area)

Related to this, a number of young women explicitly stated that their local youth provision did not provide a space for young women, and that this was a reason why they had ceased attending:

"I used to go to **** (youth club) but there's hardly ever anything on. [It was] mostly just somewhere to sit, cus they had that [a girl's space] on for us before and we liked it, but then they started bringing the wee lads in. They were taking over everything, they were taking over the games, the pool, the whole lot. So everyone just backed off and left it for themins." (Mia, aged 17 – urban area)

Finally and related to this, Nicole (aged 25 – rural area) discussed why she and some of her female friends dropped out of sports-focused youth clubs between the ages of 13 and 14 and the lack of alternatives open to them:

> **KM:** What age would you say that you really stopped going?
> **Nicole:** I suppose it woulda been thirteen, thirteen/fourteen. I woulda pushed it out as much as I could and that's cus I absolutely love sports but there was a lot of girls coming into puberty and all that there, conscious I suppose but I wasn't and I was happy enough playing with the boys ...//... I woulda dropped off and then there wouldn't a been anything else except camogie and football ...//... it's so hard in our area because like GAA is the centre of the community and if you are involved in it brilliant, and if you're not there's nothing ...//... A lot of us woulda have got involved cus we knew that if we didn't there was nothing else and you got involved even if you liked it or you didn't like it.

Nicole makes an important point here in relation to young women, puberty and body consciousness which is perhaps not fully understood when planning youth provision and when the focus is almost exclusively on sports-based activities. Furthermore, previous research among young people in rural areas of Northern Ireland has also pointed to the focus on sports and a lack of provision for young women not interested in this (Geraghty et al., 1997). Indeed, the GAA was originally founded to create a sense of masculinity "that emphasised virility, honour, strength, courage and dignity" (cited in Kitchin & Lysaght, 2004: 90). While there may be more young women involved in Gaelic football today, the young women here did discuss clear gender differences in terms of levels of funding, use of facilities (primarily owned by the men's club) and little support for the women's team.

Furthermore, while the focus on sports within youth clubs may not have been to many young women's liking, this is not to suggest that they had no interest in physical activities per se. A significant number of young women noted that they spent some or most of their free time involved in sport and/or exercise. This ranged from walking to team sports and regular visits to the gym and a number of young women when asked about their free time stated that they intended to join a gym in the near future. Sports and fitness, therefore, featured in the accounts of many young women's use of free time and was the main way in which nine young women spent their free time at the time of interview.

Overall, the lack of engaging youth provision for young women could be seen to have a very real impact on their everyday lives. As Neimh told us:

" ... **to be honest there isn't really much for us to do, especially for young girls. Like I mean there's bingo and all like, I mean bingo's loadsa granny's in it and me and my friend go, we have a laugh in it. But em, apart from that like there is nothing for us so there isn't and that's why I'm in all week, you never see me all week. Probably see me in Tesco on a Monday with my mummy getting the shopping in. Then I'm out at the weekends, you see that's the only way your life goes like, especially here, when there's nothing.**" (Neimh, aged 17 – urban area)

There is a hint of despondency in Neimh's last comment, that a routine or cycle evolves around having little to do in the area. For young women this often involved spending free time during the week in the home often helping with domestic tasks. This cycle is difficult to escape from as there is little else on offer to them.

Overall, there was little difference in the young women's descriptions of youth clubs across the three age groups and various areas. This might suggest that some forms of youth provision is still not meeting the needs of young women at a young age. While a place to meet is important, it should not be assumed that if young women do not want to play particular sports that they need no alternative activities. Such an ethos within youth clubs can effectively exclude young women from youth provision at a young age.

As well as the gender inappropriateness of youth provision, the young women also cited the age inappropriateness of provision as a factor which led them to drop-out in their early to mid-teens. Particularly with regards to youth clubs (which were often the only local provision they knew of), there was discussion of how these began to be dominated by younger groups:

"There were too many kids coming into it and started messing about and I just didn't wanna go then, so I just stopped going." (Neimh, aged 17 – urban area)

Decisions by friends to leave youth provision clearly impacted upon these young women's decisions to also cease attending. For these young women, attending youth clubs was a group activity, many noted that they were initially brought along by siblings or friends and that when friends moved on they often decided to do so too. This was sometimes despite the desire to stay but with unease about attending alone. It is possible that opportunities to volunteer and become young leaders could be more widely promoted within youth clubs and youth groups in order to encourage young women to continue attending when friends leave. More than this, however, it is also important that young women have something to naturally progress onto once they feel too old for youth clubs. As Michelle (aged 19) told us: "like from fourteen, fifteen up until eighteen there's not really anything to do ...". Notably, this was also around the age that young women were spending more of their free time on 'the streets'. This is clearly a difficult age group to capture but a small number did note the availability of more age-appropriate provision in local community centres or through other organisations and a positive experience of these. These, however, could be more actively promoted rather than leaving young women to 'happen upon' them by chance or through friends.

Perhaps some of what has been discussed here is not overly surprising – that youth provision needs to be gender and age appropriate, that a lack of youth provision is equated with anti-social behaviour, that threats to funding are ongoing, that local provision needs to be better advertised and that those in rural areas often have no local provision that they do not have to travel some distance to – yet the fact that these issues remain unchanged is very telling. Despite changes in youth provision since the 1987 policy statement it would appear that some traditional problems and divisions remain. Traditional responses have encouraged the use of single-sex work to address the needs of young women, which in itself cannot redress the imbalance of gendered activities in local youth provision. A more holistic approach to the inclusion of young women lies in the use of gender-conscious approaches to youth programming and to young people. This involves a pro-active approach to youth provision and programming which challenges gender stereotypes and provides opportunities and activities for young men and young women beyond those based on traditional gender roles and norms. In this way working towards equality of opportunity within youth provision is rooted in gender-conscious approaches, which feed into gender-conscious programming for an entire youth provider rather than merely a one-off response to 'a young women's issue'.

Furthermore, young people living in suburban areas report a complete lack of provision within their areas and feelings of isolation. It cannot be assumed that these young people are involved in other activities through schools or other clubs. Localised, appropriate and accessible provision is important for all young people. Karen shows why when talking of her younger sister:

"There's nothing for her either, I sorta feel sorry for her, like she's at the age were she can't go out and she can't, she's too young to go to other things. It would be good if there was a youth club for her to go and meet other people or whatever but there's just nothing so she would never ever go out around our way. There is a good lot of kids that would be around her age, it's kind of sad that way cos if there was a wee youth club that they could all go round to even once a week ...//... just even one night a week if they all went round even just as a confidence builder or whatever." (Karen, aged 19 - suburban area)

5.3 THE VALUE OF YOUTH PROVISION: PERSONAL AND SOCIAL DEVELOPMENT

Although of varying quality, those who attended youth facilities noted that these were local places which, if nothing else, provided "somewhere that was outta the house and [where] you were sitting with your friends" (Donna, aged 21 – urban area). Indeed Louise went further, noting that "it was good as well, just to get out and go to cos it always gave you like a routine and something to do" (aged 23 – urban area). The theme of 'getting out of the house' was strong across the accounts of all those who spent much of their free time involved in youth activities. Even if there were few options available within local youth centres etc. for young women, they were nonetheless important for providing a space/meeting place away from the family home. Thus, with regards to time spent in the home, we found that there was not so much evidence of a 'bedroom culture' (McRobbie, 2000) in terms of young women and their leisure but more of an 'invisible culture' of caring and domestic responsibilities[13]. Indeed, in a number of cases youth provision provided the only alternative to the home and the school, and was, the only time some young women had for themselves. As one young woman, who took on the majority of caring responsibilities for her younger siblings said of her involvement in a youth programme when younger:

"I liked it because it was just something to do and I wasn't in the house. And you were like always workin' towards a badge or working towards the display or something, [it] just give me something else to be thinking about, rather than thinking about looking after children all day." (Susie, aged 20 – urban area)

Thus, while youth provision was important to all of those young women who had utilised it, this was particularly the case for those who had few social outlets due to caring responsibilities or disabilities.

While most of the discussion to date has focused upon youth clubs which young women attended mainly up until the ages of 13 or 14 (but on occasion right up until 16), the remainder of the discussion focuses upon youth programmes. These, in contrast, to youth clubs, involved more structured activities, often to meet the needs of specific groups of young women (e.g. young mothers, young women who identified as other than heterosexual, young women with disabilities), or with a particular focus in mind (e.g. training, accreditation, drug awareness, sexual health, community relations, etc). Conversely, some such as drop-ins merely provided a social outlet for some groups. As previously noted, 14 young women had been or were involved in such programmes at the time of interview, half on more than one occasion and many had returned to this form of youth provision after years out of it. They were introduced to these through word-of-mouth (especially from friends and youth/community workers) and active recruitment by those who ran such programmes.

While the value of youth clubs were discussed primarily in terms of meeting friends and having fun, the value of youth programmes were much more expansive. Despite the varying nature of the programmes, six clear issues emerged as valuable across the young women's accounts: personal development and especially feeling more confident; peer support and learning; making new friends and the social aspects (e.g. enjoying themselves); learning new information and skills; shared experience and being exposed to difference. Throughout the young women's accounts and descriptions of these programmes it became clear that the core principles of youth work were being implemented and met on many occasions. That is, testing values and beliefs, personal and social development and promoting acceptance and understanding of others (DE, 2005).

---

13   See chapter 3 for more detail on the home lives of the young women, their differential levels of caring responsibilities and the domestic division of labour.

Kimberley's Experience

Kimberley was 21 at the time of interview and an in-patient in a Psychiatric Unit. Prior to this she resided in a training college for young people with learning disabilities for over a year. Some weekends, but not all, she would stay with her mother. Kimberley was often the only young person left in the college at weekends.

Kimberley moved to the Special Unit of a secondary school from 2nd to 5th year and while she described this as a positive experience, she received little or no information regarding sexual health or careers guidance. Of the latter she told us: "I had a learning disability so I didn't know anything ... I was in the Unit so they didn't really do anything". After leaving school Kimberley undertook training with a youth organisation running programmes for vulnerable young people. It was here that she received all of her careers guidance and her first work placement.

Upon leaving school Kimberley did not keep in contact with any friends and even while at school she told us that she rarely went out. From a fairly young age then, Kimberley's social networks were fairly limited, based around her immediate family, those within school or the course or programme she was undertaking at the time, yet there was generally little contact outside of these. It is perhaps for this reason that in talking of all of the courses, periods of work placement or youth programmes that she was involved in, Kimberley drew out the importance of the social aspects of these. With regards to one period of training through a youth organisation, for example, she told us that she "couldn't wait to get out [with them]".

It was during this period of training that Kimberley made the move to independent living and here we see that her experiences of extreme social isolation had a clear impact upon her mental well-being. Kimberley told us that she found the whole experience of independent living "scary" in almost every respect. She acknowledged that she did not eat well or generally look after herself and that she had little or nothing to do with her time and spent most of it in the house alone. She also did not have much of a social life at the time as she had limited finances and social networks ("I don't have any friends"), and visits from her family were rare. Asking her how she felt most of the time while living alone Kimberley told us that she was "sad and lonely".

Kimberley self-harmed seriously and made frequent attempts on her life whilst living on her own to the point of being hospitalised. Yet she talked of the value of a period of work placement (arranged through a youth provider) and her involvement in a youth programme (with another agency) after her discharge from hospital. For her the benefits of both of these were the social aspects of them and that they afforded her with the opportunity of "getting out and doing stuff". Kimberley also reinforced the importance for her of having something to do with her time in order to keep her mind busy and noted how she always looked forward to attending the current youth group she was involved with.

Those who attended groups which catered specifically to their needs talked in great detail about the value of shared experience and support, sometimes when they felt alone. This was particularly true for those who attended provision for young people who identified as other than heterosexual. Indeed, these noted the importance of having somewhere to meet that was different to the pub/club which was often their only meeting point. Of her first experience of a programme for LGBT youth, Nat (aged 24) told us:

"It had felt good to know, you know that there was some friends there that were maybe even goin' through the same thing as me ...//... So it was good to be able to talk freely about being gay to people who were gay, rather than my straight friends from school. So it was really helpful at the time."

Despite the value of this experience, Nat noted that this acted more as a drop-in and lacked direction and information, often resulting in the group ending up in the pub. She did, however, move on to another group exclusively for young women who identified as other than heterosexual which involved structured activities focusing on personal development, art and information. At the time of interview Nat was a peer educator within this group and said of this experience:

"I love it, I absolutely love it. It makes me feel like, I don't know, like I'm doin' a bitta good like and you know maybe teaching people a few things."

Susie (aged 20) was involved in three young LGBT projects at the time of interview. One as a volunteer and the others as a participant. Through these she felt that she had gained confidence and acquired new skills and knowledge. Of her experiences of these, she told us:

"I love it, yeah I really, really like it. When I only started, I used to sit and Anne [her friend] used to go [demonstrates friend nudging her]. And I used go 'Anne tell them I'm 17, Anne tell them my name's Susie'. I would never ever talk like even when we were doin' icebreakers and all, and now I can get up and like facilitate stuff and all which is good. Cus even Anne she came in, she hadn't been to **** [youth project] in about two years, and she came in and 'God it's like you're like a totally different person now'. It's really made me more confident and stuff which is good."

Despite their experiences, both Nat and Susie mentioned the initial difficulty and concern of attending these projects. While they had been encouraged to attend by friends, they nonetheless found their first experience daunting. Indeed Susie noted that the mixed-gender nature of one group meant that young women were often overshadowed and that some young people's comfort in their sexuality could be quite unnerving. For those young women who are not introduced by friends it is a lot to ask that they attend such programmes alone. Active recruitment and one-to-one pre-programme meetings in order to explain the nature of the group may alleviate some of this initial pressure/fear.

The importance of shared experience and confidence building was also evident in the accounts of young mothers who had attended programmes for this group. Again, they noted the importance of gaining new skills, training and accreditation, but it was the 'personal skills' of increased confidence and an understanding that they were not alone in their experiences which were also of great importance ("It was great, especially with the girls being young mothers themselves ...//... I really enjoyed it." – Pauline, aged 23). Furthermore, Carmel, like Nat and Susie found that she had gained confidence through her experiences and that peer learning and sharing her experiences had helped both herself and others:

"I didn't [talk] for weeks and weeks. I wouldn't open my mouth. But then I ended up and everyone was like 'oh Carmel that's brilliant'. I feel like wooo! ya know. And then I felt like 'oh god I helped someone'. That's where it started from too. So they work, they really do." (Carmel, aged 23)

Young women with learning disabilities on the other hand, while noting the importance of acquiring new skills and information, talked mostly about the social aspects of the programmes they had been involved in. Interestingly, all of those attending youth programmes noted that this was the main means through which they learned about sexual health in an informative, engaging and holistic fashion (see Chapter 7). It is important to note, however, that many of these young women were attending this provision in their late teens to early twenties and were, as such, not gaining this information at a young age when it might be most valuable.

What is interesting and important to note here is that many of the young women who had attended youth programmes had previously ceased attending youth clubs and other youth provision at a fairly young age (and for a variety of reasons). Yet with the encouragement of youth workers, health workers and friends they had returned to youth provision at a later stage in their lives and almost all reported a more positive and valuable experience of this. While the less-structured sport-based activities of youth clubs were accepted to a point in the younger years, they often provided something to do as opposed to doing nothing. This alone, clearly should not be the basis upon which youth provision is provided for young women and the mere fact that they attend (at least to a certain age), is not evidence in itself that such provision is meeting their needs. Indeed, it could be suggested that high levels of drop-out in the early to mid-teens demonstrates that this provision is not keeping them engaged. This research also reveals that as young women develop they enjoy more focused and structured programmes which are specific to their needs and interests[14]. Furthermore, despite the value of training and accreditation, most young women stressed the social skills they had developed through their experiences in youth programmes (particularly in terms of increasing their confidence) and the value of some of the information/knowledge they had acquired through these.

5.4 'STREET CULTURE' AND ALCOHOL USE

Twenty-eight young women provided details of their main leisure activities when they were around the age of 15-16. While 12 young women stated that they were still involved in sports or youth activities, the second most frequently cited past time was involvement in underage drinking on 'the streets', in parks or indoors (n=11). As previously noted, most of those who engaged in this activity related it to a lack of other appropriate or accessible youth provision in their local areas.

Throughout the accounts of all of those who had been involved in this activity, it became clear that drinking in the streets or other locations provided them with much the same as youth provision, that is, getting out of the house and being with friends. As Kim (aged 21 – rural area) said:

"There was an old derelict house out where we lived an' we all went there ...//... It was kinda gettin' outta the house as well, it was havin' a bitta time with all ma friends ...//... I could hang around with ma friends an' Ma wouldn't be complaining sort of a thing. I'd have to sneak out an' all the rest like, but it was relaxin' an' fun an' just talk rubbish."

14   See chapter 9 for a full discussion on young women's views regarding participation and their voice in youth provision.

"Standin' on street corners" (Tara, aged 19 – urban area), sitting in parks or derelict buildings often drinking or taking drugs (recreationally), has often been associated with the leisure activities of (working class) young men. Yet, a significant number of young women from different areas and socio-economic backgrounds had been involved in this activity when younger. The streets or outdoors provided a place to meet with friends away from the watchful eye of parents and was often the only such place available in areas with little accessible youth provision.

Whilst the term 'street-based' leisure is used here, it is used loosely as there were a number of places, other than street corners where the young women would meet and congregate with other young people. This included: empty buildings, around shops, behind leisure facilities, in car parks, fields and parks. The fact that young women may not be a clear visible presence on 'street corners' to the same degree as young men may be one reason why they have received less attention in this branch of literature, research and related policy (McAlister, 2007).

While not all of the young women who spent a large degree of their leisure time on 'streets' were necessarily involved in drug and/or alcohol use, most had been. The reasons they gave for being involved in street leisure are outlined above, but with regards to alcohol use, they overwhelmingly stated that this was due to lack of alternatives, boredom and following peers:

> **KM:** What kinda things did you do when you were growin' up?
> **Jemima:** Eh probably drink quite a lot out in the street (laughs), run away from the police (laughs), um maybe get caught by the police a few times drinkin' underage an' things like that there but there's really, ye know there was never a youth club for any young children an there's still not one within the local area apart from through churches an' most young people don't want to be associated with the church at ye know in their teenage years. (aged 20 – rural area)

"... what else is there just for like to have a bit of fun there's only substances, nobody offers anything better." (Karen, aged 19 – suburban area)

Again, while not all of the young women would have been causing trouble or necessarily gotten into trouble with the police or local residents, the potential for trouble to be caused or experienced was heightened because of this leisure activity (Agnew, 2003; Foster, 1990; Kennedy & Baron, 1993; Smith, 1986). While young women may have experienced risks similar to those of young men (e.g. exposure to drugs/alcohol, peer fighting and paramilitary intimidation), they also experienced further risks particular to their gender. That is, risks to their reputation and to their safety. As Fiona (aged 22) said:

"Well I know when we were younger and out having carry-outs ...//... everyone was disgusted with like girls drinking, but there was nonea that with the wee fellas. You know everybody was turning their noses up with us wee girls walking about with our carry-out or drunk or whatever."

A number of young women discussed the societal perception of young women and alcohol use, particularly drunkenness and/or drinking in public. This, they said went against what was perceived as 'feminine' and the way in which young women were 'supposed' to act:

"... it looks worse for young girls doing it, do you know what I mean, the whole lady-like, sorta thing, idiot thing." (Ellen, aged 22 – urban area)

Not only was the actual behaviour of drunkenness viewed in this manner but with this view came assumptions about young women's sexual activity. That is, that they were viewed as promiscuous or as Máiréad (aged 22 – urban area) put it "hallions" or "dirty wee bitches". In light of such perceptions, a number of young women themselves felt that women ought to know better and have more respect for themselves. Furthermore, there was a clear link made between young women, drunkenness, risks to safety and sexual health that was not evident when they discussed perceptions of young men and alcohol use. Thus, a number mirrored the societal opinion that women should not only know better because of the risk to their reputation, but also because of the risks to their safety:

"I suppose young women are vulnerable and stuff on the streets well, you know if they're seen as drinking and a man or something comes and he could do anything to them like." (Beyoncé, aged 25 – urban area)

Somewhat worryingly, notions of victim-blaming also came across in some of the young women's views:

"... girls are just puttin' themselves in a terrible position. Because wee girls are goin' out nowadays with hardly anythin' on and y'know it just takes a taxi to pull up and say, 'aye taxi 'til blah blah', 'aye no sweat jump in' and that's it." (Gráinne, aged 18 – urban area)

Many of the young women in this research, therefore, rationalised the societal perception towards young women and alcohol use in terms of vulnerability and risks to reputation, safety and sexual health. In doing so, they themselves often held views similar to those we see and hear in the popular press regarding 'ladettes'[15]. Interestingly, Griffin (2005: 10) notes that some have come to see 'ladettes' as the contemporary version of 'slags', "troublesome young women, 'folk devils' and reflections of undesirable forms of femininity" - a view not dissimilar to that expressed by some of the young women in our research.

While it has been noted that involvement in 'street culture' may not necessarily be wholly negative, young people's high visibility in public places can "result in young people being blamed for being a nuisance and seen as a problem to be solved, not a group of people who need somewhere to meet" (Dibben, 1999: 6). Furthermore, public spaces are often the only places that young people can claim as their own (Valentine et al, 1998, cited in Eubanks-Owen, 1999: 2) and in this respect they play an important part in social and emotional development (Brown, 1994, 1995; Eubank-Owens, 1999; Hall et al., 1999). While this may be the case, it should not distract from the fact that alternative options should be available. Indeed a number of young women in this research pointed to the positive impact youth provision could have in terms of providing them with something enjoyable to do and as a consequence, moving them off the streets. The potential for youth work programmes to 'break the cycle' of 'hanging about' and possibly getting involved in drugs, alcohol and other anti-social behaviour was illustrated in the case of Fiona (among others).

Aside from media accounts of 'violent girl gangs'[16] and some recent studies reporting that street-based leisure is as much a feature of young women's leisure careers as it is of young men's (e.g. MacDonald & Marsh, 2005; Shildrick, forthcoming; McAlister, 2006; Sharpe et al., 2006), this remains a relatively under-explored issue in the UK. Studies in the US, in particular, and the North-

---

15 Aside from the ITV reality TV series 'Ladettes to Ladies', recent newspaper headlines have included: 'Ladette life has Scottish girls 'among most violent in the world'' (The Scotsman, 23/01/2006); ''Ladette' drinking to increase in next five years' (The Daily Mail, 22/04/2005); 'The Ladette takeover' (The Mail on Sunday, 19/01/2004); 'Drunken schoolgirls staggering along the streets in the afternoon ... is this normal behaviour in Ireland' (Irish Independent, 18/12/2004).

16 Recent newspaper headlines have included: 'Girls lead the pack in new gangland violence' (The Observer, 15th April 2001) and 'Gangs put boot into old ideas of femininity' (The Guardian, 22nd July 1998). See Chesney-Lind (1997) and Ringrose (2005) for critical reviews of the recent focus on young women, violence and aggression.

east of England record similar findings to here in that involvement in 'street-based' leisure for young women is essentially a social activity. That is, it provides a 'social outlet' and a response to the boredom of everyday life for young people in areas where there are few leisure resources (Campbell, 1984; Chesney-Lind, 1997; McAlister, 2007). Unlike previous research, however, this research found that street-based leisure often cut across class and space and brings added risks to young women because of their gender. Furthermore, and as will be expanded upon shortly, the Northern Ireland dimension of involvement in 'street culture' for young women, like young men, in terms of paramilitary intimidation is also worthy of further examination.

Good Practice Example: Fiona's Experience

Fiona was 22 at the time of interview and living in an urban area. She worked part-time, studied part-time and was involved in a youth programme. When younger Fiona had spent much of her free-time 'hanging about the streets' of her local area with a group of other young people "drinking and sniffing". This activity, however, ceased when a local youth worker encouraged the group to attend the local youth club:

"We were brought into **** (youth club) and we were up to no good when we were standing on the street in **** (area). And leaders came round and brought us all in and then that's when we started going, using the club ...//... they (youth leaders) came round to us and says 'look there's a youth club round here, come round and use it, we want you's to come round and use', or God knows where half of us would be the day ...//... Yeah, brought us in – 'come on, we want you's, you's are good kids'. And they did, they done loads a stuff with us like".

While Fiona stopped using the youth club at age 17 as "our crowd just started splitting up" and she did not want to attend alone, she kept involved in other provision through the local community centre and a number of other youth projects. Fiona cited this instance as her 'critical moment', an occurrence in her life which she felt had impacted greatly on her or changed the direction of her life. Fiona felt that active recruitment of young people was essential to encourage them to make use of youth provision, alongside tailoring this to their needs and desires.

5.5 THE TIME AND LEISURE SQUEEZE

Despite various discussions of their use of free-time at the time of interview and when younger, a recurrent theme throughout the young women's accounts was a distinct lack of free-time. Indeed, we found that leisure time appears to be increasing 'squeezed out' in light of other commitments such as attending school, college or university; studying; domestic, childcare and/or caring responsibilities and paid employment (see Figure 1). The impact of external commitments on young women's social opportunities and the multiple realities of their lives was evident among many. Some young women such as Jo were 'juggling' all of these commitments, while others were involved in some to a greater degree than others. Overall, however, free time was scarce for many. In the case of Jo (aged 17) it was illustrated in chapters 3 and 4 that the death of her mother led her to undertake primary caring responsibly for herself, her younger brother and her father. Jo was attending a grammar school and studying for her A-Levels at the time of interview while also undertaking paid employment, as she needed an income. The difficulties and pressures she and others experienced as a result of such commitments have been illustrated throughout the chapters, but these also clearly impacted upon their leisure time. Jo, for example, found that she had little time for herself:

"If I'm not at school I'm working ...//... apart from that you sit and watch something good on TV and you drink." (Jo, aged 17)

Other young women noted the significance of drinking, particularly at a weekend, as this was perhaps the only time they had to relax in light of work and study commitments. The weekend and drinking, therefore, appeared in some ways to be a 'blow-out' or release at the end of a busy week:

"Free time? I'm mostly doing homers [hairdressing from her own or others homes] and I'm never really out during the week ...//... I'd be in my room if I'm not doing homers and just working on my folder for Tech. And then at the weekends I'm out with friends, I work on a Saturday and as soon as I get outta work on a Saturday ...//... dinner, dressed and away I go again". (Neimh, aged 17)

Not only did a significant number of young women explicitly state that they found that they had little free time, but others had often given up previous pastimes and leisure pursuits due to no longer having the time to fit them in. A number of young mothers, for example, noted that their free time often revolved around their children and was spent either with them (through family walks, outings etc.) or doing activities that their children desired. In this sense, some young mothers appeared to lack time to/for themselves. Activities outside the home even with children, however, meant time away from the home and a break in routine:

"... even though I've the children an' everyone's with me ...//... it still gets me out." (Kim, aged 21)

Leisure and free time have been found to be important for physical and emotional well-being. It is suggested that factors associated with leisure (e.g. relaxation, compensation, escapism and independence) can buffer the negative effects of stress on well-being and/or have stress-reducing properties (Iwasaki & Schneider, 2003: 109). Louise (aged 23) identified how she felt leisure, in the from of physical exercise might have helped her reduce stress at particular times in her life:

"At the minute I'm trying to get back into going to the gym because I always did before and then just this last year with being at university and I think, so much work to do, I didn't have a minute to go to the gym – which I maybe should've done because it would've ...//... helped with the stress and that." (Louise, aged 23).

Indeed, in conversations regarding how young women deal with stress, a small number pointed to physical exercise as a positive coping mechanism (see chapter 8). Aside from physical forms of leisure, however, others such as social activities and cultural hobbies have been found to have the potential to reduce stress (Caltabiano, 1994 cited in ibid.). No matter what form it takes "leisure can act as 'breathers' from stress, 'sustainers' of coping effort, and 'restorers'" (ibid.: 110).

Figure 1: The Leisure Squeeze

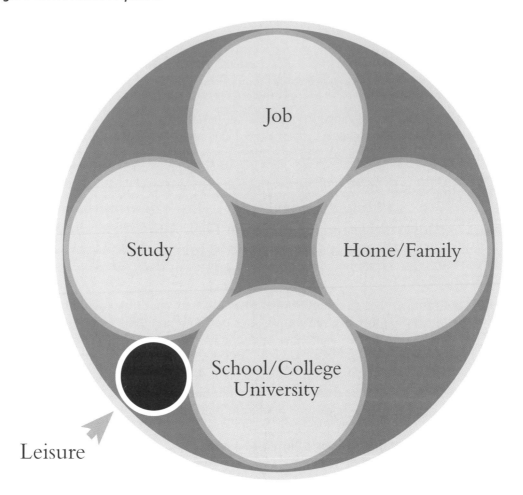

The lack of free time among young women may be a result of increasing demands and expectations educationally, increased opportunities and increasing educational costs and increased expectations of maturity. For instance, many of the young women in higher education also had part-time jobs. That said, so too did many of those who were still at school, and while this may have been a case of having to support themselves, it is perhaps most often linked to youth consumer culture. In light of the multiple realities, pressures and commitments of young women; leisure, free time and social opportunities are increasingly being squeezed out of their lives, and we must consider at what cost this is happening, particularly in light of the 'unhealthy' ways some dealt with stress and pressure (see chapter 8).

In relation to these points there are some clear challenges for work with and for young women. For example, a lack of free time may have a considerable impact upon youth provision/programmes in terms of recruiting groups, arranging times around work, study and family commitments and convincing young women of the psycho-social value of taking time for themselves and away from work and study. That said, accessible and appropriate provision should be an option and this research found that young women often return to youth provision in their late teens and early twenties when they may also be studying, working and caring/homemaking. Making such provision accessible and engaging is clearly important in enabling and encouraging young women to attend.

5.6 LEISURE AND THE CONFLICT

The conflict impacted upon young women's use of free time and leisure in a number of ways, particularly in terms of how their movements were regulated or restricted. A significant number, for instance, noted that particularly when younger, that there were certain places they were not allowed to go to, or which they knew were unsafe to go. While knowledge of perceived safe and unsafe areas was evident in the accounts of young women from all areas, the impact was more pronounced on some more than others. Nicole (aged 25 – rural area), for example, lived in an area which had a high security and paramilitary presence. While she noted that this impacted upon many aspects of her life, she talked of how she often had to stay close to her home, come home straight after school and spent most of her free-time in the home due to her parents' fears for her safety. Nicole told us:

"... I suppose the Troubles was another thing, part of that, it was so dangerous for you to be out on your own ...//... I suppose you kinda feel aggrieved, like why is this happening to me, this is not fair like we can't go out, we can't meet up or anything like that there. But then we never knew any different to it, if you get to **** [the nearest town] it's like a massive day out. Do you know what I mean? On a Saturday like your mother going shopping like, that was like a major like to do that. You woulda always been in and around home all week like. Like getting to the cinema or anything like that was brilliant do you know what I mean."

For other young women, it was the direct impact of the conflict which led them to decisions about how to spend their leisure time, where to go, when to go and with whom. Gráinne (aged 18 – urban area), for instance, who had lost a number of her family and friends through paramilitary shootings would not go out at night on her own or with others, while Neimh who had been the victim of a sectarian attack when younger would not visit her friend who lived in a predominantly Protestant area:

"I've friends and they're protestants and I've actually got a friend who's from *** [predominantly protestant area] ...//... and he's been in my house, though I've never been in his house cus of what I've experienced ...//... I wouldn't, I wouldn't go up there like." (aged 17 – urban area)

A number of young women noted that those who spent their free time on 'the streets' were as likely to experience paramilitary intimidation as young men were. Although direct experience of this within the sample was limited, knowledge of it was more widespread, yet this is an issue often discussed specifically in relation to young men and rarely young women. Of her experiences, Melissa told us:

"You'd go out on the street and you do have a laugh on the street ...//... We used to get in trouble for stuff that we hadn't even done, just because we were the people standing down the end of the street. The Provies would come over and be like, 'you were here this such, a such' and we would be like 'we've been here all night' ...//... because you were standing in the street and because you were wearing certain clothes, you were classed as a 'hood' or you were classed as a wee druggy...//... my cousin, this is a perfect example, she was out the other night and they were standing up in, it's like a parky sort of thing, there's no houses around it, it's a good place to stand because they're not annoying anybody. They were standing there

and the Provies came up, into her face, there was only three of them, and started shouting at her ...//... one of the men jumped out and started going into her face, slabbering to her and all this ...//... This woman came out of the car and started squaring up to her and all ...//... just because of what they class her, cos she stands on the street. Where else do they want you to go, there's nowhere else for you to go?" (Melissa, aged 16 – urban area)

Despite moves towards peace in Northern Ireland, division and segregation remains. As areas are often divided upon religious lines, so too can be the youth and leisure provision within such communities (Leonard, 2004). Indeed, a small number of young women stated that they desired more integrated provision within their areas while one young woman spoke of the value of detached youth workers in her local area for bringing young people from both communities together. Alongside this, conflict and sectarianism continues within communities regulating movements and thus impacting how and where leisure is spent.

5.7 CONCLUSION

The young women in this research described the various ways in which they spend their leisure time throughout the life course. While youth clubs/groups were attended by many in their younger years these remain focused on sports and physical activities and offer few alternatives to young women who have little interest in such pursuits. This lack of gender and age appropriate provision alongside the various commitments of young women in relation to employment, the home and education is impacting upon their decisions to continue attending youth provision. On a more positive note, however, we found that young women often return to youth provision at a later stage of young adulthood to undertake structured programmes which are specific to their needs and desires. Those who have experience of such programmes note their value in terms for social and personal development among other things.

The 2005-2008 youth work strategy states that:

Young people have the right to expect that it [youth work] will be accessible, affordable, high quality and flexible to meet changing needs and a changing environment (DE, 2005a: 5).

The evidence presented here would suggest that this expectation is not always being met and that in these young women's experiences youth work has not always been flexible in meeting their needs. It is important that this right and expectation is more fully recognised in the coming years in order that the next phase of research does not reveal similar experiences as some of those reported here.

5.8 RECOMMENDATIONS

- Little is known about what local youth clubs/groups are providing and whether they are meeting the needs of young women. This research suggests there is still a focus on sports/physical activities (particularly in youth clubs), which may not be meeting the needs of young women and that alternatives are not keeping them engaged. There should be an independent gender audit of provision and participation in the youth sector which should inform future funding and service provision.

- Findings would indicate that young women in the older age group will continue to be engaged with the youth sector if they can access group work and participatory activities. However, these activities are not universally available. The youth sector should ensure that good practice in this area be acknowledged and mainstreamed.

- The pressures on young women have been a recurrent theme throughout the research, which has obvious implications for their engagement with the youth sector. Yet, it is also clear that they would gain from the support which could be offered through the youth service, but also from the recreational benefits. Therefore in terms of recruitment and retention the youth sector should: re-assess their recruitment strategies; times, types and duration of programmes; provision of one-to-one support and ensure that workers have an understanding of the particular issues facing young women.

- In order to secure the full participation of young women and promote gender conscious practice youth workers need to be adequately equipped with relevant knowledge and skills. The youth work professional training curriculum needs to be revised with a greater focus on gender inequality and its implications for young women. Workers should also develop the skills to challenge sexism and inequality through their work. This should be a central focus of both initial community youth work training and continuing professional development.

- Accessibility of youth provision continues to be an issue across the board. All youth provision should be open and accessible to young women with disabilities, youth women from minority ethnic communities and those who identify as other than heterosexual. This has implications for the training of youth workers and service provision, including physical access.

- Funding for youth services has come from a range of sources and has often been short term, often resulting in threat to or closure of services. Work with young women in particular has often been funded on a project-by-project basis, leaving it particularly vulnerable. If young women's needs are to be adequately met provision needs to be mainstreamed and financially sustained.

- The targeted strategy for the allocation of resources to youth work has meant that the focus has been on disadvantaged areas to the exclusion of young people living in suburban areas/new build estates and what are often perceived as middle class areas. There would appear to be a gap in provision which could be explored through further research.

- Further research is also needed into young women and 'street based' leisure within a Northern Ireland context.

Place, Space and Time: Young Women and Leisure

Chapter Six

Community and
Social Capital

6. COMMUNITY AND SOCIAL CAPITAL

"...we are a community. We're very close, maybe sometimes too close."
(Donna, aged 21)

6.1 INTRODUCTION

It has long been recognised that people's sense of well-being and identity are integrally linked to the place in which they live (Gilroy and Speak, 1998; Glendinning et al., 2003; Hall et al., 1999; Pavis et al., 2001). Further, that where we live can impact upon our social networks, education, employment and social opportunities and our feelings of safety and belonging. One might say that the issue of place is particularly important in a Northern Ireland context as places have important meanings attached to them. As Crang (1998: 103) states:

"The place is standing for a set of cultural characteristics: the place says something not only about where you live or come from but who you are. This can be simply a matter of stereotypes but it has more to it than that."

Within Northern Ireland, place can be a key identifier of religion; one place can be inclusionary for some, and exclusionary for others. Almost 95% of social housing in Northern Ireland is segregated on religious grounds (NIHE, 2006) and 50% of the population live in areas where more than 90% of residents are Catholic or Protestant (Smyth, 2000). Census data also suggests that residential segregation has increased rather than decreased since the 1998 Belfast/Good Friday Agreement (Cairns et al., 2003). One impact of this, it is argued, is "polarisation toward political extremes and ... strengthened influence and control exercised by paramilitary organisations within local communities" (ibid: 8).

Conflict and segregation, however, can bring communities together and strengthen them (Leonard, 2004; Smyth, 2000) and it is argued that place has many 'use values' attached to it (Logan & Molotch, 1987). Our communities are often the focal point of wider activity (such as schools, services, leisure etc.) and informal social networks. Where we live can, therefore, be key to our access to opportunities, resources, services, social activities and social networks. It is of little surprise then, that the concept of community is key within policy debates. Yet, within discussions about a decline in a sense of community, enhancing social capital[17], the impact of weak community infrastructure and a lack of respect for communities among many of today's young people, the voice of young people is often missing.

Within this chapter we draw upon recent debates regarding community and social capital and examine young women's views of the communities in which they live. The chapter pays attention to the issue of locality in the more general sense and examines young women's attachment to the areas in which they live, their likes and dislikes of them and the importance of local social networks and support. On the reverse of this, however, we also demonstrate that place, strong attachment to it and strong local social capital (that is, the social relations and networks that a community/individual has access to and can potentially benefit from - Middleton et al., 2005), can have a 'downside' for young women.

---

17   "... social capital refers to connections among individuals – social networks and the norms of reciprocity and trustworthiness that arise from them." (Putman, 2000, cited in Leonard, 2004: 928)

6.2 SOCIAL NETWORKS AND SUPPORT: THE UPSIDE OF BONDING SOCIAL CAPITAL

Many of the young women we spoke to, despite an understanding of some of the problems with the areas in which they lived, nonetheless displayed a strong attachment to them. Many, for example, noted that they would like to continue living there or close-by in the future. A smaller number reported few positives about their local areas and expressed a strong desire to move from them. There was little difference in attachment to area among those living in rural and urban locales, but almost all of those living in suburban areas displayed a weak attachment to the area in which they lived.

While there were many intricacies to the young women's accounts, the main reasons given for liking the area in which they lived were strong family and social networks, familiarity with the area, the area being quiet or perceived as safe and a feeling that there was 'a good sense of community'. Conversely, the main dislikes of areas were feeling unsafe, high levels of perceived crime and anti-social behaviour, sectarianism/religious divides, lack of facilities leading to boredom, a lack of opportunities and no sense of community.

The notion of 'a sense of community' was raised frequently by young women and the themes inherent in their definitions of this were knowing people (particularly neighbours) and the community coming together for local events and in difficult times. Louise summed up the meaning of community when talking about the two areas she had experience of living in:

"Where I lived until I was about 11, it had like a real sense of community there because everyone would come round to your house if you were having a barbecue or whatever, y'know your neighbours would come round to the barbecue or even just drop in all the time and you just knew everybody ...//... and everyone was kind of working together y'know if there was something happening, an issue that would affect you all, you would have meetings in somebody's house ...//... Where we live [now], the houses, they are quite new ...//... and there has been different people moving in and out, nobody ever seems to stay for more than y'know a few years ...//... there has been so much changing and you can't really get to know people in a short space of time like that." (aged 23 – suburban area)

Despite problems with some of the areas in which they lived, this 'sense of community', knowing people, being known and coming together gave many a strong sense of attachment. Neimh, for example, noted that she would not move out of the area because of these close networks of friends and family, despite some of the area's problems:

"If I was gonna move out, I think I would just get a flat close to my mummy cus I'm a homebird. ...//... What's good [about the area] is that you've got neighbours that you know and loadsa people you like and whenever you go into the local bars you always see your friends and just there's neighbours and your family and all is close. But it's not a nice area to live in like. There's too much joy riders about and hoods standing on corners and wee girls are just as bad, lying in the middlea the roads an' all blocked." (aged 17 – urban area)

Despite the different locale, Nicole, like Neimh, also found many problems with her local area. In her case these related to its rural location, limited amenities and facilities and a lack of privacy, yet she too wished to remain living there because of the community feeling:

"Like there's one wee part that's down here with a shop and a chippy and a housing estate, but there's only eight or ten houses in it, do you know what I mean? And there's kinda like all grown ups now and retired people ...//... and everybody knows everybody else's business ...//... But I love it cus in our community aspect of it ...//... My area is very, very close, and I suppose cus we haven't got anything else and we're so spread out and it's great whenever we do come together and get involved in things. Like we would do like fun days, like sponsored walks, a sports day with kids, summer camp, all that there, all that is done. It's a very, very strong community." (aged 25 - rural area)

As expected, most of the complaints amongst those living in rural areas related to a lack of facilities, poor public transport, lack of opportunities and a lack of privacy. For those living in urban areas, their main complaints revolved around high levels of crime and anti-social behaviour (impacting on feelings of safety) and, similarly, a lack of local facilities. Yet in many cases, familiarity with the place, family networks, a strong sense of community and strong bonding social capital outweighed the negative aspects of the places in which these young women lived. Thus, while many recognised the faults with their areas, often there was not a desire to "find a better place, but to make the place they find themselves in better" (Reay & Lucey, 2000: 424).

At its most simplistic, social capital refers to the social relations and networks that a community/individual has access to and can potentially benefit from (Middleton et al., 2005). Bonding or local social capital refers to links and networks between 'like minded-people' such as families, neighbours, those of the same ethnic group etc. It "involves trust and reciprocity in closed networks, and helps the process of 'getting by' in life on a daily basis" (Stone, 2001: 22). Strong bonding social capital and social networks in these young women's lives could be seen to have value to different groups and for different reasons. For the relatively small number of young women in our sample who had made the permanent transition from family home to independent living, families remained a strong source of financial and emotional support and having them 'close-by' was often a factor in decisions about where to move (see also Catan, 2004; Jones 1995, 2002). Young mothers were another group who talked about the importance of family support and having family and extended family living close by. Indeed, as has been found in other research (see for example, Jones, 2002; MacDonald & Marsh, 2005; McAlister, 2007) it was the reliance on such networks which sometimes influenced the decisions of young mothers about where to live:

SM: So you wanted to stay local then I take it?
Hannah: Yeah, well more cos my mum does help out minding them [the children] an' it cuts down travelling just cos I was moving out on ma own and everything and I didn't want ta move [laughs] y'know too far away, and my granny just lives down *** [name of street] just as well so she's nearby (aged 23 – urban area)

Despite wanting to ideally live in 'the country', Hannah, like other young mothers was limited in her choice of place to live both by her finances and the need for emotional and practical support from the family and extended family (see also chapter 3).

The young women gave many accounts of strong bonding social capital in discussing issues around safety and trust, helping each other and coming together as a community to work towards a common goal. Donna gave a very specific example of this which is perhaps unique to Northern Ireland. Referring to a time of political unrest in her community she describes how her community came together:

Donna: The only good thing I can say about this community is that we are a community. Em, we're very close, em, maybe sometimes too close. But we understand each other and I think over the past few years we've been known as the victims. But now we're the survivors, times have changed. And em, when anything happens the community, the community is there to support it, to give a helping hand.

GN: What do you think creates that sense of community?

Donna: Em, well for me I think it was the whole **** [area] thing. That this community was shut down, there was nothing goin' in, nothing goin' out and that we had to help each other. Em, I think that's what has made us a strong community from that. (aged, 21 – urban area)

Interestingly, in her research in what may be perceived as a high conflict area in Northern Ireland, Madeline Leonard (2004: 931) found "strong community networks and a self-help ethos". She explained this as a response to years of social and economic disadvantage that stemmed from "political discrimination and the suppression of cultural identity". While the area in which Donna lived is different in many ways to the Catholic West Belfast of Leonard's study, prolonged political tension in her community had led to the community strengthening and coming together. In this respect, bonding social capital may be seen, to some degree, as having political origins. Thus, while there was often a sense of injustice, unfairness and inequality within the young women's accounts, be this in terms of high levels of conflict or a lack of facilities, Cattell (2001) notes that strong perceptions of inequality can be a uniting and/or empowering force in areas of deprivation resulting in mutual aid and solidarity.

Interestingly, however, within Donna's account she also notes that a very close community is not always a good thing. Indeed, it is acknowledged that despite the potential value of strong bonding or local social capital that it can also have a 'downside'. It is to a discussion of this and the impact upon the lives of the young women that we now turn.

6.3 LOSS OF PRIVACY AND EXTERNAL HOSTILITY: THE DOWNSIDE OF BONDING SOCIAL CAPITAL

Aside from the previously mentioned complaints about their communities (e.g. crime, lack of facilities etc.), young women's other major complaints related to a lack of privacy and sectarianism/conflict within their communities. These discussions often featured in the accounts of those young women who said that they lived in areas with a strong sense of community and, therefore, highlight some of the downsides of bonding social capital.

6.3.1 "Everyone Knows your Business"

Ironically, a close-knit or small community where 'everybody knows everybody else' was cited as both one of the most positive and most negative aspects of the areas in which some of the young women lived. The problem with such communities was a lack of privacy and 'everyone knowing your business'. Unsurprisingly, most of those who discussed this issue were living in rural areas with a smaller number living in what they described as close-knit urban communities. Indeed, Madonna felt that this was merely a feature of life wherever you lived, and that living in a smaller community merely meant that word spread more quickly:

*"... everyone knows your business here in *** [name of her town] ...//... I think it's like that anywhere really so it is. No matter where you live there's always some form of community there, within that community everybody knows everybody and you hear about things, so I think maybe cus it is smaller things will go round quicker."* (aged 25 - urban area)

The fact that these young women felt that their business was essentially community business impacted upon their lives in two main ways. Firstly, in terms of utilising some local services, information and goods, and secondly, and closely related to this, in terms of regulating their behaviour in order that they did not get a local reputation. Of the latter issue, Michelle (aged, 19) told us:

"...if you do something that's __way__ outta character like or should not be done round [here] you're always remembered ye'd be like 'that's the one that did that there'." (her emphasis - rural area)

The young women's fear of 'getting a name for themselves' or a 'bad reputation' often related to their gender and local gender expectations. Discussions often revolved around how easy it is for young women to gain a 'bad reputation' and how difficult it is to get rid of a label once it is given. As detailed in chapters 5 and 7, these discussions often related to perceptions of young women and alcohol use and young women's sexuality. An awareness of such perceptions and expectations impacted upon, among other things, willingness to access local information and advice on sexual health. A further consequence, outlined by Janine, was that young people would feel that they could not depend on privacy and thus have no support network:

"It means that really the kids are gonna think they can't trust anybody. And if you talk to someone, the next minute somebody knows your business, then it means someone else knows your business. It's gonna, they're gonna find it harder to talk." (aged 17 - urban area)

Michelle, among others, also talked of the consequences of 'jumping out of line' in her community in terms of being seen to do or be something different. Shirley gave an example of this in relation to two young men from her community who were gay. She explained their reluctance to 'come out' as partly due to community attitude but also to a lack of support structures:

"I know for a couple of fella's that would be from our area, they actually came out to be gay and they are living in England, and I haven't seen them back, you know they waited until they were away cus they can't, couldn't come out in their own area, but there's very, very little information for young people." (aged 24 - rural area)

What this short discussion demonstrates is that communities can be inclusionary for some and exclusionary for others. Also, that positions can shift and members can experience feelings of inclusion and exclusion at different times. While this is one aspect of the downside of bonding social capital, we also see that strong communities such as those described by some of the young women here can also be a constraint on actions and choices (see also Leonard, 2004). As Hall et al. note, "the very intimacy of local community can itself be experienced as something oppressive and limiting" (1999: 510).

6.3.2 Communities and the Conflict

The other main criticism a number of young women had of the communities in which they lived was high levels of community violence, religious divisions and ingrained sectarian attitudes. Nineteen young women spoke specifically about the impact of the conflict in relation to the areas they lived in with many noting heightened community tension around the 12th of July[18], and how they felt more anxious or aware of the legacy of the conflict at this time of year.

18   The 12th July is an annual Protestant celebration commemorating the Battle of the Boyne in 1690. Members of the Orange Institution stage parades throughout Northern Ireland on this date.

Beyond this, however, the young women reflected upon growing up in areas of religious segregation. Many, like Kim, who grew up in a predominantly Catholic or Protestant area positioned beside an area disproportionately populated by 'the other religion', told us that when they were growing up "Catholics play with the Catholics" and vice versa. A number of those who discussed this felt that it led children to grow up with a lack of exposure to 'difference' and became an unquestioned way of life. Residential segregation and sectarian attitudes, some firmly believed, went hand-in-hand, and it was the passing down of these attitudes rather than direct experiences of violence that was the main impact of the conflict on young people today.

Indeed, so religiously segregated were the lives of a small number of young women living in rural communities that they noted that it was not until the age of 18, when they went to university outside their local area, that they first (knowingly) met someone of 'the other religion'. Kelly, now aged 21, reflected on the influences on her attitudes and experiences when growing up, demonstrating the early, perhaps subconscious, entrenchment of sectarian attitudes that some young people experience because of where they live:

"[My community] is a Protestant community and if you go over that bridge it's the Catholic part of it. Like I know, like I'm living next year with two Catholic girls, like one of the girls actually whenever I was in high school got on our bus and nobody spoke to her because she was a Catholic. Like looking back on it like, me and her are really good friends now and we are like looking back on it, it was just so silly. It was just the way you were brought up and you weren't supposed to speak to them because they were a different religion which, which was daft."

As illustrated here, Kelly, among others in this research, positively shows how these attitudes do not necessarily pertain over time and that young people can resist them (see also Leonard, 2007). That said, there were many examples given by these young women of how their communities could oppress and exclude because of religious divisions. Jemima, for example, told us how places around her had became 'exclusive':

"I suppose you've got your Protestant housin' estate an' your Catholic housin' estate ...//... ye know they would be very Protestant, no Catholic would go into it an' no Protestant would go into the Catholic one an' it's jus', that's jus' the way it's been over time." (aged, 20 - rural area).

What we see here are processes of exclusion working at a very local community level and the downside of strong bonding social capital. As Forrest and Kearns (2001: 2107) note "strong in-group loyalty may also create strong out-group antagonism".

Presenting a more in-depth glimpse into some of the areas where these young women lived and grew up may help to contextualise their experiences and understandings of the entrenchment of sectarian attitudes and exclusion of 'the other'. Some of the areas in which they lived were interface areas[19] where political violence has and continues to be high or areas which have/had a strong security or paramilitary presence. Such experiences of violence and conflict will inevitably impact upon community attitudes and indeed feelings of safety and well-being.

---

19   Interface areas are usually located in working class areas and are characterised by sporadic outbursts of violence between the Catholic and Protestant residents who live at either side of the interface (Davey et al., forthcoming).

Growing up in an area which had a high security presence and thus paramilitary activity, Nicole told us, impacted on every aspect of her life from going to school to her use of free-time. While Nicole talked in great detail about this aspect of growing up, we feel that it is worthwhile quoting her at length in order to highlight the very real impact of the conflict on the everyday life of some young women:

" ... the troubles woulda been very much at a height at that time whenever I was growing up. Am, and then because I live in an area, do you know what I mean, that there's very much heavy police presence in it ...//... and there's look out posts, and helicopters, police stations everywhere like ...//... going to school on the bus we had to go through a police presence, where they stop the bus and might even search the bus or get on the bus as such, having to go to school and you had to go through like a barrier going to school and coming out of school. I felt that was very, very unfair on us ...//... Like we were never kinda like down the town as such, we were at school, you stayed in school because there was that whole thing if there was an explosion or a bomb or there was a shooting which could happen at any other day at any hour. ...//... even in the evenings you went straight home, it wasn't a case you went down the local town as such because it was deemed to be far too dangerous do you know what I mean to do that.

>   KM: And so what sort of effect did that have then on you growing up?
>   Nicole: I suppose in some ways I kinda didn't know any the wiser, do you know that way? Like you are just prone to living and just get on with it. Am, I suppose you kinda feel aggrieved, like why is this happening to me, this is not fair like we can't go out, we can't meet up or anything like that there. But then we never knew any different to it ... (aged 25, rural area)

While Nicole lived in a rural area, those living in urban areas that experienced high levels of conflict and violence discussed similar experiences. In her response to a question regarding the impact of the conflict on her life, Neimh (aged 17) told us that she had 'experienced a lot' because of where she had, until recently, lived. She had been locked in a local chemist and beaten up by paramilitaries, regularly witnessed high levels of street violence and rioting (and on occasion had joined in on these herself), and was aware that there was a strong paramilitary presence in the area. Having only recently moved from the area she told us that things had not changed a great deal over time:

>   Neimh: ... see livin' there it puts you under stress ...//... I'm glad I'm away from down there like cus you get a good nights sleep now. I feel sorry for anyone living close to where all troubles are going on.
>   GN: Do you think times are changing and it's getting better? Or is it still the same?
>   Neimh: No, I think it's still the same like. Cus, it can quieten down an' all and you think it's getting better, but it just comes up again. It quietens down for a while and then it's all goin' mad again, so to me times haven't really changed, they're just, in a way sometimes they can feel like they're just getting worse and not getting any better.

As shown here and experienced by others in the research, the conflict was very much still a feature and reality of the everyday lives of some young women.

Those living in high conflict areas talked of feelings of safety. Five mentioned the prominence of members of paramilitary groups in their communities, with three explicitly stating that despite the view that these protected the community that this was far from their experience. Janine, for example, told us that within recent months violence had flared up in her community again. Street riots and shootings were not uncommon and she firmly believed that it was the culture of violence and paramilitarism endemic within the area that was to blame:

"... half of them [young people] are quite mad, but you can't blame them for that and you can't put it down to their parents either cus it's not what they're living in, it's what they're coming up in. And at the minute there's a lot of trouble going on in the area ...//... the likes of shooting and all too, and the likes of the rioting and all in the **** [area], they'll all go up to it ...//... It's just, well it scares me, I don't like it. The paramilitaries were brought into the community to help the community, but they're not, they're just letting the community live in fear which is wrong. They're shooting their own men so they are ...//... they [young people] have the pressure too, they get pressured to join it when really they don't want to. And a lot of women are living in fear at the minute." (aged, 17 – urban area)

The theme of fear ran throughout Janine's account. As a result of being sexually abused when younger she felt unsafe around men and tended to restrict her social movements to her own area, yet she revealed here that she does not even feel safe in the place in which she spends most of her time.

What is revealed through the above discussions is that while some level of peace may have been achieved in Northern Ireland, this is certainly not experienced in the everyday lives of young women living in high conflict or, what might be described as, enclave areas. Yet, even recently, it has been reported:

It is often residents in enclaves that have experienced the most intense effects of the Troubles. Sectarian attacks are commonplace on the boundary of such areas, and it is young people, particularly young males, who are most often involved, both as victims and aggressors (Smyth, 2000: 6).

While this may be so, the almost exclusive focus in research, literature and programme development on the impact of the conflict on young men, with little specific mention or recognition of the lives of young women, makes young women 'invisible victims'. Their experiences, worries and fears often go unheard. While this research has revealed that the conflict and its legacy permeates all areas of young women's lives, the long-tern consequences of this remain unknown.

6.4 CONCLUSION

Perhaps borne out of a history of conflict, discrimination and segregation, Northern Ireland has many strong communities and a vibrant community sector. Many of the young women in this research talked of living in close-knit communities characterised by strong social and familial networks, reciprocity and, at times, common community goals or causes which served to strengthen attachment and belonging. Despite noting many problems with the areas in which they lived, most of the young women, because of this feeling of belonging, had little desire to live anywhere else. Yet the power of such strong bonding social capital in engendering attachment to area, can ironically also serve to be limiting or restricting. A desire to remain close to family and friends may serve to restrict or limit opportunities and aspirations. So for example, job aspirations and opportunities may be restricted to the local area and attitudes heavily influenced by those of the local community, such as perceptions of women and their roles.

Aside from this, one of the main problems young women identified with living in close-knit communities was a lack of privacy. This, it has been shown, could impact upon their ability and willingness to access services and restrict their actions and movements. Further to this, many were aware that the religious segregation of the areas in which they lived impacted heavily upon the attitudes and experiences of young people growing up there. Communities could be strong and accepting of those who 'belonged' or 'fit in', but exclusionary and hostile to 'difference'. Within a Northern Ireland context, the most obvious consequence of this is the continued transmission of sectarian attitudes, a lack of exposure to and acceptance of 'difference' and continued violence within many communities.

While it is encouraging that within the course of this research that Northern Ireland's first religiously integrated social housing estate was developed, in the context of these young women's lives, and indeed the next generation of young women, we are unlikely to see any great effect as many areas remain heavily segregated. This research has revealed that as a consequence of this that many young women continue to experience and witness high levels of community violence. Further, that the more 'hidden' or indirect impact of the conflict in terms of the transmission of sectarian attitudes as a consequence of residential segregation is a legacy that will be difficult to remove. Within a Northern Ireland context then, one might say that the conflict, and all that goes with it, has played a part in creating strong communities and strong bonding social capital, and in turn this strong bonding social capital now plays its part in maintaining or perpetuating attitudes and activities related to the conflict.

6.5 RECOMMENDATIONS

• The impact of the conflict on young women is not fully understood yet it emerged as a strong theme running through the accounts of young women. Further research is needed to clearly differentiate the experience and impact of conflict on young women and young men.

• In light of the fact that many young women have a strong attachment to the areas in which they live and spend much of their time, it is important that they play a key role in the design and development of local services and are encouraged and enabled to have a greater, more visible stake in their own communities.

• There appear to be few 'safe spaces' for young women within their own communities. This is of particular concern given that the resourcing of the Community and Youth Sector is traditionally short-term, unstable and potentially under greater threat through the Review of Public Administration. Consideration should be given by the Community and the Youth Sector, and those who fund them, to the creation and maintenance of 'safe spaces' (with a specific focus on young women).

• Cross-community/community relations work is central to the development of a peaceful society in Northern Ireland. Yet young women's accounts are not reflecting the scale of funding targeted towards this. Opportunities, in both the formal and informal education sectors, must be maximised for meaningful contact to be developed between people from different religious backgrounds

Chapter Seven

Hush Hush:
Sex, Sexuality and Gender

"HUSH, HUSH"[20]: SEX, SEXUALITY AND GENDER

"It wouldn't be talked about. Sex would be a quiet word ..." (Carmel, aged 23)

7.1 INTRODUCTION

While there is some debate about the precise meaning of the term sexuality and it is often used synonymously with sexual orientation, we employ a broader definition of the term here. Employing the World Health Organisation's working definition:

Sexuality is a central aspect of being human throughout life and encompasses sex, gender identities and roles, sexual orientation, eroticism, pleasure, intimacy and reproduction. Sexuality is experienced and expressed in thoughts, fantasies, desires, beliefs, attitudes, values, behaviours, practices, roles and relationships. While sexuality can include all of these dimensions, not all of them are always experienced or expressed. Sexuality is influenced by the interaction of biological, psychological, social, economic, political, cultural, ethical, legal, historical, religious and spiritual factors (http://www.who.int/reproductive-health/gender/sexual_health.html).

Laws and policies relating to sex and sexuality differ in Northern Ireland in comparison to other parts of the UK. There are, for example, no mandatory requirements for schools on the teaching of sex education, the age of sexual consent is 17 years of age (as opposed to 16 in the rest of the UK) and abortion is legal in Northern Ireland only under certain (extreme) circumstances (e.g. where there is evidence of serious physical or mental risk). These laws are further reinforced by the social and religious pressures brought to bear within Northern Ireland. Two of the main sites of sexual health and family planning advice within the country are picketed by pro-life campaigners on a regular basis, as is the annual Belfast Gay Pride Parade by some religious groups, and it took a further 15 years after homosexuality was decriminalised in England and Wales – and a ruling by the European Court of Human Rights – for the same to happen in Northern Ireland. The religious discourse of sexuality in Northern Ireland can not only be seen within such policies and practices but continues to play an important role "in shaping moral values of Northern Irish society and in the maintenance of ethnic identity" (Kitchin & Lysaght, 2004: 86).

The teachings of both Catholic and Protestant churches on sexuality (and which are often adopted within the ethos of Northern Irish schools[21]), is "rooted in long standing moral conservatism" and "discourses of sin, shame, guilt and familism" which are evident within the teachings of both (ibid.: 86). This discourse can be seen in moral and legal debates regarding abortion and the teaching of sex education in schools. With regards to abortion, while it is noted that the Belfast/Good Friday Agreement (1998) makes a commitment to issues of women's equality and participation that "the language used to promote peace and social progress, when juxtaposed against that used to frame the abortion debate, shows how far the latter fails to address either women's reproductive agency or equality" (Fegan & Rebouche, 2003: 222).

---

20 Carmel's description of the way that sex is dealt with in the home and society in general.

21 See chapter 4 for an explanation of the maintenance and governance of schools in Northern Ireland.

Against this legislative and cultural backdrop are worrying trends and experiences. Northern Ireland, for example, has one of the highest teenage pregnancy rates in Europe (CCEA, 2001). Research on Northern Irish young people's sexual attitudes and behaviour found that less than a quarter of those aged 14-25 could name any STI other than HIV/AIDS and further research found many parents reporting that they never discussed sexual issues with their children (cited in FPA/HPA, 2005). Additionally, while abortion is to all intents and purposes illegal in Northern Ireland, except under extreme circumstances, Northern Irish women do seek abortions "either through illegal and often dangerous means or through travel (mostly in secret and at great cost) to clinics in Great Britain" (Fegan & Rebouche, 2003: 227).

In relation to the teaching of Relationships and Sexuality Education in schools (i.e. sex education), there is no uniform provision but rather guidelines from 1987 which are open to differential interpretation and implementation. While schools are expected to have a written policy on sex education, the guidelines provide much latitude in stating that RSE:

Should be taught in a sensitive manner which is in harmony with the ethos of the school and in conformity with the moral and religious principles held by parents and school management authorities (DENI, 2001: 2).

The religious ethos of schools, therefore, can clearly impact upon the nature of RSE school children receive. So for example, a survey of Northern Irish school children in 1996 found that that almost half of fifth form males reported never receiving information of STIs (other than AIDS) or explanations of menstruation, one in four never had lessons on puberty and one in eight girls never had a class explaining menstruation or puberty. Furthermore, personal relationships were less likely to be discussed than contraception and pregnancy (cited in CCEA, 2001: 10). Another survey in the same year reported that 81% of primary school teachers and over one half of post-primary teachers stated that they had received no specific training in the teaching of sex education (cited in FPA/HPA, 2005). More recent research carried out in 2002 with 14-25 year olds revealed a core criticism of the sex education they received in schools was a lack of focus and openness on the emotional aspects of sexual feelings and issues relating to sexual orientation, abortion and sexual pleasure. This study also revealed that pupils at Catholic maintained schools were less likely to be taught about contraception and safer sex (Schubotz et al., 2003; Rolston et al., 2005). More generally, it was concluded that:

Underpinned by a particular traditional and conservative strain of Christian morality, sex education in Northern Ireland schools is marked by conservatism and silence and by the avoidance of opportunities for informed choice in relation to sexuality on the part of young people (Rolston et al., 2005: 217)

Thus, while the more recent guidance on RSE is encouraging and suggests the inclusion of what may be religiously sensitive and contentious issues such as contraception, abortion, STIs and sexual orientation (see CCEA, 2001 & DENI, 2001), it remains questionable whether the wide-reaching personal and social benefits of RSE teaching is understood and embraced by schools. For as the guidance suggests:

RSE can have a positive effect on self-esteem. Schools can help to develop their pupils' self esteem by creating a climate of trust and acceptance in which each person is valued and respected and encouraged to feel good about themselves. Pupils are encouraged to recognise their individual needs, to respect the needs and wants of others, and to develop the skills and self esteem to become confident adolescents (CCEA, 2001: 1).

Hush Hush: Sex, Sexuality and Gender

Within this context, this chapter examines issues surrounding sex and sexuality for the young women involved in this research. It offers an overview and examination of the sources they utilise to gain information about sex and sexuality and their views and perceptions of the value of these. It also examines these young women's understanding of wider societal attitudes regarding gender and sexuality and examines the impact of this, along with the nature of information sources they use, on their sexual behaviour and their ability to access further information, advice and services.

The chapter demonstrates that the themes of embarrassment, fear and shame are strong throughout the young women's accounts and that this is a result of the way in which gender, sex and sexuality is dealt with through various social institutions within Northern Ireland. As in previous chapters, examples of good practice will be discussed in order to illustrate what young women themselves define as useful.

7.2 SEXUALITY, GENDER AND SOCIETY

The intersection of both age and gender within debates and discussions of sex and sexuality has meant that much of the focus has been upon young women. Within political and public debates the attention on young (teenage) mothers and female promiscuity linked to binge drinking has many moral undertones. The young women involved in this research were aware of societal messages surrounding young women and sex and particularly the labels that might be attached to them because of their behaviour and sexuality. While there were many examples of this, the young women most often discussed this in relation to the differential views and attitudes towards young men and sex and young women and sex:

"...if you have a couple of one night stands you'd be branded a slut or a whore where men can just go out and do what they want and have one night stands and they're branded as being good." (Beyoncé, aged 25)

Indeed, a number also noted the problems with young women carrying condoms because of the negative assumptions that went with it:

"She would be seen as a bit of a tart or a slut I think. I think there's like a negative perception of that and if you go out and like you pull a guy, 'why are you carrying that? Did you go out with the specific purpose of bringing a guy back?'" (Louise, aged 23)

Further to this, the fact that the Brook Advisory Clinic continues to be picketed by pro-life demonstrators on a regular basis gives a clear message to young women regarding Northern Irish society's views of women, sex and the body. The impact of this is clear in at least one respect:

"... outside the Brook Clinic, there'd always be a loada protests outside it ...//... but I don't see why there should be protests because it's not like they're doing any harm, they're just helping young girls. They're there for the young girls who need the help. But people just don't wanna go, they see the protests outside it, they'd be scoundered walking in or in case anybody sees them." (Neimh, aged 17)

These wider societal views not only impact upon young women's behaviours but also their own attitudes towards young women, sex and sexuality. This was clear in their descriptions and discussions of other young women's sexuality. These young women, despite their protestations about the 'branding' of sexual behaviour were indeed guilty of this themselves as they talked of how young women were having sex at a younger age today, were having a number of sexual partners and did not 'respect' themselves. Morally conservative views, therefore, have permeated into the beliefs of young women themselves, although this was always with reference to 'other' young women, not themselves.

As will be discussed in the next section, negative or at least morally laden views and attitudes towards sex and sexuality in a Northern Ireland context are reinforced in many of its social institutions. The potential impact of the social construction of sex as 'wrong' or 'immoral' at a young age has been alluded to here but will be given fuller attention in the final section of the chapter.

7.3 SOURCES OF INFORMATION ON SEX AND SEXUALITY

The young women reported various sources of information on issues regarding sex and sexuality. While all noted having some form of sex education at school, those sources of information that they noted as most valuable were:

- Informal education/youth provision (n=7)
- Schools (n=6)
- Friends (n=6)
- Magazines and the internet (n=6)
- Mothers (n=3)

7.3.1 Informal Sources: Mothers, Magazines and Friends

While a small number of young women (n=3) reported that their mothers talked openly and honestly about sex and had supported them in accessing information and contraception, most noted that their mothers were often embarrassed talking about sex, gave limited information and/or advocated a 'don't do it approach':

"My mother I suppose would have been very old fashioned and would never kinda be able to talk about things like that. Not that we hadn't a fantastic relationship, but just couldn't communicate those sorts of things ..." (Nicole, aged 25)

"My mother's just, em, like she's just like 'don't be at it', that was what I got and like you know that was it." (Molly, aged 20)

Furthermore, young women felt that if mothers and families were more open in talking about sex that young women would be less embarrassed about the issue and less fearful of 'being judged' or 'letting their family down' if they were to gain knowledge of their sexual behaviour. Indeed it was the fear of their family, and particularly their mothers finding out that they were having sex or considering becoming sexually active, that many young women cited as a barrier to young women accessing contraception.

Mothers and the family are a clear starting point of information for young women, yet it cannot be assumed that these will provide sufficient information, or the type of information that young women require in order to make informed decisions. In research on young women and menstruation, Kissling (1996) has noted that a mother's embarrassment and discomfort in discussing the issue with her daughter can create a similar sense of secrecy and shame among them. The 'communication taboo' around menstruation may reflect how the information on sex and sexuality is passed from mother to daughter. The embarrassment and discomfort of the mother can have a similarly deep impact upon the young woman's own attitudes and behaviours to sex and sexuality.

Hush Hush: Sex, Sexuality and Gender

Friends, on the other hand, provided a form of information and talk that some young women felt more comfortable with and it was through their (sometimes older) peers or siblings that a number of young women felt they had gained most information about sex. Indeed, Erin (aged 19) noted that she would have known nothing about contraception and how to access it if it had not been for her two older sisters. In other cases it was friends who had given information about where family planning centres were located or had supported their friends in taking them to these. More generally, however, young women noted that they had merely 'just picked up' information on sex from their friends in a fairly informal way:

"your friends mostly ...//... see your friends like, just, everybody just sorta, I don't know really, everybody seemed to just know, nobody was ever taught it or asked it but everybody knew like" (Karen, aged 19)

The quality of information that young women receive from their friends obviously differs, and again we cannot assume that it is always good or accurate information. That said, friends were often a clear source of support particularly for providing an open and comfortable forum for discussing sex and for providing information with regards to contraception and service provision

Likewise, the quality of information that young women receive from magazines and the internet is questionable, but its appeal is clear. These provide a faceless means of gaining information and the young women who cited these as their most useful sources of information were clear about their benefits. When we asked Jo (aged 17), for example, where she got most of her information regarding sex from, she replied:

"I thoroughly believe in the bible, which is Cosmopolitan."

Jo's mother had died when she was a child and she told us how she had to learn everything from books and magazines because she had found her sex education at school very limited. Despite the value for Jo, messages regarding women's sexuality in magazines are somewhat confusing and contradictory (see McAlister & Neill, in press), and Relationships and Sexuality Education (RSE) in schools or beyond would provide a perfect forum for examining these messages more critically. Indeed, Jo herself told us that although she had been sexually active for a number of years that she knew little about STIs:

"I'm 17 and I've been having sex for years, so if I don't know anything about it [STIs] a 13 year old having sex for her first time isn't going to know anything about it"

Thus, while young women's magazines may provide some information, they may not necessarily provide it in a holistic and informative way. Furthermore, the magazines young women read at a time when they are considering becoming sexually active may not necessarily be those which have accurate and useful information.

The internet also provided a useful source of information for young women, particularly those who identified as other than heterosexual. These young women noted that there was often no other means open to them, that it was not discussed at school or in the home and that unless they attended very specific youth provision that they had to find out for themselves. Nat (aged 24) who had been doing some research on the internet around lesbian sexual health for her part-time job as a Peer Support Worker, had found a wealth of information that she had not known about. Despite the value of the use of this medium, however, Nat felt that some of the information was so important that it needed to be talked about more and that young lesbians should not be expected to find this out for themselves:

"There's so much information on the internet and if it's presented in the right way it could be really useful, em but stuff needs to be talked about more. Like tons of stuff needs to be talked about more."

7.3.2 Formal Sources: Post-primary Education

Thirty-eight young women discussed the nature of the sex education they received within their schools. Table 1 provides a breakdown of their general views regarding this in relation to the type of schools they attended. This shows that only six young women (16%) described the sex education they received in school in their own terms as 'good', with the remaining 32 (84%) describing it in various ways as 'poor'. Furthermore, no young women attending Catholic maintained schools described their sex education as good and only 20% of those attending State Controlled schools found it good.

The average age of those who described good sex education was 22 years, while the average age of those who described poor or limited sex education was 20 years. This would suggest that the quality of sex education in schools (from the viewpoint of those receiving it) is, overall, still fairly poor, even for those still in compulsory education, or recently out of it. Indeed, despite the new guidance on the teaching of RSE in post-primary schools (see CCEA, 2001 & DENI, 2001), the findings presented here would suggest that little has changed with regards to young women's experiences of sex education in Northern Irish schools.

Table 1: Quality of Sex Education by School Type

	Good	Poor	Total
State Controlled (Protestant)	3 (20%)	12 (80%)	15
Roman Catholic Maintained	-	16 (100%)	16
Other[22]	2 (67%)	1 (33%)	3
Unsure[23]	1 (25%)	3 (75%)	4
Total	6 (16%)	32 (84%)	38

Other general findings regarding the young women's sex/sexual health education within compulsory education included:

- 23 young women reported that it was delivered only by teachers (average age = 21);
- 7 young women reported that someone external to the school had delivered all or part of their sex education (average age = 19);
- 15 young women reported that their sex education was limited to part of their science/biology class;
- There were mixed views on whether sex-education was best received within single or mixed sex groups;
- Young women reported receiving little information on periods. A number discussed a 'one-off talk' that focused on the physicalities or 'mechanics of it';
- Young women talked of feeling embarrassed during sex education and discussions of menstruation at school;
- Only one young woman reported that relationships other than heterosexual were discussed in her sex education.

22   This includes Integrated, Independent and Irish Medium schools.

23   This refers, in the main, to voluntary grammar schools where young women did not explicitly state that these were Catholic in ethos.

While this offers a quantitative overview of the general findings with regards to sex education in schools, a detailed qualitative analysis allows for a fuller examination of the factors relating to the young women's definitions of 'good' or 'poor' sex education within their schools. Furthermore, it allows us to highlight examples of good practice and to provide an understanding of what young women themselves say they want and need from their sex education within schools.

Perhaps one of the most frequently used phrases by young women when discussing the sex education they received was that it had provided 'just the basics'. By this they explained that there had been an almost exclusive focus on the biological or reproductive aspects of sex and in many cases, no information regarding contraception or STIs was provided:

"...it wasn't like specifically a sex education talk it was just more to do with like the biology of it." (Hannah, aged 23 – Grammar, controlled, co-ed)

"...it didn't go through diseases or nothin' or stuff like, y'know sexually transmitted infections an' all, it didn't go through none of that it just kinda give you the basics." (Gráinne, aged 18 – Secondary, RCM, single-sex)

As can be seen, this was not only the experience of some of the older young women in the sample, but also among those who had attended school more recently. Related to this, over a third of young women (39%, n=15) told us that all of their sex education had been received in science or biology classes, leading to an exclusive focus on the physical aspects of sex. While some of the older young women (i.e. aged 22-25 years) told us that this had primarily taken the form of a video which they sat through quietly, others with this experience described the use of diagrams and a biological talk:

"Well the only sex education that we got woulda been in science, which was basically this is what happens, you know when you have sex, and have a baby, blah, blah, blah." (Ellen, aged 22 – Grammar, RCM, single sex)

Within all school types and age groups, a major criticism of sex education was that it was 'too moralistic'. Some young women talked of a culture of secrecy where some teachers would give information in a private manner, suggesting that it should not be repeated outside the classroom. Many others reported that either implicitly or explicitly the teaching they received made them aware that sex was viewed as 'wrong', 'bold' or that it was 'frowned upon'. As Karen put it:

"I think in our school you would have been made to feel bad, they wouldn't have done it directly but I don't know, it was sort of frowned upon." (Karen, aged 19 – Grammar, RCM, single sex)

Jo and Madonna on the other hand, felt that the moralist and 'don't do it approach' was much clearer in their respective schools:

"Sex is all for having kids, sex is for no other reason but having kids. But it's not because everybody knows that sex is about showing love and all this. It's a lot more than just reproducing, it's a lot more than the basic primate, man woman make child. It's a lot more than 'at but you weren't told that, you were told that anything other than reproducing is bad, cos you're not supposed to have sex". (Jo, aged 17 – Grammar, Voluntary, co-ed – her emphasis)

"... it wasn't actually sex education, sex was bad. Sex isn't allowed..."
(Madonna, aged 25 – Grammar, Voluntary, co-ed)

There are many dangers with this approach to sex education and previous research has shown no strong evidence for the effectiveness of abstinence approaches (FPA/HPA, 2005: 3). The impact of this moralist approach to sex education became clear in Carmel's account when she talked about the treatment of a young woman at her school who had had an abortion:

"Abortion, we done that because we had a Vice Principal who was a nun, who was very anti-abortion. ...//... she sat us down and put us to watch these very vulgar videos of ya know abortion. An' eh it was in our heads never to have an abortion, never ever. Have an abortion, guilty and go to hell (laughs) ...//... Stuck right in us ...//... there was a girl that ended up getting bullied in my class in em grammar school, who had an abortion an' she had to leave cos we bullied her an' I can admit that now. That was years and years of putting that in our heads. Nowadays I understand it's the person's choice. Situations are different in every circumstance, doesn't matter like. Years ago I thought it was 'you're going to hell, I can't believe what you've done, you've kilt your baby. You murderer'."
(Carmel, 23 years – Secondary, RCM, single sex)

The impact of the religious ethos of schools on the teaching of sex education was discussed by many who attended Catholic maintained schools none of whom had felt that their sex education had been of value. It was described in various ways as limited, poor and moralistic and few reported having received any information on contraception and STIs. While similar criticisms were found in some of the experiences of young women attending other school types, they were most evident and pronounced amongst those attending Catholic schools. Overall, however, and as a group, these young women's main criticisms of the sex education they received in school was that it failed to cover issues relating to the emotional aspects of sex and sexuality:

"I feel quite strongly that it shouldn't just be about the physicalities and it should be about the mentalities of it and you should be told that there is emotional involvement here no matter what, no matter who you see or what you see..."
(Sue, aged 25 – Grammar, voluntary, co-ed)

While there is value in highlighting the criticisms young women made of their sex education, it may be of more value to highlight instances of positive experiences or good practice. Indeed, the examples of good practice to come to the fore in the research, and the factors young women noted as making it a positive and valuable experience, were in direct contrast to some of the experiences noted above. At a general level, the factors which young women highlighted as making their sex education good or of value included: it was not limited to one-off sessions; they felt comfortable enough to ask questions; it was holistic and expansive; it was enjoyable/fun and there were no moral undertones. While there were components of these in the accounts of the six young women who reported good sex education in their schools, there were only a few cases which stood out as incorporating all of these.

Good Practice Example: Jill's Experience

Jill was 17 at the time of interview and attending a single-sex, controlled grammar school. She received sex education every year she had been at post-primary school. Jill believed that the school had taken the issue of sex education seriously, demonstrated by the fact that they had pre-arranged and structured workshops spanning six week sessions which were delivered by experts in the field rather than teachers. These sessions were backed up in Religious Education and pastoral care, where issues relating to abortion and HIV were discussed in more detail. Of the sex education she received in school, Jill told us:

"We had different people coming in and different talks ...//... it would be workshops like, six week things. The school would have it set out, it wouldn't be like 'aw we'll give them this', it's all in their plan of whatever. Aw you know it was quite good, it was fun ...//... they [those delivering the sessions] know what they are talking about more, maybe, I suppose. Like that's what they do, they go round and they have all the resources and stuff you know, they know how to make it a bit more fun and stuff."

Jill's final point about the value of sex education being delivered by those other than teachers was shared quite heavily across the board. Many young women felt that teachers were not qualified to teach the topic area, were embarrassed and thus made the pupils embarrassed, made the topic stale and sometimes moralistic and that pupils often did not feel comfortable enough to open up and ask questions. In discussing what they felt would be useful for future sex education in schools, nearly all of the young women stated that it would be better taught by experts who were independent to the school.

While only two young women reported having discussed any form of intimate relationship other than heterosexual relationships within sex education or related lessons, there was overwhelming support for the inclusion of this issue. This was felt important on the basis of raising awareness and acceptance. Those young women who identified as other than heterosexual felt that these discussions could have helped them understand and accept themselves at difficult points whilst growing up and in highlighting information and advice points. Despite concerns about the discussion of homosexuality within schools, Tara (aged 19) clearly illustrates the reality of the nature and value of it:

"...it wasn't like a promotion of homosexuality ye know by any means, but it was basically like more of eh a relaxed opinion that nobody has any right to put you down for your sexuality ye know if you have any problems about ye know 'I don't know what my sexuality is' ye know we can put you in touch with people an' whatever else ye know they did have the support there for you ..."
(Secondary, controlled, co-ed)

Susie's Experience

Susie was 20 at the time of interview and identified herself as a lesbian. She had attended a single-sex controlled grammar school until the age of 16 but had a poor record of attendance due to caring responsibilities and domestic violence within the family home. Susie's sex education at school consisted of a video and a discussion of teenage pregnancy. She received no information on STIs or any form of relationship other than heterosexual relationships.

At school Susie was openly gay with a number of her friends, and teachers, to varying degrees, had knowledge of this. As part of her Religious Education class Susie and her classmates were given a picture "of a man sitting on a chair in a garden, and another man was behind, but he had his hand on his shoulder". They were invited to write about what was 'wrong' about the picture and discuss their views in class. On listening to the views of her classmates and the teacher regarding homosexuality and 'sodomy' being 'wrong', Susie became increasingly upset and frustrated and decided to express her own views on the matter.

"My essay near got me booted out of that school, I just went flying off on one and the teacher was tryin' to shut me up ...//... all these girls were goin' 'oh it's wrong' and all this and I was like 'hello, I'm standing here and you're my friend, why are you getting on like that?' ...//... I was not just gonna sit there and let the whole class say I was wrong and let him [the teacher] tell me I was wrong for being gay."

In standing up for herself Susie had effectively 'outed herself' to her whole class (and potentially the rest of the school) and risked being excluded because of the way in which she had approached the issue. Despite this, however, Susie felt that she had done the right thing because she recognised that there might have been other people in the class who were gay or unsure of their sexual orientation and that the discussion would make them feel that it was 'wrong' and create more difficulty in coming to terms with their sexual orientation. While Susie's actions are brave, they are likely to be an exception to the rule. Indeed, her willingness to put herself in this position may have been a result of her 'disengagement' with school as she was a poor attender and felt that she was unlikely to achieve well academically as a result of this and her associated family problems.

Finally, while our sub-sample of young women with disabilities is small and we do not wish to make sweeping generalisations, we feel that it is important to note that all of these young women displayed some level of embarrassment in discussing the issue of sex with us. When asked if she received any information in school around sex or relationships, Avril (aged 21), for example got embarrassed and laughed. When this question was followed up with "did you learn about having babies", Avril was unsure. Avril was the only young woman to use one of the pass cards she had been provided with[24] and choose to do so when discussing sex education. Vanessa (aged 21) also indicated that she did not want to discuss the issue of sex further by waving her hand and saying "don't ask". Kimberley on the other hand told us that she had received sex education at school but that she had not understood much of it:

---

24   See chapter 2 for a full discussion of the methods employed in the research.

"It was funny cos it was personal an' it was funny because I didn't understand anything so it was funny." (Kimberley, aged 21 – Special Unit, Catholic maintained, single-sex)

Given the limited information these young women were willing to offer regarding sex education within their schools it is difficult to make definitive statements or suggestions. Having said this, it is imperative that sex education for young women with learning disabilities is pitching at an appropriate and understandable level[25]. Kimberley, for example, had received no other sex education or information on sexual health since leaving school, and it was rather worrying that when we asked her about the good and bad things about being in a relationship that she cited sex as a bad thing. In light of her experiences of sexual abuse when younger this is of great concern.

In conclusion, schools are the main site where all young women could access information regarding sex and sexuality, yet it is clear that many schools are failing to provide them with accurate and holistic information in a manner which is appropriate to their needs. Despite the potential positive effect of RSE on pupil's self-esteem, some of the information presented here would suggest that this is not fully realised. These young women's experiences, in the main, show little evidence of a "climate of trust and acceptance in which each person is valued and respected and encouraged to feel good about themselves" (CCEA, 2001: 1). The limited nature of the sex education some receive may not only impact upon their ability to make 'informed choices' but moral undertones of sex as 'wrong', 'bad' and/or 'embarrassing' does little to instil a positive sense of self.

7.3.3 Filling the Gap? Informal Education and Youth Provision

Those young women who were involved in youth provision were among those who tended to have the greatest awareness and knowledge of sexual health, available services and a more holistic understanding of sex and sexuality beyond the biological. Indeed, a number of young women noted that it was through these programmes that they realised how little they had previously known:

"I got well clued up on it, whenever, one day we had a speaker in the group. An' eh, I was amazed ...//... An' I could see other girl's faces in the group goin', 'what's that? Diaphragm, wha?' (laughs), didn't have a clue." (Carmel, aged 23)

The fact that a number of these young women were in their 20s and felt that they had only recently received good and holistic information on sexual health and sexuality is not only concerning, but it highlights the continued need for this provision. Most interestingly, young women who identified as other than heterosexual noted that it was only through specific youth programmes tailored to their needs that they had ever been given information regarding lesbian sexual health. Some of these noted the misconceptions many young lesbians were under regarding sexual health as they had never been provided with adequate information. This had led to the decision among one such group that one of the young women attended to develop a sexual health resource pack for young lesbians by young lesbians. Furthermore, Wonder Woman (aged 21) noted that it was through a youth employment project for young people with disabilities that she had received most of her sex education, and that this had been both interesting and fun.

For specific, perhaps more marginalised groups, then, youth provision can fill many gaps left by schools in providing young women with holistic and appropriate information concerning sexuality

---

25   The UN Convention on the Rights of the Child states that every child has the right to access information to enable them to make decisions and choices in their lives and that this information should be presented in a form which is meaningful to them (Art. 17, UNCRC). Furthermore, RSE guidance states that "the provision of RSE is an equal opportunities issue. All pupils have a right to an education which adequately prepares them for adult life, and good RSE plays an integral role" (CCEA, 2001: 1).

and sexual health. Beyond this, however, and at a general level, the factors that young women identified as positive aspects of the sex education received through informal education/youth provision were that it was holistic, covering emotional as well as physical issues, was tailored to the needs and interests of the young women involved, was open, relaxed and fun and was delivered by experts. While it was clear that youth provision is filling a gap in knowledge, it should not be suggested that it can or is capable of doing this alone. Indeed, there are difficulties for youth workers whose knowledge and training in the sexual health field may be limited as it is seen as a specialism rather than a core occupational requirement. Furthermore, where the young women are under 16, parental consent must be explicitly gained before sexual health education can take place, which can exclude those most in need. Additionally, the strong connection of much youth service provision to religious institutions can rule out sex education from the youth programme entirely.

Cultural barriers, as Nicole (aged 25) found out in her work, are also hard to overcome in a youth work setting when wishing to do work with young women around sexual health:

"I think even workers themselves is very conscious do you know what I mean, don't have experience or the knowledge kinda way to talk about it ...//... In some ways I suppose because like me living in a predominantly Catholic area like the whole sex thing, people would lose their life the minute you open your mouth or if you were thought you're gonna do like sex education, do you know what I mean?"

That said, young women who had been involved in Alternative Education Programmes and youth programmes were unanimous in the view that the information they received here was of more value than that they had received in schools.

7.4 BEING KNOWN AND NOT KNOWING: BARRIERS TO ACCESSING CONTRACEPTION & ADVICE

In light of the views and teachings around young women, sex and sexuality in Northern Ireland, it is of little surprise that the themes of embarrassment and fear were a key part of the barriers to accessing sexual health information, advice and/or contraception. Twenty young women identified embarrassment or fear of being found out, seen or talked about as the main barrier to accessing information, services and advice on sexual health[26].

These themes were intrinsically linked with *a fear* of being judged by doctors if asking about contraception, *a fear* that advice and information might not be confidential and a fear that members of their community may see them entering family planning or sexual health clinics. These perceptions did not necessary tally with the young women's own experiences. While some talked of their discomfort and embarrassment on entering sexual health and family planning clinics or accessing contraception, none of them talked about actually *being* judged. This is not, however, to take away from the potential impact of these perceptions, for as will be illustrated, these could be strong enough at a young age to act as barriers to accessing contraception and advice. What we should be examining is the origins and impact of the message which maintains that young women's sexual behaviour is something to be hidden, while young men's is something to be celebrated.

---

26   It is important to note that many of the young women in the sample referred to experiencing these feelings when younger and put these forward as reasons why younger young women (particularly those under 18 years) may find it difficult to access information and particularly contraception.

While this fear and embarrassment of being seen entering sexual health clinics and accessing contraception is most often discussed in relation to young women living in rural areas, we found little difference of opinion and experience across all areas. That said, additional barriers were evident for young women living in rural areas in so far as actually getting to their local doctors or closest family planning centre may necessitate getting a lift from parents, hence increasingly the risk of being 'found out'. As Shirley (aged 24) told us:

"... my local doctor would be eight to ten miles away from us ...//... if it's a young person who had to go to ask for a lift from their parents, 'I've to go to the doctor, I'm sick', 'why what's wrong with you, are you sick?' It would be tough you know."

With regards to the barriers to accessing information, advice and particularly contraception, Erin summed up the views of many when she said:

"... they'd be afraid to go an' ask for it or think they're gonna be judged" (Erin, aged 19)

Related to the fear of being judged by others was a fear of parents finding out if young women were to access information or services regarding sex at a young age. While only two young women were of the belief that doctors would have to inform parents if a young person under the age of 16 years was to access contraception, there was a general lack of mistrust regarding doctor-patient confidentiality. Some young women, for example, noted that they would know their family doctor well or others who worked in their health centre or local chemist, and thus felt that there was the potential that their family might find out. Thus, as Susie (aged 20) put it:

"... although they know it's confidential, they don't trust adults and stuff".

The result of this was that embarrassment had led a number of young women to not accessing contraception and others to go outside their local areas to do so. Indeed, Ellen (aged 22) said that if her doctor had not suggested she take the pill that she "wouldn't have had the nerve to ask ...//... because I was young, because it's seen as bold ..."

What we see here in relation to the theme of embarrassment and fear of being judged relates to society's perceptions of young women, sex and sexuality. While women and their bodies may be highly sexualised in the media, and it is suggested that young women are more sexually liberated today, there is a clear risk attached to this 'liberation'. Such views and images give a sense of 'false equality' among young women in that they find that the talk of sexual liberation does not meet with their experiences. Thus not wholly unexpected, and as illustrated earlier, was the focus of many conversations on the social construction of young women as 'sluts' and young men as 'studs' when it came to sexual behaviour. As Kitzinger (1995: 193) notes, and as rings true of the opening quote from Carmel:

the tenaciousness of terms such as 'slag' speak, in part, of the continued absence of a discourse of female desire. Women must not speak about, or act openly in the pursuit of, their own sexual pleasure.

Those who talked of this clearly saw these labels as unfair and to all intents and purposes, socially constructed and inaccurate, yet despite the unfairness and inaccuracy of them they were fully aware of the affect of "getting a name" by being labelled as a 'slut' or 'tramp'. The risk to young women's reputations and long-term consequences are illustrated by Neimh (aged 17):

"It's not nice that girls should have that name, for it's not nice for any girl to have

that name on her. Cus if you have that name once it's gonna stick with you for the rest of your days ...//... That's why you just try and respect yourself like. That's one of the worst worries like in my life it would be to respect myself, cus I wouldn't want a name like that. To walk up the road and have to keep my head down."

Because of the risk to reputation, young women controlled/regulated their sexual behaviour, or in many ways did not speak openly about it particularly when younger. Furthermore, the persistence of these constructions and stereotypes and the risk to young women's reputation as a result of their sexuality impacts upon their sexual health. After all, to ask for contraception is admitting that you are sexually active (or intend to be) and there is a judgement and risk that goes with this. Indeed, the impact is more far reaching than this because a number of young women reported having no knowledge of STIs and that contraception was used expressly for the purpose of preventing pregnancy. Furthermore, a small but significant number of young women noted that they had a lack of information about the correct use of the pill. Beyoncé (aged 25), for instance, told us:

"I started using the pill, but I only started using it, and I wasn't really sure if I was doing it properly or not so I think, cos I missed one day and then I took two the next day I thought I would have been ok but I wasn't."

From their conversations then, it is evident that young women not only find it difficult to ask for any contraception when young but there is further difficulty in asking for advice on the proper use of it and a lack of knowledge of options other than the pill and the importance of protection against STIs.

In sum, many of the barriers to good sexual health In Northern Ireland are cultural rather than structural or spatial. The way in which Northern Irish society deals with the issue of sex at a societal level and in our homes and schools has constructed young women's sexuality within a discourse of shame and immorality, which impacts upon young women perceptions of their own sexuality and their sexual health.

While cultural barriers are clear and may be difficult to change quickly, the young women in this research noted a further (related) barrier which may be easier to tackle. Ten young women, for instance, felt that there was simply a lack of information about what services did exist, where they were located and the facilities they offered. While some of these young women were aware of local services themselves, they noted that they had only come by this information through youth provision, the internet or other means of actively searching. These young women felt that greater advertising was needed and some advocated that the best place for this to start was schools where information leaflets should be available. Susie (aged 20) and Tara (aged 19), for example, both noted that despite the fact that many would have heard of the Brook Advisory Clinic or FPA in Belfast, few would know where they were located or their opening hours. Similarly, of her area, Donna (aged 21) felt that a lack of provision was not the problem but a lack of knowledge of its existence:

"There's enough places to go to, but you need to know where to get the information ...//... as for advertising there's nothing."

Having to seek out information and services rather than being offered the information again goes back to the issue of putting an onus on young women to admit that they are sexually active.

That said, Susie and other young women who identified as lesbian did note the lack of information, advice and services for them regarding sexual health and the belief among their peers that sexual health was of little concern. While two young women noted the value of the internet for providing information on lesbian sexual health, others stated that it was only through youth provision that they had received sexual health information tailored to their needs. The value and importance of this information and such programmes was highlighted by Susie who spoke of the views of her peers:

"There's a lot of women who wouldn't know anything about anything, they'd just be floatin' along thinking 'oh we can't get anything' ...//... even if we're talking about it, and they're like 'oh sure we cant catch anything' ...//... they just think that if you're having heterosexual sex or whatever you can pass things on, but you don't see it and because you can't get pregnant so it doesn't matter, don't need to use protection ..."

'Not being able to get pregnant' may give a degree of greater 'freedom' to non-heterosexual young women, but the dangers associated with this are clear in that there may be the assumption that there is no need to practice safer sex. Furthermore, the fact that same-sex relationships are rarely mentioned in RSE in schools further reinforces the notion that these are 'bad', 'wrong', 'shameful' and should be hidden or secret. Related to this, it was noted that there was a sexual health drop-in for gay men in Belfast but no equivalent for women. Indeed, specific youth programmes appear to be the only providers of sexual health for young women who identify as other than heterosexual. Only a small number of young women, will, however, attend such programmes/groups leaving many others in the 'blissful' ignorance that Susie describes of her peers.

7.5 CONCLUSION

Sources of information regarding sexuality for young women remain piecemeal and difficult to access. The religious and moral discourse surrounding young women and sexuality in Northern Irish society appears in many ways to be legitimised and perpetuated in schools (Rolston et al., 2005), the main site where all young women could be provided with accurate and holistic information. Rolston et al. (2005: 217) note the absence of a 'discourse of desire' within sex education in schools particularly for young women where the risk of desire is closely aligned to pregnancy, abortion and STIs. Added to this is the risk to young women's reputations and this "mixture of secrecy, lack of knowledge and negative media messages confuses young people and encourages poor self esteem, resulting in uninformed choices being made" (FPA/HPA, 2005: 3). While youth provision and sexual health services do, in these young women's experiences, offer more valuable, holistic and less moralistic information, difficulties remain in terms of accessing them and the numbers of young women they can reach.

The major challenges regarding young women and sexuality in a Northern Ireland context are primarily cultural; engrained, reproduced and replicated in many of its social institutions. What is required is more trust in young people's abilities to make informed choices when given the appropriate information rather than a 'fear' or reticence of giving full information. This, Rolston et al. (2005: 232) suggest would aid in the "replacement of silence and avoidance with open discussion of dialogue" - something which Jo (aged 17) firmly echoed:

"Kids aren't as stupid as what so many people make them out to be, we can act responsibly, there obviously are exceptions to this. We can act responsibly, we do know the consequences of what we're doing, regardless of whether or not we take them into account what the consequences are [laughs] or whether or not we stop doing what we're doing. Well, there's a lot more trust that could be put into us by parents and people could be talked to about sex, by parents, a lot earlier".

7.6 RECOMMENDATIONS

Within a society where issues regarding sexuality are often hidden and taboo, sexual health services face many barriers in terms of advertising their services to young people. This, however, adds to the mystery and misconceptions around them and the following strategies should be employed to make these more transparent, particularly in explicitly putting across the message that these services are confidential:

- Those working in the women's sector and particularly with and for young women should continue to challenge cultural attitudes regarding young women. Sex, sexuality, a 'discourse of desire' and the realities of sex should be built into all forms of sex education through the formal and non-formal education sectors;

- In many cases contraception is seen primarily as a form of pregnancy prevention rather than as an integral part of healthy sexual relationships. Schools, youth and health promoters should continue to challenge the purely functional and mechanical aspects of contraception and promote a more rounded discussion

- Young women note the difficulties in carrying condoms and asking male partners to wear them. A nationwide 'carry a condom' campaign targeted at young women and young men could begin to challenge some of these stereotypes and begin to 'normalise' contraception use;

- The emotional as well as the physical and biological aspects of sex and sexuality should be part of all forms of sex education;

- There is a lack of recognition of non-heterosexual relationships in all forms of sexual health and sex education. This can result in young people feeling marginalised and prejudiced within the school setting and beyond. Schools, health and youth providers should more fully build sensitive discussions of non-heterosexual relationships into their work. This could best be done through consultation with young people who identify as other than heterosexual;

- There is a need for specific sexual health programmes and services tailored to young women who identify as lesbian or bi-sexual who feel that current provision is not relevant to them or that safer sex may not be a concern for them. The adoption of the Out and About Sexual Health Pack (in partnership with YouthAction Northern Ireland, FPA and Brook) currently being produced by a group of young women who identify as other than heterosexual may prove an invaluable resource;

- There is a need to inform and educate young women about sex at an earlier age and to build their confidence in discussing sexual matters in a non-embarrassed way. This needs to be taken forward in a number of ways, firstly within youth provision and schools as outlined below in discussion of RSE curriculum but also in work with current and future parents;

- Young women have positive experiences of sexual health/education teaching by professionals in the field and note a desire for more of this within schools. The pressures on teachers to teach sex education should be more fully recognised and greater school support and training offered to them. Furthermore, schools could more widely utilise independent experts in the field within the school environment;

- CCEA (2001) and DENI (2001) guidance on the teaching of RSE in schools are an excellent starting point, providing guidance on issues to be included in RSE, the rationale for this and useful resources. These should be implemented more widely and holistically within all Northern Ireland's schools. As a starting point for this, the DE should commission research which more fully examines how RSE guidelines are or are not being put into practice in Northern Ireland's schools and to address difficulties and challenges that schools continue to face.

- The youth service needs to develop a framework for sexual health education which meets the needs of young people. This should provide workers with clear guidelines on: age and maturity appropriate information; appropriate boundaries; sexual health issues for young women with disabilities and the impact of personal values on the delivery of such information.

- Finally, we endorse and reiterate the recommendation of Shubotz et al. (2003: 112, their emphasis) resulting from their research on the sexual attitudes and lifestyles of young people in Northern Ireland:

Policy makers and those responsible for implementing policies should trust young people. Good accessible information will not lead to promiscuity or irresponsibility. Ignorance will not protect young people physically or emotionally and neither will it enable them to build relationships on what they themselves identify as the key ingredient – trust.

Chapter Eight
Health & Well-being

8. HEALTH AND WELL-BEING

"I think there's just an awful lot of celebrities are like really skinny. Especially young girls, whenever they buy them magazines ...//... we have to be that thin because like Victoria Beckham is that thin or you know am, Renee Zelwegger's that thin and that's the way it should be. We could be like that, and I just think there's a lot of pressure from that side of it that they have to look the part."
(Kelly, aged 21)

8.1 INTRODUCTION

In 1994 Charles and Walters conducted an exploratory study into the health concerns of women prompted by the observation that there was a limited understanding of lay health concerns and by the recognition that definition of women's health issues seemed to be closely bound to traditional definitions of appropriate roles for women. Few studies had placed women at the centre of analysis or focused on women's own perspectives and priorities. They argued that even where research had sought to articulate the views of ordinary women it had often duplicated the emphasis found in medicine such as childbirth, pregnancy, infertility etc. Although the sub-samples according to age group were small, for most of the women interviewed reproductive and gynaecological problems were not among the most frequently reported health issues in their study. We aimed to give young women the opportunity to talk about the key health issues for them.

Concerns about public health have gained momentum in the UK and health policy has increasingly focused on the need to prevent ill health and promote well-being (DOH, 1999; DOH, 2002 ; DHSSPS, 2002). Since 1997 targets have been set in relation to key areas including reducing rates of smoking and alcohol intake, increasing physical activity rates and promoting mental health. However, there has been relatively little emphasis on the health of young people (McDonagh and Viner, 2006). This is perhaps not surprising given the common perception that young people are rarely ill. Yet there are distinct continuities between adolescent health and adult health. Where attention has focused on young people it has tended to be about addressing negative behaviour. Coverage in the UK and Ireland has continually highlighted concerns about levels of smoking, drinking and drug taking, growing rates of obesity and increasing suicide rates, especially among young men.

We asked young women about their perception of their own health and about what they thought the key health and well-being issues were for young women in Northern Ireland. This included discussion of motivations for smoking and alcohol use. In view of current debates we explored attitudes to body image and what factors they felt influenced their own and other young women's perceptions. The findings discussed in this chapter highlight the prominence of stress in many young women's lives. Their views, looked at in the context of issues discussed in other chapters in this report, demonstrate the need to take into account the totality of young women's lives.

8.2 PERCEPTION OF OWN HEALTH

In terms of views on their own health a variety of responses emerge. Most of the young women referred to being reasonably healthy – but talked of the need to improve health, for example, by eating a healthier diet or taking more exercise. However, a significant minority (n=8) said they did not regard themselves as healthy. In a number of cases this was due to the circumstances of their life such as living in a hostel. Where young women felt they were unhealthy or could improve their health, there was little evidence that this was because they lacked awareness or understanding of factors contributing to good or bad health. On the contrary, many were knowledgeable about health related advice regarding diet, smoking, exercise etc. The availability and appropriateness of health related information for young people was raised. The main points were that information in doctor's surgeries and other general health settings tended to be targeted at a broad audience and there was nothing specifically focused on issues of concern to young people and that health professionals were not specifically trained/ skilled in working with young people. Other research has identified that few youth services exist, although there is evidence that young people avoid using services not designed for them (Jacobsen et al., 2001). Despite the high level of awareness of public health related information there was a lack of acknowledgement of the long-term implications of unhealthy lifestyles. This may be due in part to the general difficulty of foreseeing health problems when you feel well, but also to the lack of control which some young women feel they have over their lives.

8.2.1 Smoking

As noted earlier there has been much discussion about increasing levels of tobacco and alcohol use among young women. An overview of equalities and inequalities in health and social care shows that the percentage of male smokers decreased from 39% in 1983 to 27% in 2002/03 while the decrease among women has been less marked (29-26%) (DHSSPS, 2004). A survey of 16 year olds looking at the main influences on their attitudes to alcohol, sex, smoking and illicit drugs, found the main factors to be peer pressure, boredom, having nowhere to go and nothing to do (Hannaford, 2005).

"I think cos wee girls, girls have more things on their mind and I think smoking makes them feel calmer and relaxed more ...//... if I have an argument with **** [boyfriend] I smoke two or three fags after the argument and then when I'm friends with him again ...//... I wouldn't really bother with em"

The above quote from Gráinne (aged 18) reflects the views of a number of young women. A few talked of smoking more when under stress (during examination times for example). Even those who did not smoke themselves suggested that smoking may be a way of coping with the stresses of children or depression.

While many of the young women we spoke to saw peer pressure as an important factor in young women starting to smoke, overwhelmingly smoking was linked to body image. Frequent references were made to smoking as a way of staying thin. Kim (aged 21) spoke of how her younger sister smoked a lot but would go weeks without eating much in case she put on weight. Others made reference to smoking substituting for food. Crisp et al. (1999: 669) considered the evidence for an association between body-weight/shape concerns and smoking in females. They suggested that despite the fact that there was a significant literature concerning the relationship of cigarette smoking amongst females to their concerns about their shape, that this literature was largely ignored, probably, they argue, because its implications for intervention are too challenging.

8.2.2 Alcohol

Contrary to societal and media perceptions, few of the young women in our study said they drank a lot. Again, they tended to be aware of information on safe drinking guidelines. Donna (aged 21) said:

"...when I drink I binge drink ...//... like one of my drinks would probably be four units. So I'm binge drinking all the time, but it wouldn't be every night, it's not."

As with smoking, peer pressure was cited as a reason for young women starting to drink. This was seen to be particularly the case for those who started drinking in their early teens. Interestingly, a number of young women who cited peer pressure as their main motivation for starting to drink said that while they drank quite a lot when they were in their early to mid-teens they drank much less as they got older. Reference was also made to alcohol being used to enhance confidence. Karen (aged19) referred to it as being "a confidence thing", adding that: "if I was going to meet a fella there's no way I could go without a drink".

Coleman and Carter's (2005) study of 14-17 year olds, and why they get drunk cited mostly 'positive' reasons for getting drunk. These were the increased confidence it gave them on social and sexual situations; getting drunk to 'escape' and forget problems, and something to do. Almost all of the young people in the Coleman and Carter study saw getting drunk as completely normal. The influence of friends as a leading motivation was often mentioned but interestingly, the authors point to instances of peer pressure being rare in their study and reports of peer pressure being much more common.

In response to a question about some of the dangers/implications for young women drinking, a few references were made to a link between alcohol use and unsafe sex. Anna (aged 18), for example, felt that women growing up in "rough estates" were more likely to become teenage mothers. When asked why, she said that they were the ones involved in binge drinking and hence did not know what they were doing.

It is interesting to reflect on the different ways in which women and men's drinking behaviours are viewed - the fact that women drinking in public are frowned on to a greater extent than men, that young women are seen to place themselves in danger by drinking too much - and the extent to which these media and societal perceptions influence young women's thinking. An article in the Irish Independent (O'Doherty, 2004), on young women and alcohol highlights how perceptions of young men and women abusing alcohol are very different. It is difficult to imagine the following language being used to describe young men. Describing a young woman the writer refers to:

... a bloated body already shows the signs of routine alcohol abuse ... a swollen belly bulges from her hipster skirt ... a group of Dublin 4 schoolboys shouts out "slapper" but she gives them the eye nonetheless. Like an ageing prostitute she lifts her miniskirt to reveal a thighful of puppy fat.

The article, in the vein of much popular reporting, goes on to blame the 'ladette culture', arguing that girls are no longer drinking at a younger age to impress boys but to endear themselves to other females. However, as a range of research has identified, peer pressure in relation to behaviour such as smoking and drinking has always been an issue.

When the discussion of health and well-being was broadened beyond their own health young women tended to discuss body image and/or emotional well-being as being the main health concern of young women generally.

8.2.3 Body Image and Self Esteem

In Northern Ireland research commissioned by the Health Promotion Agency in 2001 reported that 47% of young people said that they worried about their appearance. This was the case for 66% of females compared to 28% of males, with women in the youngest age group (16-19) most likely to report worrying about their appearance. The pressure on young women to be thin was raised by many of the young women we spoke to. The most frequently mentioned source of this pressure was the media and the perception of some celebrities as the 'ideal'. Failure to live up to this ideal was linked to low self-esteem. Susie (aged 20) felt many young women perceived the 'ideal' as "the perfect size 10, blond hair and all this". Victoria (aged 22) felt that image was very important saying:

"It's a big competition isn't it? Like who can be the skinniest and the brownest and the best hair and make up …".

In a similar vein, Nicola (aged 20) noted that:

"Even in school like all the popular girls are the skinny blonde …".

Some young women linked the pressure to be thin to eating disorders. The language used by Janine (aged 17) in the following quote illustrates how thin is seen to equal 'good':

"… they all want to be thin…//… they all want to look the way celebrities do. …//… they want to fit in with the crowd, to be nice and skinny".

Rachel (aged 25) said that she thought:

'… everybody wants to be thin …//… I think a lot of people starve themselves to be thin …//… cus I used to do it you know".

A number of studies have explored the extent to which female self worth can be linked to appearance. In a study of 235 adolescents' views on eating attitudes, self-esteem, reasons for exercise and their ideal versus current body size and shape, only girls associated body dissatisfaction with the concept of self-esteem (Furnham et al., 2002). Clay et al. (2005: 452) demonstrated that, controlling for family cohesion and stressful life events, there was a pronounced and progressive drop in girls' self- esteem from 12-17 years. Boys' self-esteem was much more stable. Their findings showed that viewing ultra thin or average-size models led to decreases in body satisfaction and self-esteem in girls age 11-16. Research links have also been made between exposure to thinness and a rise in eating disorders among teenage girls (Stice et al., 1994; Cattarin et al., 2000), an association made by a number of young women in our study in relation to bulimia and anorexia.

8.3 EMOTIONAL WELL-BEING

8.3.1 Views on Causes and Levels of Stress

Higher levels of poor mental health among young women in Northern Ireland have been identified in previous research. In 2001 the Health Promotion Agency for Northern Ireland concluded that while many of the young people who took part in their survey on mental health of young people regarded themselves as healthy, a significant number, especially girls, had a relatively negative view of their health compared to those in other European countries.

In 2004 the Northern Ireland Young Life and Times survey included a number of questions relating to the mental health of Northern Irish 16 year olds. The measure of mental health was the 12 item General Health Questionnaire. Analysis of the data (Cairns and Lloyd, 2005) showed that significantly more females than males – 30% compared to 16% – fell into the psychologically distressed category. The most frequently mentioned stressor for females and males was schoolwork with 62% of males and 73% of females citing this as the main cause.

When we asked young women about the levels of stress experienced by women and men many of the young women made reference to the fact that women were more likely to experience stress because of the need to juggle work and family responsibilities. The number of young women in our study reporting stress and poor emotional well-being was striking. For a number of young women stress was a fairly constant feature of their lives and was identified as a current issue by fifteen young women. Several other young women gave examples of times in their past when they had experienced considerable levels of stress. Many of the young women also made reference to how often their friends felt stressed. Beyoncé (aged 25) said that her:

"... whole life has been a stress, I think that's why I had the burst ulcer as well, cause they put it down to stress, I can't just say one thing cause there's a lot of things."

Rachel (aged 25) talked of "feeling stressed every day". Her description of her 'typical' day revealed a packed schedule consisting of looking after her child, going to work, a range of domestic responsibilities including looking after her uncle and her mother who has been ill.

For some young women the main causes of stress were events in their life such as bereavement, abuse, homelessness, living in a hostel, coming to terms with their sexuality or negative reactions to their sexuality. The impact of child abuse and domestic violence on young women is discussed fully in chapter 3. Our findings show that in the absence of appropriate and timely intervention the impact of abuse is long lasting.

The pressure on young women to achieve academically was discussed in chapter 4 and examinations and pressure relating to school was highlighted as a common source of anxiety and stress. For some, the stress was constant, resulting in sleeplessness, crying and considerable worry about how their results in examinations would shape their future.

Tara (aged 19) provided a vivid description of what she sees in the hostel she is currently living in and the mental health problems of people she has met there. She is clearly living in a stressful environment which, because of the restrictions of hostel living, has implications for her physical as well as her emotional well-being. She spoke of how she has thought about suicide, but said that it scares her so she wouldn't. Her situation is indicative of the multiple stressors faced by some of the young women we spoke to. The impact of emotional well-being on physical health was apparent in other young women's stories. Beyoncé discussed how she believes stress contributed to her stomach ulcer. Susie (aged 20) said that although she eats properly she gets sick a lot. She has eczema, which worsens when she is stressed. She explained:

"... I don't go out and drink loads and I don't sit in every night drinking and all. I eat proper food and stuff ...//... I just get really sick and the doctor doesn't know why either. And mostly, sometimes it's due to stress and all as well ..."

8.3.2 Self Harm

Two young women in our sample had self-harmed but many more talked of the extent of self-harm among young women. Studies of self-harm in the UK have shown that while experts are reluctant to talk about the profile of a 'typical' self-harmer, patterns have emerged from research. Girls are seven times as likely as boys to harm themselves; self-harming usually starts in adolescence, although a study by the Bristol Crisis Service for Women in 2002 reported that a third of 76 women who took part in their study had begun harming themselves as children. Nat (aged 24) talked of how she had started self-harming when she was 11 or 12. She feels the reason for this was that she felt she needed "punished for something". She strongly objected to the way in which suicide and self-harm is sometimes linked, arguing that it would deter her from using a service if it was titled 'self-harm and suicide'. Nat said that her most recent experience of counselling had helped her a lot. She has not self -harmed for a year and a half although she pointed out that "I still want to do it". Janine (aged 17), who used to self-harm regularly, but who feels she has also gained from counselling, said that "you felt you were cutting the pain away".

In Northern Ireland in 2004/2005 hospital admissions from self-harm numbered 4,705 although this figure no doubt under-estimates the problem (*Belfast Telegraph*, 10 May 2006). In 2004 the Mental Health Foundation and the Camelot Foundation launched an inquiry looking into self-harm in young people. It reported in 2006 and findings showed that the UK has the highest self-harming rates in Europe. A key factor identified as exacerbating self-harm was social isolation. The study suggested that school based work appears to be one of the most promising areas where the prevention of self-harm can be tackled.

In 2004 the National Institute for Clinical Excellence released new recommendations for dealing with self-harm, stressing a non-stigmatising approach. In Northern Ireland reference is made to self-harm in the Northern Ireland Suicide Prevention and Action Plan (2006-2011) (DHSSPS, 2006) and recommendations have been made relating to positive mental health and well-being training, including how to deal sensitively with disclosure of self-harm. This is cited as a priority for teachers and youth workers and other relevant workers.

8.3.3 Coping with Stress

Research by the Health Promotion Agency for Northern Ireland (HPANI, 2001) into the emotional and mental health of young people reiterated the frequently aired belief that there are differences in how young men and young women express their concerns and cope with emotional difficulties. This view suggests that young women are more likely to communicate their worries and use social support to help themselves whereas males keep problems to themselves or ignore them. This view of how women and men cope with stress, anxiety and depression has also been discussed as a possible factor in the number of suicides among young men.

The HPANI research identified the main issues concerning young people as school, work or career and lack of money. The three main coping strategies reported by the young people who took part in the survey were listening to music, talking to friends, and arranging a night out with friends. Males and females chose the same top three activities. More formal routes of coping, such as talking to another adult, youth leaders or teachers, came bottom of the list for males and females.

In our research coping mechanisms tended to fall into two main categories – ignore it/block it out or talk to family/friends but mainly the former. For many, the way of coping with stress was just to get on with things or to hide problems. These are some of the phrases used:

Coping by ***"being detached"*** (Karen, aged 19)

"Pushing it all to the side" (Nat, aged 24)

"I wouldn't really be one to talk a lot about my feelings" (Nicole, aged 25)

"... everything just gets pushed into a wee box and I just kinda float along. Something's gonna happen" (Susie, aged 20)

So while a number of young women expressed the view that women and men dealt with stress and depression differently, with men being more embarrassed to seek help and women coping by talking to friends, many accounts, including some of their own, suggest this is not the case. For example, in a discussion about stress and coping, Jo (aged 17) talked about the importance of friends as somebody that you can talk to and how she felt that "women cope with stress pretty well nowadays" and how they were more willing to talk about their feelings. Yet she also said that she herself was often reluctant to talk about her problems.

A number of accounts suggest that getting on with things was perceived as a strength or conversely, to ask for help would be a sign of weakness. Gráinne (aged 18), while having to face real challenges and difficulties, pointed out that she would never feel so stressed that she would have to get medical advice "cos I'm that strong minded". As discussed in chapter 3, there was evidence in some young women's stories of a 'survivor mentality' with a reticence to talk about problems, as this would be an admission of vulnerability.

The desire to address and cope with stress runs through a number of accounts. Susie, for example, expressed a need to understand and address her emotional health. She had been prescribed medication for stress in the past but had stopped taking it on the grounds that she felt it would be better to find out why she was stressed.

A few young women mentioned other coping mechanisms. Tara talked of how she coped by writing things down and by writing poetry. Others mentioned going running or going to the gym. As noted earlier, smoking was perceived by some to be a coping mechanism.

To an extent the strong focus on male suicide has skewed the discussion on mental health away from the issues facing young women. Young women themselves made frequent reference to the suicide among young men and, were obviously directly affected when it was a friend or a relative - although this largely goes unrecognised. The myth that women cope better because they are more likely to talk to friends is perpetuated even by young women themselves. Yet, if this goes unchallenged it is unlikely that appropriate support will be provided to young women.

8.3.4 Experience of Counselling

From the experiences of the young women some issues regarding counselling can be identified. Many of those who had sought support or advice had fairly negative experiences. Reference was made to counselling being a waste of time or to counsellors being patronizing. There were concerns about confidentiality, not just from some of the young women who had used services, but from others who perceived the lack of confidentiality as a problem. It is also clear from a number of young women's accounts that there are issues around expectations from counselling in that they are expecting solutions to their problems or for someone to make their problems go away. This raises a question about whether counsellors are explaining their role to young women in a way that they can fully understand.

There were also some examples of good practice. Janine (aged 17) had a traumatic childhood; one of the outcomes of this was that she started to self-harm on a regular basis. She couldn't talk to her family. She did however receive support from a school counsellor, as a result of which she disclosed her experience of child abuse. She feels strongly that there should be more counsellors and more access to support through locally based youth services.

Good Practice Example: Oscar's Experience

Oscar (aged 17) had experienced considerable stress as a result of a bereavement. Her mother had then taken an overdose which Oscar found hard to cope with. She found it difficult to understand why her mother wanted to kill herself when she had her children. The issues were never discussed within the family. Oscar was offered counselling by the school but initially refused saying that she did not want to talk to anyone about it. However, after breaking down in school she did end up talking to her Year Head, whom she felt had been very supportive. She did not feel that she gained anything from the first counselling session, but she did go back to the counsellor a few weeks later and she did find it useful. She identified the positive factors as having someone to talk to apart from your best friends, someone who was mature and understood what she was going through.

Oscar's story highlights a number of important points about good support: the counsellor was based in her school but was independent from it; the school had identified that there was something wrong with her and the Head of Year had offered ongoing support in a way which did not make her feel pressurised.

8.4 CONCLUSION

The young women who took part in this research focused much of their discussion about health and well-being on emotional and mental health. While the research sample spanned an age range from 16-25 there were few discernible differences in views relating to age.

A number of young women perceived stress as leading to physical ill health. Ways of coping with stress included unhealthy responses – smoking is a good example – even though the young women were aware of the harmful effects on health. This has been identified in much research on women's health, including work by Hilary Graham (1994). These findings suggest that health promotion campaigns which simply point to the detrimental effects of behaviour such as smoking, are unlikely to be successful. Rather, there is a need to tackle the factors contributing to stress such as the various cited pressures on young women, the multiple demands on their time and the limited control some of them have over aspects of their life.

The extent to which stress can be directly linked to ill health is subject to debate. One school of thought is that although stress may be important – its effects may be more indirect than direct – such as influencing drinking, smoking etc. Siegrist (2000) refers to psycho-social stressors such as relative income deprivation, in terms of work and housing, restricted social mobility and freedom, social isolation and exclusion. He notes that strong relative feelings of anger and hopelessness are associated with prolonged exposure to such stressors which in turn contributes to the development of physical and mental disease. This argument, at least to some extent, is supported by Wilkinson (2001) who argues that a lack of social cohesion is implicated in health effects through mechanisms such as shame, social anxiety and perceptions of inferiority.

A number of the issues raised in this chapter have also been identified in other research and investigations. The Bamford Review of Mental Health and Learning Disability in Northern Ireland (2006) recommended that mental health promotion and prevention in the school setting should be developed across all schools to include Independent School's Counselling Services and pastoral care initiatives. It also stressed the need for practitioners in education to be given the necessary skills and knowledge to address young people's mental health needs and foster positive mental health in the classroom. It would seem sensible that this also needs to be an important feature of youth service provision.

8.5 RECOMMENDATIONS

- The government strategy to secure general improvements in population health does not focus sufficiently on age or gender. For this strategy to have a long-term sustained impact there is a need to refine and develop health quality indicators specifically for young people which take account of gender differences.

- Health promotion as it currently stands tends to be 'taught' in classes such as PSE, Home Economics and pastoral care. This undermines the importance of health and well-being to every other aspect of living and also the way in which health is affected by a whole range of external factors. To encourage a more holistic understanding of health and 'wellness', health promotion should be embedded in multiple areas of the school and youth service curriculum.

- Body image and weight are generally viewed as diet and food issues rather than being related to self-esteem and the product of social and cultural factors. Young women therefore need to be supported to deconstruct and challenge the societal influences they encounter in relation to body image and weight. This should be a feature of health promotion curriculum for schools and youth provision.

- Young women said that too often health related information and services were generic rather than specific to young people. Age specific information, while currently available in particular settings such as some schools or youth agencies, is not widely accessible in a wide range of public settings. There needs to be better dissemination of existing material where all young people can access it. Staff working in health related areas need to be specifically trained in the issues facing young people and responding sensitively to their needs.

- The current policy discussion and strategic planning clearly identifies many of the mental health issues facing young people. Recommendations made in the Bamford Review relating to the mental health needs of children and young people need to be implemented and adequately supported by the allocation of sufficient inter-departmental resources.

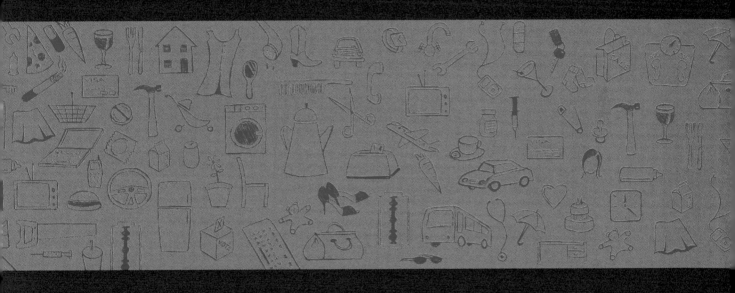

Chapter Nine

Politics and Participation

POLITICS AND PARTICIPATION

"...what's the point in me voting, cus it's got nothing to do with me." (Neimh, aged 17 on politics)

"...it makes us feel we are doing something" (Ruth, aged 17 on school councils)

9.1 INTRODUCTION

Historically women have been under-represented in electoral politics in Northern Ireland and in appointments to the public bodies which are responsible for administering and delivering key public and social services. These include the Education and Library Boards, Invest Northern Ireland, Health and Social Services Boards and Trusts, the Youth Council and the Policing Board. Northern Ireland has the worst track record in the UK in terms of women's representation.

Decades of conflict has meant that government and political parties have focused on parity of esteem between two major political/religious blocks, not integrating women and other under-represented groups into political and public life (Hinds & Gray, 2005). Political parties in Northern Ireland have consistently opposed introducing specific actions to tackle the under-representation of women and the treatment of representatives from the Women's Coalition by some male colleagues less than a decade ago highlights continued misogynist attitudes. Of this, Fionola Meredith (2003) reported:

At the peace talks which led to the Good Friday Agreement, when the two representatives of the newly-formed Women's Coalition took their seats at the negotiating table, Pearl Sugar and Monica McWilliams were met with a variety of sexist and sectarian insults, not least the suggestion from leading Democratic Unionist Party members that they would be far better employed 'staying at home and breeding for Ulster.'

This may seem difficult to understand given that political arrangements in Northern Ireland in relation to the Assembly are designed to protect cross-community parity, but it illustrates the low priority that has been attached to gender equality in politics and in social policy.

In the most recent elections to the Northern Ireland Assembly (March 2007), out of a total of 278 candidates, 52 were women. Of the 108 MLAs elected, 18 were women: no increase on the 2003 results. Furthermore, seven constituencies in Northern Ireland have no women elected. Following the 2005 local government elections in Northern Ireland, women held 22% of council seats. This reflected an increase at each of the last three local government elections - from 14% in 1997 to 22% in 2005 (Hinds & Gray, 2005). Following the implementation of the Review of Public Administration the number of councillors in local government will be considerably reduced. This could mean that the already inadequate number of women councillors could considerably diminish.

This continued under-representation of women in decision-making in Northern Ireland is even more striking given that the European Union and the United Nations have stressed that women are integral to building and sustaining peace and democracy. The United Nations passed UN Resolution 1325 in 2000, a central focus of which is to increase the participation of women in conflict resolution and peace processes. Women and children are disproportionately affected by conflict and by the consequences of peace-building, so must be centrally involved in establishing new conditions in post-conflict society. Yet, an overview of many of the institutions in Northern Ireland reveals a distinct lack of women. The UN Resolution is an important tool to press for women's equal representation. The UK government has regularly articulated its commitment to UN Resolution 1325 and in 2006 published an Action Plan on it (FCO, 2006). The Gender Equality Strategy for NI (OFMDFM, 2006) cites UN Resolution 1325 as one of the International Commitments to be met, alongside the obligations on national governments set down by the Convention on the Elimination of Discrimination Against Women (CEDAW). These also include equality in decision-making.

With regards to young people's involvement and interest in Northern Ireland politics and voting, figures from the 2006 Young Life and Times study reveal that 16 year old young women are less interested than young men in politics (YLT, 2006). That said, 2005 data found that young women were more likely to say it was worth voting and that everyone has a duty to vote. Also, although young men regarded themselves as slightly more knowledgeable about politics, young women were slightly more likely to answer the questions on elections correctly (Schubotz, 2005). Despite young people's interest in politics, research continues to find that they feel that politicians do not make enough efforts to listen to them or to make politics relevant to them (Institute of Conflict Research, 2006). In light of this, the Chief Electoral Officer recommended in 2004 that the process of elections and electoral registration be part of the curriculum in the latter years of school and in universities (Kilkelly et al., 2004: 47). The introduction of citizenship education into post primary schools is one mechanism through which such information can be passed onto young people and through which young people may be encouraged to become more involved in the democratic process (ICR, 2006: 10).

Participation, however, goes beyond an informed interest and understanding in politics and there has been much discussion on the value of youth participation in all areas of life. Youth participation, it is suggested, can enable young people to exercise their rights, play their part in knowledge creation, prepare them to be active citizens and strengthen social development (Checkoway & Richards-Schuster, 2003). Young people's participation in policy, practice and research is increasingly being implemented in many areas today but with varying degrees of success (Hill et al., 2004). Indeed, Hill et al. (2004: 82) among others caution that to consult with young people is not enough and that children and young people "make clear that ... their views should have an impact". Related to this, research with over 1,100 children and young people in Northern Ireland concluded that:

The conclusion that Northern Ireland does not listen to its children or, worse, that it affords them only minimalist, tokenistic opportunities to participate and engage with adults is a theme which cuts across all themes within the research ... by far the most pressing issue to emerge was having limited influence on the decisions that affected them (Kilkelly et al., 2004: xxii).

Article 12 of the UNCRC (ratified by the UK in 1991) provides children and young people with the right to express their views on matters concerning them and to have their views given due weight, yet the aforementioned research suggests that this is not the experience of many children and young people in Northern Ireland. That said, significant developments have been made in an attempt to ensure the greater participation of children and young people in schools (through school councils), in the youth sector (through youth forums) and in the policies and practices of many agencies. Many individual groups and agencies have children and young people panels or specific initiatives or policies to ensure the inclusion of the voice of young people, yet the degree to which this is implemented across the board and the level of success of these is unknown. Some reports of schools councils, young people's involvement in policy formation and consultation, however, remain disappointing (see for example, Include Youth, 2003; Kilkelly et al., 2004; Schubotz & Sinclair, 2006; YCNI, 2001).

The advocacy of a participatory approach in many areas of life while young (family life, school life, leisure, community and the framing of local policy) can prepare young people for full participation in adult society. In other words, it can prepare them to be full and active citizens with the recognition that citizenship is about the:

right to symbolic presence and visibility (vs. marginalisation); the right to dignifying representation (vs. stigmatisation); and the right to propagation of identity and maintenance of lifestyles (vs. assimilation). (Pakulski, 1997, cited in Kitchin & Lysaght, 2004: 84)

Picking up on a number of the points discussed in this introduction, we felt it important to gauge the attitudes of young women in relation to Northern Ireland politics and their participation in decision-making. Given the under-representation of women in political life and public bodies, we felt it important to consider the impact of a lack of female role models on young women's views and interest in politics. Also, to consider young women's views on and experiences of decision-making within their own lives. Thus, in the latter part of this final chapter we attempt to locate young women's voices in schools, communities, youth provision and political life.

9.2 NORTHERN IRELAND POLITICS: VIEWS ON VOTING AND LOCAL POLITICS

While many young women said they had no interest in Northern Ireland politics, their responses to a number of questions around the issue suggested differently. These young women held many views on the political situation in Northern Ireland, and despite sometimes feeling disillusioned, they showed great knowledge of it and discussed in detail its meaning or otherwise for themselves and their peers (see also ICR, 2003).

In response to a direct question on their interest in Northern Ireland politics, 17 young women declared no interest. Yet, ten of these told us that they currently voted or intended to do so when they turned 18. In total, 18 young women voted or intended to do so, and despite many complaints about the system, they noted various reasons about why they did/would vote. These included:

- Pressure/influence by community, parents or peers (n=7)
- To make changes at a local/community level (n=4)
- To exercise their right/have a voice (n=3)
- Because women fought for the vote (n=2)

The small number of women (n=5) who stated that they did not or would not vote gave a number of reasons also, and the most often cited were:

- They did not understand politics (n=3)
- Voting would make no difference (n=3)
- Voting was based on religion not social issues (n=2)

Although 18 young women voted or intended to, they had many complaints. Eight felt that despite voting they thought it would make little difference to Northern Ireland society and eight complained about politics being based on religion, about there being a lack of focus on social issues and a lack of relevance to young people.

While this offers a general overview of the young women's attitudes towards politics and voting, we want to take a little more time to discuss some of these issues in a little detail.

9.2.1 To Vote ...?

A significant number of young women informed us that their decision to vote was based on some form of pressure or influence from friends, partners, family or the community. Within the accounts of these young women it was clear that this influence took two forms. Firstly, someone impressed the importance of voting in terms of exercising their right, influencing decisions or ensuring that the right person was in place so that local/community issues were dealt with adequately. Secondly, and more reflective of this group, was that someone actually influenced the young woman's voting preference. In other words, they told them how to vote. Key to both discussions was that young women were not making fully informed personal decisions when it came to voting. Kelly (aged 21), for example, told us that she voted because a friend phoned her the day before to remind her to do so. While Kelly told us that she voted "because it's my right to vote", on reflection she felt that she perhaps should not vote as she did not understand the process or necessarily know why she voted for particular candidates:

"... I know like our local elections, I don't understand any of it, but I'm told I have to go because it's my right to vote but I'm like 'I don't care' ...//... I just don't know who I voted for and why I voted for them. It's not, it's not what I am interested in. I do vote but I really shouldn't, cus I don't know what I'm voting for." [her emphasis]

Like Kelly, some of the young women we spoke to who had not yet reached voting age told us that they would vote when they reached 18 years of age simply because they could. It was something new in that they now had the right so might as well exercise it, rather than this being based on any genuine interest or understanding of politics and party politics. Indeed, a number of these young women said that they would probably just vote for the same people as their parents and would make their first legal vote but were unsure if they would bother after that. As Ruth (aged 17) told us:

"I'll vote the first time yeah, but I don't plan to vote any other time, it's a waste, it doesn't seem to make any difference ..."

Others, who were older continued to vote in line with their parents. As Kim (aged 21) and Louise (aged 23) both reveal in the following extracts:

> **GN:** ... do you vote when there is a general election
> **Kim:** I did for the first time last year
> **GN:** And did that come from a kind of –
> **Kim:** No, my Ma [mother] told me ...//... My Ma [mother] told me, 'go in an' cross this box an' that box' and I was like 'ok'.

"I just vote for, this probably sounds quite bad, my Mum and Dad, who they vote for and I would just say 'I'll vote for them cos my Mum and Dad vote for them'."

What was interesting about Louise's account is that she had formerly lived in Scotland as a student and told us that she had always voted while living there. She read all the leaflets that came to her home at the time of local elections and noted that she was "able to make a decision based on their policies." She was also delighted, yet somewhat surprised to find that the party had managed to achieve some of the things they said they would, such as a local park in the area. The point here is that Louise made an informed decision based on good information about local policies while living in Scotland in a way that she felt unable to do in Northern Ireland. The result, as with a number of other young women, was that Louise ended up basing her vote on the views of her family or community background - an established pattern that many felt was hard to break in light of the many religious divisions in Northern Ireland society:

"... everything seems to be based on religion now ye know where ye have to vote, if you're a Protestant you vote for a Protestant an' you don't vote for the Catholic ..." (Jemima, aged 20)

"... it depends on how they're brought up and stuff as well. It's like, if they're comin' at it from a religious point of view, then their parents are gonna say, they've been brought up to say 'we have to vote this'" (Susie, aged 20)

9.2.2 ... Or Not to Vote?

While many noted a lack of knowledge of politics and of the voting process, this had led only a small number to decide not to vote. Nat (aged 24) told us:

"... I've never voted, because one I don't know how to, and two I don't know who to vote for, I've never been interested enough in it and I'm not about to go and vote for somebody just because everybody else is voting for somebody."

It is difficult, however, to see how we could define Nat's and others decisions not to vote as informed decisions. If, after knowing all of the facts, young women were deciding not to vote, then we might say it was an informed choice, but for many, these facts were simply lacking (see also section 9.4.4).

Aside from this, perhaps one of the most interesting points to emerge in the accounts of those who did not or would not vote was that voting for them was seen in some ways as 'taking sides.' This is of little surprise in that Kitchin and Lysaght, among others, note that "Political identities, positions and their associated political parties in Northern Ireland cannot be disconnected from the religious inspiration which underpins them" (2004: 93). For these young women, it appeared that to declare no interest in Northern Ireland politics and not to vote was essentially declaring no interest or side in the religious conflict. Voting, because of the nature of the political system, signified to them having an allegiance and defining oneself as Nationalist/Republican or Unionist/Loyalist. Not voting was one of the ways in which they distanced themselves from these identities. The use of phrases like "I don't really wanna take anything to do with it" (Neimh, aged 17) and "if they wanna fight amongst themselves and get people to do this, I'm like 'whatever!'" (Susie, aged 20) was how they expressed this distancing.

Indeed, some young women felt that the religious divisions and conflicts in Northern Ireland were perpetuated by the political system and that the only way to move forward as a society was a complete over-haul of this system. In the words of Karen:

"Like I would never ever ever care about anything like that [religion], but then there is people who do and it's fuelled by the politicians because ultimately they are their leaders and they are voting for them and obviously they're taking in what they are saying whether they want us to or not." (aged 19)

9.2.3 Voting and the Future of Northern Ireland: 'What Difference Do I Make?'[27]

Whether young women voted or not, there was the overwhelming view that their vote essentially made little difference. There was a strong feeling that politics was based on religious or sectarian divisions and that local politicians were not taking the concerns of the people into account. While there was a general desire for change in Northern Ireland, young women were fairly disillusioned with the political situation at the time of the research. As previously noted, the Northern Ireland Assembly had been suspended for some time and this caused a great deal of annoyance, especially among those who had bothered to register their vote in the hope that it would be restored. Madonna and Jill illustrate this general sense of frustration:

"What do they [politicians] do? I mean we vote people in and they won't talk to each other, sit at the table, we don't have an Assembly and they're getting paid to do it. How, you can't defer power to somebody like that, you can't support that cus they're just sitting on their fat asses fighting. It gets to the stage where I don't care what you's do." (Madonna, aged 25)

"MP or MLA ...//... [sighs] they get off with so much. I don't know, they're pretty useless in this country." (Jill, aged 17)

Thus, even when young women did vote they felt that their vote made little difference and was unlikely to. The clear concern is that if young women continue to think that their vote will make little difference this could lead to those who currently vote, deciding not to in the future.

In sum, among this group of young women there was a great desire for change, yet a somewhat despondent attitude in that they were increasingly beginning to think that they had little control or say over the future even when they did bother to vote. Many advocated a move away from tribal politics and a move towards a political system and political parties based on the everyday issues that effect young people, their families and their communities. In the words of Karen and Kim, it is time for Northern Ireland to move forward:

"... like there's a whole lot more issues out there apart from a Northern Ireland peace process. I mean when do we ever hear about anything that concerns real people everyday? Like there isn't flipping fighting everyday and I know it's a problem and all but there's bigger things going on now than just that." (Karen, aged 19)

"... if everybody wud just forget the past an' get on with now, there'd be no arguments, no war, no nothin', everyone'd be fine even if we all had different religions or whatever, just get on with it." (Kim, aged 21)

The Northern Ireland Assembly is due to be restored shortly after the launch of this report and this signals what many see as a new era in Northern Ireland politics. Local politicians have a responsibility to listen to and act upon what young people who vote for them require of them, and to make greater efforts to engage with young people and make politics more young people friendly (see also Kilkelly et al., 2004).

---

27   Nat aged 24.

9.3 WOMEN AND POLITICS

In order to gauge the views of young women on the place and role of women in politics, we asked their views on the under-representation of women in Northern Ireland's political parties and their views on the difference, if any, greater representation of women might make. It is perhaps revealing that in response to both questions, a significant number of young women answered that they did not know or had not considered it. This in itself may suggest that young women have become accustomed to the under-representation of women in politics, as this is simply a fact of life and the way in which things have always been. Indeed, this may well have been one of the first times that this fact was actually brought to their attention.

While a substantial number of young women felt unable to offer an opinion, 19 young women did offer comment. Out of these, only one did not see any gender imbalance. Máiréad, as discussed in section 9.4.4, attended a school where a number of teachers were ex-political prisoners and where one of her female teachers was an MP. Of her school, she told us:

"My French teacher's a MP now. We were always, as I say we were never really from like a segregated women-men, it was always, always mixed, no matter what." (aged 22)

While it is encouraging that Máiréad was provided with a female role model and a real life example of how women can and do become involved in politics, in some respects, it may have served to conceal the historical position of women in politics and the continued inequality in representation and barriers to involvement.

9.3.1 The Under-Representation of Women in Northern Ireland Politics

While Máiréad's is a very specific example, other young women noted that there were still no female candidates within their constituencies and they offered a number of reasons why they felt women were not involved in politics in Northern Ireland. The main reasons put forward included:

- That it was always a male dominated profession
- That women were less interested or not encouraged to be interested in politics
- That women were not/would not be taken seriously
- That the history of politics in the country was hard and aggressive and that this left little place for women

Northern Ireland politics, and indeed politics more generally, was recognised by young women as a male dominated profession that was difficult for women to get involved in. Carmel likened this profession to other positions of authority where women are under-represented ("men get into authority that's it, women aren't perceived that way because of society"), while Donna noted that "for years it's always been men" and Karen felt that women would be put off and intimated "having to go in somewhere that's predominately male."

Linked to this, a number of young women noted that there were always a greater number of young men taking politics as a subject in their schools. And Kelly told us of how this pattern appeared to follow through into universities where her female friend was one of only three young women in her politics degree. While some felt that this merely symbolised that young men were more interested in politics than young women were, others felt that it was a reflection of what was seen/understood as open to them. In response to a question on her thoughts on why few women in Northern Ireland were involved in political parties, Louise explained:

"Maybe it's more difficult for them [women] to get into because it's always been seen as like a male dominated profession and even when we were at school, I mean stuff like politics – it was all boys did politics in my school and eh I really think it is because all the politicians you see are men and I would never have thought 'oh I want to be a politician' cos it's like a man's job." (aged 23)

This is linked to the fact that, as Karen said, young women are "not encouraged" to take an interest in politics or to consider it as a profession and that because as a number of young women noted, male politicians are always seen on television and people have begun to think "guys know more". Clearly, encouraging young women to take an active interest in politics and increasing female political role models is one way in which these stereotypical views can begin to be broken down. Schools are a prime site to begin the process of opening up politics to young women (see also section 9.4.4).

In addition to these points, a number of young women felt that women were simply not taken seriously when it came to politics. They explained this primarily in relation to widely held stereotypical views of men and women and to the attitudes of men. Ruth, for example, said that "males think it's their thing, they know it best and they can do it best." Kelly felt that people may think "men are better at arguing" and Michelle noted that involvement in politics is "really hard work an' like a lotta people might think like oh women aren't up to the job, like it should be a man". All of these points link to traditional stereotypical views of 'men's jobs' and 'women's jobs' and to the perceived characteristics of men and women. In essence, some felt that women would simply not be taken seriously and that they would find it difficult to secure votes, especially from men. As Carmel said:

"Votin' wise (pause) who's gonna vote for a woman if they're a man (laughs). Right I don't know it's just different sexes, it's nothin' to do with what they're speakin' about, it's nothing to do with their opinions, it's nothing to do with what they're gonna do for our community or their community. ...//... I wouldn't see my father goin' down an' votin for Monica [McWilliams, leader of the Women's Coalition] or ah, ya know I wouldn't see my father goin' down and votin for any [women] ya know." (aged 23)

There remain barriers to women entering politics and while a number of the young women we spoke to had some understanding of what these may be, a substantial number felt unable to offer any reason. In light of this, there is a need to open opportunities to better inform young women of the historical position of women in Northern Ireland politics. While the presented case example (below) of Madonna's understanding is put forward as a way in which women can be better informed, it is important to note that her understanding based on research and reading is not wholly different to some of the views expressed by other young women. Yet an important part of Madonna's understanding is missing in the accounts of all of the other young women we spoke to, namely the important role that women have historically played at a grassroots level in the political history of Northern Ireland. What Madonna is talking about is the invisibility of women in Northern Ireland politics. This information is now being increasingly written into accounts of Northern Ireland politics, but it is not necessarily filtering down to young women despite the potential empowering effect it may have. There is still a need as Margaret Ward (1989) notes, not just to rewrite women into Northern Ireland's history but to understand the motives of why they were left out (cited in Dowler, 1998: 159).

Madonna's Experience: Enhancing Opportunities to Inform Young Women of the Historical Position and Role of Women in Northern Ireland Politics

Madonna was 25 at the time of interview and a recent graduate in International Politics "working part-time in a bar until I get a proper job".

As part of her course Madonna had undertaken research on women in Northern Ireland politics and had found it an enlightening exercise that had ultimately increased her interest in the area. Based on her research she now firmly believed that the under-representation of women in Northern Ireland political parties "basically came down to the image of women." Within the Nationalist community, women were seen as 'homemakers' and within the Unionist community they were seen as 'tea makers'. From all sides, however, the historical view was that women "shouldn't be involved in politics, politics is a man's job ...//... it's no place for someone who's maternal, maternal instincts don't come into politics."

While Madonna did acknowledge that the situation had changed somewhat over time, and that at the time of fieldwork Sinn Fein was the party with the largest number of female candidates, other parties continued to lag behind:

"DUP's the worst, Ulster Unionist, they don't think there's a place [for women]. Paisley himself came out with some statement saying how God made man and man's all this, until God says so women won't be involved in politics."

Madonna blamed the demise of the Women's Coalition and the continued under-representation of women in other political parties on male politicians treatment of members of the Women's Coalition, noting that their views were constantly demeaned and their jobs made difficult. In her view this reflected the attitude of many male politicians that "they're just not open to having women in politics in Northern Ireland."

When asked if she felt that greater numbers of women involved in politics would make any difference, Madonna informed us that:

"Women have made a big impact in politics in Northern Ireland on the ground but people don't realise, from local groups set up in Belfast in the late '60s and early '70s so they have. They've done a lot of work to push things forward but the politicians believe women's issues shouldn't come to the forehead until the Northern Ireland question, but the Northern Ireland question is also about women, but em, you know women have done a lot at a grass roots level, they're not allowing them to move up the spectrum into broader politics."

9.3.2 The Impact of Greater Political Representation of Women

Young women were asked if they thought that greater representation of women in political parties would have any impact. Again, some felt unable to comment and a few felt that it would have no impact because:

- The 'Northern Ireland question' would always take precedence no matter who was involved
- They wouldn't be taken seriously by male colleagues
- They take on 'male characteristics' to be taken seriously/fit in, so it makes little difference

Others, however, felt that greater female representation had the potential to make a difference. At a basic level it would make representation more equal, which was seen as a positive thing, and, more specifically, it would ensure women had more rights, provide a voice for women and greater recognition of issues specifically impacting upon women. Interestingly, two young mothers felt that it would provide the potential for issues relating to them as mothers to receive greater political attention. Erin (aged 19), for example noted the potential for:

"... more weemen organisations an' like babies an' stuff, for there'd be more nurseries an' stuff like if weemen were involved an' that, whereas men don't have a clue how to put weemen's rights first if ye know what I mean. ...//... They should have childcare but you shouldn't have to really, I mean ye should have to pay for it but like a fiver a week ...//... weemen could get out there an give their [women's] point if ye know what I mean."

Others referred to the potential of more women in politics to bring 'women's issues'/'caring issues'/'social care' to the political agenda. By this they invariably meant issues which related primarily to women as the main carers in society and issues relating to women's health. Molly, after some thought, felt that a local woman councillor might have helped in the fight to keep women's health services in her area open:

*"Like you know where I'm from like they've closed the, I know men can get it, but it's very unlikely. The breast cancer screening, they've closed it in both **** [area] and **** [area]. Maybe if there was a woman [councillor], they'd be pushing it more".* (aged 20)

While these are indeed important points, it is interesting to note that only one young woman talked of the more general potential for providing more of a voice for women in all areas.

9.4 YOUNG WOMEN'S VOICES/PARTICIPATION

The previous section focused specifically on young women's views and voices in relation to Northern Ireland politics and this theme of voice and participation is further discussed here. Reflecting back on a number of the issues raised in the report, in this final section we consider where young women's voices are located in schools, youth provision, communities and politics and their level of participation within these areas.

9.4.1 School Councils: A Useful Mechanism for Inclusion?

Few young women reported that their schools had school councils. Unsurprisingly, the four who did have these were in the younger age group and all aged 17. That said, others within this age group, or only a little older, did not have any knowledge of school councils within their schools.

While most had no experience of a school council they felt that it would have been useful and was a good idea in principle. A small number, for varying reasons, felt that it would not have worked in their school at the time that they were pupils there. Overall, however, the young women, either through experience or perception, identified both positive and negative aspects of having a school council. As can be seen in Table 1, the positives far outweighed the negatives.

Table 1: Views of School Councils

Positive	Negative
Cuts out teacher as first point of contact Peer support Faceless complaints Pupils have a say/voice Pupils empowered through efforts and change Teaches young people leadership skills	Tokenistic: not listened to, waste of time Pupils put forward silly ideas

There were examples of both good and poor practice of school councils in the young women's accounts. Jill (aged 17), the Assistant Secretary on her school council told us:

"... there's a day in October where you go and learn things about committees and stuff like that, team building exercises for everybody. Then you have meetings once a month and then we get to put points across, issues in school, stuff like that." (Grammar, controlled, single-sex)

Through this mechanism Jill felt that they had managed to successfully negotiate a healthy school tuck shop and a gardening programme to brighten up the school grounds. From the experience, she felt that she personally had learned leadership skills and that the pupils in general had been given a say in their own school and as a result were more appreciative and took pride in it (e.g. the school garden/grounds). This view backs up the findings of recent research in Northern Ireland which found that those pupils who had an "active and working school council had a greater sense of ownership of their school" (Schubotz & Sinclair, 2006: 3).

Janine (aged 17), however, from her experiences felt that the school council within her school had been of little value as:

"... sometimes teachers don't look into it. So really it's a waste of the pupil's time doing it." (Secondary, controlled, single-sex)

It is clear then, that for school councils to be effective that young people must be listened to and their concerns addressed - even as Jill said, if things did not change, to know that they had been considered and reported back on made pupils feel that their views were included and taken on board.

Overall, most of the young women in this research felt that school councils had value as a means of peer support, a place to voice opinions without fear of reprisal and for putting forward and representing the views of pupils, even if these were not always acted upon. In the words of Ruth (aged 17):

"... it makes us feel we are doing something, cus we're putting something forward ..."
(Grammar, controlled, co-ed)

For these young women, school councils, if run appropriately and taken seriously, had the potential to act as an important mechanism for pupils to express their views and to feel part of the school and the decisions made within it. The experience could, therefore, be an empowering one, as it was in the case of Melissa (aged 16) who had been involved in a five-month battle with the Board of Governors to allow girls to wear trousers as part of the school uniform. This involved writing various letters to them, highlighting issues around young women and body consciousness and engaging other pupils in the debate. The Board finally agreed that girls could wear trousers if they wished and Melissa felt that this was one of her greatest achievements in the school.

While more schools are making use of school councils, Schubotz and Sinclair (2006) found in their recent research that there was still not a culture of pupil participation in many schools and that some schools councils were ineffectual. They note the potential value of these and other mechanisms of pupil participation for improving the school culture, attachment to school and the framing of inclusive and meaningful policies (such as anti-bullying policies).

9.4.2 Participation: A Defining Feature of Youth Provision?

Few young women reported having any say in the youth provision they were provided with or the clubs/projects they attended. In most cases, it was the leaders who decided the activities or in some instances the older or 'more responsible' young people or the boys. On other occasions, young people were given some level of control or choice, yet the nature of this was constrained in that it was within certain confines of an already established programme. Thus, the choice as described by one young woman was that they did not have to do the activities if they did not want to, but no alternatives were offered.

Those who felt that they had not been consulted, did, in hindsight, think that this was a good idea. Michelle (aged 19) explained why in the following manner:

"Because if young people are gonna be usin' the facilities like then it should be what the young people want. Like there's no point in settin' up things an' then the young people turning around goin' 'I don't wanna do this' an' they'll not do it so it's a waste a time an' it's a waste a money. So it's better to ask them like."

Four young women stated that they had an input in their clubs or programmes. Fiona said her group were asked regularly what they wanted to do and steered in the direction of it. Susie said that her group regularly carried out evaluations and needs analysis and, where there were things they wished to do, these were always included in the programme. All of these young women felt it was important to consult with young people in order to meet their needs and Nicola (aged 20) also noted that it gave some form of control and ownership over projects and clubs. Of her local drop-in centre she told us:

"... whenever it opened an' all, we took part in paintin' it an', y'know it made it feel more like oh this is our place ye know." [her emphasis]

Clearly, young women still have a lack of say in the provision available to them and in the nature of the programmes/clubs/projects etc. they attend. Those who did feel that they were asked their opinion and had it taken into account, recounted experiences of feeling a sense of ownership, control and pride in the projects they were involved in and a sense that these were meeting their needs.

One of the key principles of youth work which is imbedded within the youth work curriculum, is participation. This principle is of such primary importance that recent youth service initiatives have been set up and resourced to improve the participation of young people in the youth sector. In policy terms the youth service liaison forum has established a participation sub-group to feed into the youth service strategy for Youth Work for Northern Ireland. However this research suggests that participation for young women involved in youth clubs and programmes is limited. While some clearly felt more involved than others, the overall experience (particularly of youth clubs) was that young people were not active participants in decision-making. Such a finding is of significance to a youth service that strives to be inclusive and participatory. Also significant is the benefits which the young women could articulate arising from their active participation in projects. This offers opportunities for models of inclusive practice to be widespread and mainstreamed throughout the youth sector.

9.4.3 Women: An Invisible Voice in Our Communities

Young women were asked if they felt that young people were valued within their communities and included in local decision-making. Only one young woman felt that women were valued members of her community. Donna noted that during recent events in the area where there was heightened security and sectarian violence that women were actively involved in this and had in many respects held the community together:

"I think women were sick of feeling that they were not superior, you know, that it was just the men. The men were out working, women were looking after houses. But now, it's women that are the strong ones that are holding the community together you know. They were out there doing their bit, that it wasn't just the men." (aged 21)

While this is a very particular example it raises the issue of the position of women in conflict related situations and, despite the views and experiences of some, Donna firmly believed that women played a key role in her community at this particular time.

On a more general level, young women provided us with many examples of feeling ignored and excluded within their own communities. The resounding view was that young people were viewed as a nuisance and trouble and that it was not worth asking their opinion. As Janine said of young people in her community:

"They're judged before they're asked. Everybody just judges them." (aged 17)

Indeed, Fiona noted that it had taken high levels of joyriding, drug use, glue sniffing and increases in suicide among young people in her area before the community decided that they needed to do something for the young people of the area.

With regards to young people being represented on local forums or committees or involved in local decision-making, examples of this were minimal. Indeed, Rachel summed up the experiences of many with regards to local events when she said:

"You'd probably get a leaflet through, you'd never be asked ..." (aged 25)

Others who had been asked their opinion felt that this was merely tokenistic and a means of pacifying young people, but that essentially their views were still ignored. Furthermore, it was noted by one young woman that young people's views had been sought but nothing had been done. This led her to believe that their views had been ignored and consultation tokenistic. While this may well have been the case, it may equally have been the case that it was difficult to implement the requests of young people. It is important, therefore, that when young people are consulted that they are reported back to in order to show them that their views had been taken into account in decision-making.

Kim (aged 21) discussed the difficulties she had of getting onto her local community committee in order to represent the views of young people. Even when she did get to put her views across she felt that these had been ignored and that there was a lack of interest in young people:

> **Kim:** ... they wouldn't let me on the committee or nothin' I think the youngest person there's about 40 maybe. They're all older an' like it's a mixed area too an' I think it really needs, cus the Catholics play with the Catholics an' the Protestants like, I think they need like a youth group to take both of them together or somethin', there's no rows or nothing it's just there's separate parts
> **GN:** An' did they give you any reasonin' behind why they didn't want to do -
> **Kim:** Couldn't be bothered with the hassle (laughs) more or less that's just what they said.

Not dissimilarly, although Nicole had managed to get young representatives on the committee of her local youth club, the committee of the community centre (where the youth club was based) would not allow young people on their committee. A youth leader representing the views of young people, however, had brought some benefits but she felt that it had been a long and difficult process with more challenges in store. Despite the difficulties Nicole was not, as yet, discouraged:

"I've been a part of it in my local youth club, they have got young people on as youth delegates and kinda putting across your own views. Now to me you're still no more listening, you might as well talk to the wall, they kinda still think you're none the wiser. We have had a lot of problems and a lot of barriers with the management committee in the resource centre and the youth club, in the fact that they see the young people as a lot of trouble ...//... they blame the youth club for everything even though they do nothing and I think it's only now they're starting to realise well there actually is good work going on there. Em, there's like a representative from the youth club on the management committee but she's a leader but we're kinda trying to push now two young people to represent rather than the youth leader but it's kinda hitting the brick wall. But do you know what I mean? We'll encourage it and keep pushing for it". (aged 25)

Nicole, working within her local youth club was preparing young people for having a stake in their community. Shirley also worked with young people and provided an example of good practice that is of value in highlighting how young people can be encouraged and supported to have a more active role in their communities and hence feeling more 'included':

" ... we would work with young people in rural areas ...//... Sort of giving them more of a role in their communities, get them more involved in their community associations, give themselves a greater sense of empowerment because there would be a renowned problem of young people in rural areas, sorta once you get to a certain age, they move out, they move to the towns, cities to go to university, to get work and they don't really come back. So, the expectation of young people being a problem in rural areas, we're trying to get them to see the benefits of their own area". (aged 24)

Politics and Participation

9

163

As a final, but interesting point, when asked how she felt young women were valued in her community, Máiréad (aged 22) answered in terms of young women's ability to provide care:

> **KM:** ... So how do you think young people and really young women are valued by adults in your community?
> **Máiréad:** If you're a girl you have to babysit your kids first wouldn't you

9.4.4 Informed Choices? Young Women's Political Voices

A key aspect of ensuring full participation is ensuring that young people have accurate and full information upon which to base their decisions. It was illustrated previously that a number of young women told us that they did not vote as they did not understand politics and/or the voting process. Furthermore, a substantial number of young women who did vote told us that they were not necessarily interested in politics and based their voting preference on the views of others. It is clear, therefore, that young women lack full and accurate information regarding politics and voting in order to make informed decisions.

In light of these discussions, we asked young women if they learned about politics and voting in school (aside from through taking GCSE or A-Level Politics). Only four young women reported having experience of this, and while the value they placed on it varied and one young woman's experience was worrying in light of the one-sided nature of the information she received, Ruth's experience demonstrates how schools can make this an insightful, interesting and engaging part of learning.

Good Practice Example: Ruth's Experience

Ruth was 17 at the time of interview and attending a state controlled grammar school. Ruth felt that she had learned about politics and elections through two main processes in school: elections for and representation by a school council and the running of mock political elections. Of the latter, she demonstrates how young people can become informed about politics and the process of voting in an engaging and inclusive manner:

"In January we held our own elections. We got people to represent each em, party. And then we'd vote for them, they'd make a wee speech and we vote for them. ...//... It was interesting (giggles). The teachers were more involved and they were talking about what, em, the parties stood for, then the people, then we'd vote for them."

Importantly, Ruth notes how the whole class as well as teachers were engaged in this activity and demonstrates how through it there was the opportunity to learn about party policies, democracy and the voting process.

While Ruth felt that this was a useful and positive experience she noted that she still lacked interest in politics as she, and others, did not see its relevance to them. Ruth felt that young people needed to know how politics and different policies would impact upon their lives as young people. In doing so, she sends a clear message to political parties:

"I think it's [politics] boring ...//... there's no interest in it, there's no, they're not trying to do nothing for us, it's all their generation type thing that they're affecting, we need information about it and things like that."

A number of young women involved in the research felt that it would be useful for schools to inform young people about politics and voting. While a number of reasons were put forward for this, the main one was that it was felt that it would provide better understanding and allow for informed decisions to be made. Pauline's view was reflective of others:

"It would be useful, cus then you'd know sort of who you want to vote for and what benefits you would be getting if you voted for this particular party." (aged 23)

Related to or inherent within these discussions was again the view that young people tended to vote based on the preferences of their family and friends or their community background. To learn about all parties and their policies within school, some felt, would encourage people to make informed choices and not those based on tradition and culture. Explaining why she feels it would be good for schools to teach young people about politics and voting, Jemima offers a detailed insight into a worrying trend in voting in Northern Ireland that may be set to continue without further input from schools and other agencies:

"Yeah I think it would be good ...//... because like I go out an' vote an' sometimes I say to myself 'why am I votin' for?' ye know an' then I think 'well I suppose I've the right to vote so why shouldn't I?' ...//... but at the end of the day I don't really know what I'm votin' for ye know what I mean. An' I think an awful lotta young, more young people needed [to know] ...//... this is what the SDLP'll do for me, or this is what Sinn Fein'll do for me, or this is what the DUP'll do, ye know that kinda way that if people were actually informed to know [that] such an' such a group will help bring money to the homeless or whatever ye know jus' for an example, then ye might think 'well maybe I will vote for that group because they're doin' somethin' good for other people' ye know that kind of a way. But I don't have a clue what any of them do, I jus' know one's Catholic, one's Protestant, an' one's em a mixture of both, um I couldn't tell ye what the rest of them do." (aged 20)

Young women were clearly aware that voting should be about more than exercising a right and that a decision should be made based on all of the information. This information, however, appears to be lacking and a number of young women felt that providing it could actually increase the number of young people voting through highlighting to them why it was important and what their vote means:

"...more people would vote if they knew what it was gonna do ..." (Molly, aged 20)

"... I think there should be a bitta basic knowledge y'know on what happens if you don't vote or does it really matter if you vote." (Nicola, aged 20)

Here we have discussed the teaching of politics and voting within the context of schools. This is not to suggest that the full onus be on schools but, aside from the home, this is the place where young people spend the majority of their time. There are of course difficulties, Ellen, for example, cautioned of how teachers could pass on their own political views to pupils and Máiréad's experience demonstrated this in practice. There is space for the youth service, voluntary and statutory organisations to carry out work in schools and communities regarding politics. An element could be built into EDI training for young people, agencies such as Women into Politics or the Electoral Commission could carry out sessions within Citizenship Education or PSE within schools and in youth and community programmes. This, as shown in the experience of Donna, can have a radical impact.

Good Practice Example: Donna's Experience

Donna was 21 at the time of interview and living in a predominately Catholic interface area. In the five years prior to fieldwork, the area in which Donna lived had been the site of political tension, conflict and violence particularly around the 12th of July. As noted in previous chapters, Donna cited these experiences as strengthening her community. One impact of this, however, was that when Donna gained the right to vote she gave little thought to party politics and felt that she should naturally vote in line with the majority preference of her community. She told us:

" ... when I got my first vote, I voted for who my community wanted me to vote for. Em, I never read any of them manifesto's or what they were offering me. I voted for (political party) because that's who everybody else was voting for."

Donna told us that in the year prior to us meeting her that she had been involved in a piece of research with the Electoral Commission. The process, it appears, informed Donna about politics and voting rather than merely focusing upon collecting her views as part of a research project. The value of this process was clear in that Donna told us:

"But now, that I took part in a piece of research with the Electoral Commission last year and I voted, and I voted for who I wanted to vote for, who was offering the best for me. Em, and I think that, I think it's, I think you need to have more of this, more research done, young people think around political issues that young people can air, you know sort of get everything off their chest."

9.5 CONCLUSION

It has been illustrated here that young women are not being afforded the opportunity to fully participate in many areas of their life because of a lack of good information, a lack of voice, or a lack of visibility. Within the research, however, there was some evidence of a changing climate, instances of good practice and individual experiences which may provide useful lessons for others.

There now also appears to be a change in the political climate in Northern Ireland. The data presented here were collected at a time when the Northern Ireland Assembly was in suspension, and the views of the young women here are reflective of the political climate of the time. The Northern Ireland Assembly is due to be functional again shortly (May 2007) and the mood of these young women may well be different now. Yet, in light of the young women's general views of not feeling included in the political process and in many areas of their lives, this is a prime opportunity for all institutions to bear in mind the advise of the Special Representative of the United Nations Secretary General for Children and Armed Conflict (2001) that "Northern Ireland will have a far better chance for a durable peace if young people are a priority in that process." (cited in Kilkelly et al., 2004: xvi).

9.10 RECOMMENDATIONS

- While there has been an increase in the number of female political candidates and some political parties fare better than others, clear inequalities remain. The onus remains on political parties to actively promote and encourage women to take on visible/public roles.

- Opportunities should be increased to inform and educate young women of the historical role and position of women in Northern Ireland history and politics through the school curriculum and the youth service.

- School councils hold the potential to act as one mechanism for the voices of young people to be taken into account within schools. Continued expansion and evaluation of these is necessary to ensure that they genuinely facilitate and encourage participation rather than being tokenistic.

- There is little evidence that young women are uniformly involved in decision-making relating to youth policy and provision at a meaningful level. More effective mechanisms are required to ensure that the principles of participation are implemented and practised by all agencies involved in youth service provision.

- Political parties need to do more to engage young people, particularly young women. This might take the form of specific sections within manifestos that clearly inform young people, in language appropriate to them, how voting for that party would impact on them as young people and for their future.

- There should be a greater emphasis on politics and voting education in schools and youth groups. This would help increase the political voice of young people and assist them to make informed decisions. Kilkelly et al. (2004: 49) have suggested that: "We need an integrated approach to 'political literacy' where young people receive this as part of citizenship education."

.

Chapter Ten
Concluding Comments

CONCLUDING COMMENTS

This research has provided a holistic view into the lives of young women in Northern Ireland. The issues raised were analysed thematically and the inter-related nature of themes is striking. The way, for example, in which a disrupted and difficult home life adversely affects education and subsequent labour market opportunities and how problems and difficulties not dealt with in childhood continue to affect young women in adolescence and later life. The young women's accounts show that in many areas of their lives - home, school, work and community – their choices, opportunities and actions are influenced by the persistence of discrimination and gender inequality. However, while they acknowledge differences between the opportunities and choices open to men and women they do not see these as being rooted in gender discrimination, but rather as an inevitability. For example, expanded opportunities in terms of educational and career choices were not linked to the need for new types of family arrangements. Instead, many young women accepted that they would carry the bulk of domestic responsibilities while also working outside the home.

This raises questions about young women's views on equality and the relevance of feminism to their lives. Many acknowledged that they have benefited from feminism and the women's movement through enhanced access to education, employment and social welfare provision – especially in relation to working rights for pregnant women etc. But, among many of the young women we interviewed there seemed to be little desire to press for further change. Those who did tended to be well informed about gender issues as a result of their studies or very individual life experiences. In some respects this could paint a pessimistic view of ambivalence towards gender equality and feminism but we need to place these young women's experiences and views in the context of the social, political and cultural environment in which they have lived.

As a result of economic and social change, young women in their twenties have been exposed to a rhetoric of individualism, to values of autonomy and individual choice. Rich (2005) argues that gender inequalities are often masked through a neo-liberal position, which she says, paradoxically feels empowering to young women. So success may be about educational achievement, having a good income etc., all things perceived to be in the control of the individual. This may go some way to explaining the tendency for young women to also individualise problems and difficulties, even when these had obvious structural causes. It may also help to explain the sense of pointlessness attached to voting or to collective action and political participation.

For young women in Northern Ireland there are additional reasons why feminism may carry little meaning. Little (2002) points out that there have been a number of constraints on feminism in Northern Ireland, including traditional and conservative views of women, a narrow definition of what is political where politics is mostly understood as being related to issues of nationality and religious identification (an issue raised by young women in this study), and a scepticism about political ideas in an environment where political discourses have been dominated by practical problems of political reality and conflict. Over decades, political debates in Northern Ireland have been dominated by the constitutional question. During Direct Rule social policy was made at Westminster and amended for implementation in Northern Ireland so there has been little opportunity for young women to see 'normal politics' in action. The lack of women involved in electoral politics has also meant that they have had few role models.

One could point to the development of extensive equality legislation in Northern Ireland and expect that this should have contributed to gender equality. UK gender equality legislation has tended to focus on work issues such as Equal Pay and measures to address Sex Discrimination. One of the consequences of the Northern Ireland conflict has been the development of strong anti-discriminatory and equality legislation in relation to religion. As a result of the Good Friday/Belfast Agreement new equality legislation, Section 75 was introduced. This identified nine categories (including religion, race, age and gender, against which public bodies have to 'proof' policy). A number of observations can be made about the success of legislation in addressing equality. Certainly, it is important to have strong anti-discriminatory legislation, but it is interesting to note that gender discrimination has never been tackled with the same legislative vigour as religious equality. It would seem that the implementation of Section 75 has often got bogged down in procedure and paperwork, but also that it has in some respects seemed to have had the perverse incentive of reducing women's equality to one-ninth of an equality agenda. While accepting the need for strong legislation and appropriate redress mechanisms, what is clear from this research is that considerable attitudinal change is required before significant advances in relation to gender equality can be achieved.

Acknowledging this context, and further reflecting on some of the reasons why young women do not acknowledge their circumstances to be the product of inequality, a number of points can be made. Is it that young women have to experience inequality to understand it? Do they need to encounter the barriers before they can see the relevance of feminism or the need to challenge discrimination? Aronson (2003) raises this point in her study of women's perception of feminism, when she notes a comment by one participant that - nothing had happened to her to make her a feminist.

A second point arises from the desire of many young women not to be perceived as victims but to be in control. Would young women perceive engaging in feminism as a sign of weakness? Would it seem to them to be admitting to having a problem or being treated unequally/differently, and thus undesirable on those grounds? In relation to a number of the issues discussed in this report we note how the idea of a 'survivor mentality' runs through many of the young women's accounts. The concern about being seen as vulnerable, weak or a victim deters them from seeking help. Yet, as noted earlier, there is little potential for these problems to be addressed through individual agency given their structural base.

Finally, we wish to draw out two further strong and cross-cutting themes which have emerged from the research: the pressure on young women in terms of their time and their perception of how the conflict has/has not impacted on their lives. As young women attempt to juggle school or college with work and/or family and caring responsibilities the thing most likely to be squeezed out of their lives is their leisure time – although they themselves did not articulate this as a problem but accepted the fact that they simply had little free-time. This is an issue which has frequently been discussed in relation to older women in terms of having adverse implications on health and well-being. The fact that this pattern is establishing itself at such an early stage in the lives of young women is concerning and highlights the need to address these pressures through a multi-agency approach. These are not just issues that can be tackled by individuals or families but require co-ordinated support from health and social care, youth, education and housing agencies.

Finally, and perhaps a fitting place to close this report in light of current political developments in Northern Ireland is in relation to the impact of the conflict on the lives of young women. Only those young women with direct experience of the conflict (i.e. personal violence or bereavement) said that it had affected them. Yet, its impact and legacy could be seen in almost all of the young women's accounts and is highlighted throughout the report. It is evident that the way in which the conflict has impacted upon young women is not fully understood and there is a need for greater recognition of the fact that:

Existing inequalities between women and men, and patterns of discrimination against women and girls, tend to be exacerbated in armed conflict (Annan, 2002).

Now emerging from over 30 years of conflict, Northern Ireland has to make-up for inequalities which have, to some degree, gone unchecked due to the focus on constitutional and conflict-based issues. We believe that this is a prime time to re-ignite debates regarding gender equality and to start afresh with awareness and consciousness raising. This report is the first, of what we hope, is many small steps in bringing the issue to the forefront of the political and social agenda in Northern Ireland.

Chapter Eleven
References

REFERENCES

Agnew, Robert (2003) An Integrated Theory of the Adolescent Peak in Offending. *Youth and Society*, Vol. 34, (3), pp. 263-299.

Armstrong, David and McVicar, Duncan (2000) Value Added in Further Education and Training in Northern Ireland, *Applied Economics*, Vol.32,(13), pp1727-1736

Aronson, Jodi (1994) A Pragmatic View of Thematic Analysis. *The Qualitative Report*, Vol. 2, (1).

Aronson, Pamela (2003) Feminists or "Postfeminists"? Young Women's Attitudes toward Feminism and Gender Relations. *Gender and Society*, Vol.17, (6) pp903-922

Babor, T., Caetano, R. and Casswell, S. (2003) *Alcohol: No Ordinary Commodity*. Oxford: Oxford University Press

Barter, Christine & Renold, Emma (1999) The Use of Vignettes in Qualitative Research. *Social Research Update*, Issue 25.

Beck, Ulrich (1992) *Risk Society: Towards a New Modernity*. London: Sage

Brayton, Jennifer (1997) *What Makes Feminist Research Feminist? The Structure of Feminist Research within the Social Sciences*. Source Unknown.

Breitenbach,Ester and Galligan,Yvonne (2004) *Gender Equality Indicators for Northern Ireland*. Belfast: OFMDFM

British Sociological Association (2002) *Statement of Ethical Practice for the British Sociological Association*. www.britsoc.co.uk

Britton,Liz; Chatrik,Balbir; Coles,Bob; Craig, Gary; Hylton,Carl and Mumtaz,Saira (2002) *Missing Connections: the Careers Dynamics and Welfare Needs of Black and Ethnic Young People at the Margins*. York:JR

Broad,Bob (2005) Young People Leaving Care: Implementing the Children Leaving Care) Act 2000? *Children and Society*, vol.19, pp371-384

Butler, Ian, Scanlan, Lesley, Robinson, Margaret, Douglas, Gillian & Murch, Mervyn (2003) *Divorcing Children: Children's Experience of their Parent's Divorce*. London: Jessica Kingsley

Cairns, Ed, Van Til, Jon & Williamson, Arthur (2004) *Social Capital, Collectivism-individualism and Community Background in Northern Ireland*. Proceedeings of the Researching the Voluntary Sector Conference. Belfast:OFMDFM

Cairns,Ed and Lloyd,Katrina (2005) *Stress at 16*: Research Update from data collected in Young Life and Times Survey 2004. www.ark.ac.u

Camelot Foundation and the Mental Health Foundation (2006) *Truth Hurts: Report of the National Inquiry into Self Harm Among Young People*. London: Camelot Foundation and the Mental Health Foundation

Campbell, Anne (1984) *The Girls in the Gang: A Report from New York*. Oxford: Basil Blackwell.

Campbell, Rebecca & Wasco, Sharon (2000) Feminist Approaches to Social Science: Epistemological and Methodological Tenets. *American Journal of Community Psychology*, Vol. 28, (6), pp. 773-791.

Carroll, R. (1998) 'Gangs put boot into old ideas of femininity'. *The Guardian*, 22nd July.

Catan, Liz (2004) *Becoming Adult: Changing Youth Transitions in the 21st Century*. Brighton: Trust for the study of Adolescence.

Cattell, Vikki. (2001) Poor people, poor places, and poor health: the mediating role of social networks and social capital. *Social Science and Medicine*, Vol. 52, pp. 1501-1516.

Charles,Nikki and Walters, Vivienne (1994) *Women's Health, Women's Voices*. Health and Social Care, vol.2

Checkoway, B. & Richards-Schuster, K. (2003) *Youth Participation in Community Evaluation Research*. The American Journal of Evaluation, Vol. 24, pp. 21-33.

Chesney-Lind, Meda (1997) *The Female Offender: Girls, Women and Crime*. Thousand Oaks: Sage.

Clay, Daniel, Vignoles, Vivian and Dittmar,Helga (2005) Body Image and Self Esteem Among Adult Girls: Testing the Influence of Sociocultural Factors. *Journal of Research on Adolescence*, vol.15 (4) 451-477

Coleman,L and Cater,S (200) *Underage 'Risky' Drinking: Motivations and Outcomes*. York: JRF

Coles,Bob (1995) *Youth and Social Policy*. London: University College London

Collins,Katrina; McAleavy,Gerry; Adamson,Gary (2004)
Bullying in Schools: A Northern Ireland Study. Educational Research, Vol.46 (1) pp55-72

Connolly, Paul (2003) *Ethical Principles for Researching Vulnerable Groups*. Belfast: OFMDFM.

Connolly,Paul (2004) *Evaluation of the Pilot Programme of the Media Initiative for Children in Northern Ireland*. Unpublished Report prepared for the Peace Initiative Institute

Council for the Curriculum, Examinations and Assessment (N.I)(2001) *Relationships and Sexuality Education: Guidance for Post-primary Schools*.

Costley, Debra (2000) 'Collecting the views of young people with moderate learning difficulties' in Lewis, Ann & Lindsay, Geoff (eds.) *Researching Children's Perspectives*. Birmingham: Open University Press.

Crang, M. (1998) *Cultural Geography*. London: Routledge.

Crisp,A Sedgwick,P Halek,C Joughin,N and Humphrey,H (1999) *Why do Teenage Girls Persist in Smoking?* Journal of Adolescence, 22

Davey, Ciara, Dwyer, Clare, McAlister, Siobhán, Kilkelly, Ursula, Kilpatrick, Rosemary, Lundy, Laura, Moore, Linda, & Scraton, Phil (2004) *An Analysis of Research Conducted with School Children into Children's Rights in Northern Ireland: School's Report*. Belfast: NICCY.

Davey, Ciara., Dwyer, Clare. & McAlister, Siobhán. (forthcoming) 'Researching Children's Rights in the Context of Northern Ireland' in Tisdall, K., Davis, J. & Gallagher, M. (eds.) *Listening to Children*. London: Sage.

Dearden,Chris and Becker,Saul (2004) *Young Carers in the UK, the 2004 Report*. London: Carers UK and The Children's Society.

Department of Education Northern Ireland (1987a) *Policy for the Youth Service in Northern Ireland*. Northern Ireland: DENI.

Department of Education Northern Ireland (1987b) *Northern Ireland Youth Service: A Review*. Northern Ireland: DENI.

Department of Education Northern Ireland (1997) *Youth Work: A Model for Effective Practice*. Northern Ireland: DENI.

Department of Education Northern Ireland (2001) *Relationships and Sexuality Education (RSE)*, Circular Number 2001/15. Bangor: DENI.

Department of Education Northern Ireland (2005a) *Strategy for the Delivery of Youth Work in Northern Ireland 2005-2008*. Northern Ireland: DE.

Department for Education in Northern Ireland (2005b) *Participation in Full-time Education and Vocational Training by 16 and 17 year olds in Northern Ireland*. Belfast: DENI

Department for Employment and Learning (2001) *Review of Careers Education and Guidance*. Report of the Review Group. Belfast: DEL

Department of Health (1999) *Saving Lives: Our Healthier Nation*. London:DOH

Department of Health (2002) *Cross Cutting Review on Health Inequalities*. London:DOH

Department of Health, Social Services and Public Safety (2002) *Investing for Health Strategy*. Belfast: DHSSPS

Department for Health, Social Services and Public Safety (2004) *Equalities and Inequalities in Health and Social Care in Northern Ireland: A Statistical Overview*, Belfast: DHSSPS

Department of Health, Social Services and Public Safety (2006) *Project Life: A Shared Vision, the Northern Ireland Suicide Strategy and Action Plan*. Belfast: DHSSPS

Department of Enterprise Trade and Industry (N.I) (2006) *Statistical Bulletin: Women and the Northern Ireland Labour Market*. Belfast:DETI

Detheridge, Tina (2000) 'Research involving children with severe learning difficulties' in Lewis, Ann & Lindsay, Geoff (eds.) *Researching Children's Perspectives*. Birmingham: Open University Press.

Dibben, Pauline (1999) *Young People and Social Exclusion: Speaking Out Against a Culture of Blame*. Paper presented at the International Conference on Young People and Social Exclusion, University of Strathclyde, Glasgow, 9th – 12th September 1999.

Dowler, L. (1998) 'And they think I'm just a nice old lady': Women and War in Belfast, Northern Ireland. Gender, Place and Culture, Vol. 5, (2), pp. 159-176.

Duncan,Simon and Edwards,Ros, (1999) *Lone Mothers, Paid Work and Gendered Moral Rationalities*. Basingstoke. Macmillan

Eubank-Owens, Patsy (1999) *No Teens Allowed: The Exclusion of Adolescents from Public Spaces*. Paper presented at the International Conference on Young People and Social Exclusion, University of Strathclyde, Glasgow, 9th – 12th September 1999.

Equal Opportunities Commission (2005) *Working Below Potential: Women and Part-time Work*. Manchester:EOC

Family Planning Association & Health Promotion Agency (2005) *Relationships and Sexuality Education in Schools Factsheet*. Northern Ireland: FPA & HPA.

Fegan, Eileen & Rebouche, Rachel (2003) Northern Ireland's Abortion Law: The Morality of Silence and the Censure of Agency. *Feminist Legal Studies*, Vol. 11, pp. 221-254.

Fenton,C; Bradley,H and West,J (2003) *Winners and Losers: Employment Trajectories*. Research Report. London: ESRC

Finch, Janet (1984) ''It's great to have someone to talk to': the ethics and politics of interviewing women' in Bell, Colin & Roberts, Helen (Eds.) *Social Researching: Politics, Problems, Practice*. London: Routledge

Ford,J Rugg,J and Burrows,R (2002) Conceptualising the Contemporary Role of Housing in the Transition to Adult Life in England. *Urban Studies*, vol.19, (2),pp.2455-2467

Foreign and Commonwealth Office (2006) Action Plan on UN Resolution 1325, London:FCO

Forrest, R. & Kearns, A. (2001) Social Cohesion, Social Capital and the Neighbourhood. *Urban Studies*, Vol. 38, (12), pp. 2125-2143.

Foster, Janet (1990) *Villains: Crime and Community in the Inner City*. London: Routledge

Francis,Becky (2000) The Gendered Subject: Students Subject Preferences and Discussion of Gender and Subject Ability. *Oxford Review of Education*, Vol.26,pp35-4

Furlong,Andy and Cartmel,Fred (1997) *Young People and Social Change*. Buckinghamshire: Open University Press

Furnham,A Badmin,M Sneade,I (2002) Body Image Dissatisfaction: Gender Differences in Eating Attitudes, Self Esteem and Reasons for Exercise. *The Journal of Psychology*, vol.136(5)

Gatenby, Bev & Humphries, Maria (2000) Feminist Participatory Action Research: Methodological and Ethical Issues. *Women's Studies International Forum*, Vol. 23, (1), pp. 89-105.

Gershon, K (2003) Moral Dilemmas, Moral Strategies and Transformation of Gender. *Gender and Society*, Vol.16 (1) pp8-28

Gilroy, R. & Speak, S. (1998) 'Barriers, Boxes and Catapults: Social Exclusion and Everyday Life', in Madanipour, A., Cars, G & Allen, J. (eds.) *Social Exclusion in European Cities: Processes, Experiences and Responses*. London: Jessica Kingsley.

Geraghty, Teresa, Bleakey, Caroline & Keane, Teresa. (1997) *A Sense of Belonging: Young People in Rural Areas of Northern Ireland Speak About Their Needs, Hopes and Aspirations*. Belfast: YouthAction Northern Ireland.

Glendinning, A., Nuttall, M., Hendry, L., Kloep, M. & Wood, S. (2003) Rural Communities and Well-being: a good place to grow up? *The Sociological Review*, pp.129-156.

Government of Northern Ireland Youth Welfare Act (1994) Belfast: HMSO.

Graham,Hilary (1994) Gender and Class as Dimensions of Smoking Behaviour in Britain: Insights from a Survey of Mothers. *Social Science and Medicine*, Vol 38 (5)

Graham and McDermott (2006) Qualitative Research and the Evidence Base of Policy: Insights from Studies of Teenage Mothers in the UK. *Journal of Social Policy*, Vol.35, pp21-37

Gray,Ann Marie and Robinson,Gillian (2004) *What Women Want? Women and Gender Roles in Northern Ireland*. Research update 24, www.ark.ac.uk

Gray,Ann Marie and Carragher,Lucia (2006) *Possibilities: the views of Lone Parents on Childcare in Northern Ireland*. Belfast: Gingerbread

Gray,Ann Marie and Carragher,Lucia (2007) *Possibilities: The Impact of Poverty on the Health and Well-being of Lone Parents in Northern Ireland*. Belfast: GIngerbread

Gray, Louise (2006) 'Ladette life has Scottish girls 'among most violent in the world''. *The Scotsman*, 23/01/2006

Griffin, Christine (2005) *Impossible spaces? Femininity as an empty category*. ESRC Research Seminar Series: New Femininities. 8th July 2005.

Hall, T., Coffey, A. & Williamson, H. (1999) Self, Space and Identity: Youth Identities and Citizenship. *British Journal of Sociology of Education*, Vol. 20 (4), pp. 501-513.

Hancock, Beverley (2002) *Trent Focus for Research and Development in Primary Health Care: An Introduction to Qualitative Research*. Trent Focus.

Hannaford, Sarah (2005) *Drinking, Smoking and Sexual Intercourse – Education and Influences for Young People in Northern Ireland*, Research Update, 37. www.ark.ac.uk

Harman, Colm and Walker,Ian (2000) Education and Earnings in Northern Ireland. Belfast: DEL

Hazel, Neal (1995) Elicitation techniques with young people. *Social Research Update*, Issue 12.

Health Action Zone (2004) *The Little Book of Stuff*. Belfast: HAZ.

Hester,Marianne and Westmarland,Nicole (2005) *Tackling Domestic Violence: Effective Interventions and Approaches*, Home Office Research Study 290. London: Home Office

Hill, M., Davis, J., Prout, A. & Tisdall, K. (2004) *Moving the Participation Agenda Forward. Children and Society*, Vol. 18, pp. 77-96.

Hinds, Bronagh and Gray, Ann Marie (2005) Women and the Review of Public Administration in Northern Ireland. Unpublished Research Paper prepared for Review of Public Administration

Hine, Julian & Grieco, M. (2003) Scatters and clusters in time and space: implications for delivering integrated and inclusive transport. *Transport Policy*, Vol. 10, pp. 299-306.

Hope,A Dring,C and Dring,J (2005) *College Lifestyle and Attitudinal National Survey*, Dublin: Department of Health and Children

Include Youth (2001) *'Our Rights' Commissioner for Children in NI: A Young Person's Response*. Belfast: Include Youth.

Institute of Conflict Research (2006) *Youth participation in the democratic process*. Belfast: ICR.

Institute of Conflict Research (2003) *Young People and Politics in North Belfast: An outline of a survey by North Belfast Community* Research Project. Belfast: ICR.

Itzen,Catherine (2006) *Tackling the Health and Mental Health Effects of Domestic and Sexual Violence and Abuse*. London: Home Office and DOH

Iwasaki, Yoshi & Schneider, Ingrid (2003) Leisure, Stress, and Coping: An Evolving Area of Inquiry. *Leisure Studies*, Vol., 25, pp. 107-113.

Jarman, Neil (2005) Teenage Kicks: Young Women and their Involvement in Violence and Disorderly Behaviour. *Child Care in Practice*, Vol. 11, (3), pp. 341-356.

Jones, Gill (1995) *Family support for young people setting up home*. JRF Findings no. 70. York: JRF.

Jones, Gill (2002) *The Youth Divide*. York: JRF/York Publishing Services.

Jones,Gill and Bell,R (2000) *Youth, Parenting and Public Policy*. JRF Findings no.241, York: JRF

Kemp,Peter, and Rugg,J (2001) *Young People, Housing Benefit and Risk Society*. Social Policy and Administration, Vol.35, (6), pp.688-700

Kilkelly, Ursula, Kilpatrick, Rosemary, Lundy, Laura, Moore, Linda., Scraton, Phil, Davey, Ciara, Dwyer, Clare & McAlister, Siobhán (2004) *Children's Rights in Northern Ireland 2004*. Belfast: Northern Ireland Commissioner for Children and Young People.

Kirby, Perpetua (1999) *Involving Young Researchers: How to Enable Young People to Design and Conduct Research*. York: Joseph Rowntree Foundation.

Kitchin, Rob and Lysaght, Karen (2004) *Sexual citizenship in Belfast, Northern Ireland*. Gender, Place and Culture. Vol, 11, (1), pp. 83-103.

Kitzinger, Jenny & Barbour, Rosaline (1999) 'Introduction: the challenge and promise of focus groups' in Barbour, Rosaline & Kitzinger, Jenny (Eds.) *Developing Focus Group Research: Politics, Theory and Practice*. London: Sage

Kilpatrick, Rosemary (1997) *Scoping Study on Children/Youth in Making Belfast Work Areas*. Belfast: Graduate School of Education

Kissling, Elizabeth (1996) Bleeding Out Loud: Communication about Menstruation. *Feminism and Psychology*, 6 (4), pp. 481-504

Kitchin, Rob & Lysaght, Karen (2004) *Sexual Citizenship in Belfast, Northern Ireland*. Gender, Place and Culture. Vol, 11, (1), pp. 83-103.

Kracen, A (2003) *Mental Health Initiative: A Resource Manual for Mental Health Promotion and Suicide Prevention in Third Level Students*. Dublin: Trinity College and the Northern Area Health Board

Leach, Fiona (2000) *Gender, Education and Training: an International Perspective. Gender and Development*, Vol.6 (1) pp9-18

Leonard,Madeine (1999) *Gender and the Transition from School to Work in Belfast.* Women's Studies International Forum, Vol.22, (6), pp619-630

Leonard, Madeline (2004) Bonding and Bridging Social Capital: Reflections from Belfast. *Sociology*, Vol. 38, (5), pp. 927-944.

Leonard, Madeline (2007) *The Three Rs: Reiteration, Resilience and Resistance in the Lives of Young People Growing Up in Divided Belfast*. Paper presented at School of Sociology, Social Policy and Social Work Seminar Series, Queen's University Belfast, 04/03/'07.

Lister, Ruth (1997) *Citizenship: Towards a Feminist Synthesis.* Feminist Review, Vol.57 (1) pp28-40

Little, Adrian (2002) *Feminism and the Politics of Difference in Northern Ireland.* Journal of Political Ideologies, Vol.7 (2) pp163-177

Little, Jo & Panelli, Ruth (2003) *Gender Research in Rural Geography*. Gender, Place and Culture, Vol. 10, (3), pp. 281-289.

Livesay,C (2005) 'The Hidden Curriculum 1' www.sociology.uk.org. Accessed 01/02/05

Logan, J. & Molotch, H. (1987) *Urban Fortunes: The Political Economy of Place*. Berkeley: University of California Press.

MacDonald, Robert & Marsh, Jane (2005) *Disconnected Youth? Growing Up in Britain's Poor Neighbourhoods*. Houndsmill: Palgrave.

MacDonald, Robert & Shildrick, Tracy (forthcoming) Street Corner Society: Leisure careers, youth (sub)culture and social exclusion. *Leisure Studies*.

MacDonald, Robert & Marsh, Jane (2005) *Disconnected Youth? Growing Up in Britain's Poor Neighbourhoods*. Houndsmill: Palgrave.

Marsh, Beezy (2004) 'The ladette takeover'. *The Mail on Sunday*, 19/01/2004.

Middleton, Alan; Murie, Alan and Groves, Rick (2005) Social Capital and Neighbourhoods that Work. *Urban Studies*, Vol. 42, (10), pp. 1711-1738.

McAlister, Siobhán (2007) *An Ethnographic Investigation of 'Underclass Youth': A Case Study of Blossom Hill: Teesside*. Unpublished PhD thesis. University of Teesside.

McAlister, Siobhán & Neill, Gail (in press) *Young Women's Positive and Negative Perceptions of Self in Northern Ireland*. Child Care in Practice.

McAlister, Siobhán & Neill, Gail (2005) *Different Worlds: The Differential Impact of Family Support and Social Networks on the Lives of Young Women*. Paper presented to The Equality Commission for Northern Ireland, 27/09/2006.

McCartan, Clare (2004) *Conducting Research with Peer Researchers*. Paper presented at European Conference in Educational Research. Greece.

McCarthy,Helen (2004) *Girls in High Places: How Women's Networks are Changing the Workplace*. London: DEMOS

McRobbie, Angela (2000) *Feminism and Youth Culture*. Houndsmills: Macmillan Press Ltd.

McGlynn,Clare; Niens, Ulrike; Cairns,Ed and Hewstone,M (2004) Moving Out of Conflict: the Contribution of Integrated Schools in Northern Ireland to Identity. *Journal of Peace Education*, Vol.1 (2), pp147-163

McKie, Linda; Bowlby, Sophie and Gregory,Susan (2001) Gender, Caring and Employment in Britain. *Journal of Social Policy*, Vol.30, pp233-258

Meredith, Fionola (2003) 'Why so scared boys? Irish Politics is still hamstrung by sexism'. *The Observer*, 26th July 2003.

Middleton, A., Murie, A. & Groves, R. (2005) Social Capital and Neighbourhoods that Work. *Urban Studies*, Vol. 42, (10), pp. 1711-1738.

Millar,Jane and Gardiner,Karen(2006) How Low Paid Employees Avoid Poverty: An Analysis by Family Type and Household Structure. *Journal of Social Policy*, Vol.35, pp351-369

Mooney,E McDowell,P and Taggart,K (2004) *Briefing Paper on Northern Ireland Care Leavers (2002/03)*. Belfast: DHSSPS

Mullen,Christine, Rollock,Fiona, McAlister, Siobhán, and Fitzsimons,Lelia (2007) *"Don't Be So Formal We're Normal". A Research Report on the Mental Health of Looked After Children/Care Leavers in Northern Ireland*, Belfast:VOYPIC

Mullender, Audrey (2001) *What Works in Reducing Domestic Violence*. London: Home Office

Morrow,Vic, and Richards,M (1996) *Young People's Transitions to Adulthood*. JRF Findings no.98, York:JRF

National Children's Bureau (2006) Guidelines for Research. www.ncb.org.uk

Northern Ireland Commissioner for Children and Young People (2006) *A Northern Ireland Based Review of Children and Young People's Participation in the Care Planning Process*. Belfast: NICCYP

Northern Ireland Housing Executive (2006) *Mixed housing scheme is launched – 30/10/06*. http://www.nihe.gove.uk/news/news.asp?Id=1221 (accessed, 01/11/06)

Northern Ireland Office (2005) Tackling Violence at Home: A Strategy for Addressing Domestic Violence and Abuse in Northern Ireland. Belfast: NIO

Oakley, Ann (1988) '*Interviewing women: a contradiction in terms' in Roberts, Helen (Ed.) Doing Feminist Research*. New York: Routledge.

OFMDFM (2006) *Gender Equality Strategy for Northern Ireland*. Belfast: OFMDFM

O'Doherty, Gemma (2004) 'Drunken schoolgirls staggering along the streets in the afternoon ... is this normal behaviour for Ireland'. *Irish Independent*, 18/12/2004.

References

Pateman,Carole (1992) 'Equality, Difference, Subordination: the politics of motherhood and women's citizenship' in G.Bock and S.James (eds) *Beyond Equality and Difference*. London: Routledge

Pavis, Stephen, Hubbard, Gill & Platt, Stephen (2001) *Young People in Rural Areas: Socially Excluded or Not? Work, Employment and Society*, Vol. 15, (2), pp. 291-309

Rake, Katherine and Davies,Helen (2000) *Women's Incomes Over the Lifetime*. London: Cabinet Office and stationery Office

Reay, D. & Lucey, H. (2000) "I don't really like it here but I don't want to be anywhere else": children and inner city council estates. *Antipode*, Vol. 32, (4), pp. 410-428.

Reid, Colleen (2004) Advancing Women's Social Justice Agendas: A feminist action research framework. *International Journal of Qualitative Methods*, Vol. 3, (3). Article 1. Retrieved 21/06/06 from http://www.ualberta.ca/~iiqm/backissues/3_3/html/reid.html

Reinharz, Shulamit (1992) *Feminist Methods in Social Research*. Oxford: Oxford University Press.

Rich, Emma ((2005) Young Women, Feminist Identities and Neo-Liberalism. *Women's Studies International Forum*, Vol.28, pp495-508

Ringrose, J. (2005) *A New Universal Mean Girl: Examining the empty objects and contradictory discourses of girl's aggression and violence*. ESRC Seminar, 23rd March 2005.

Rolston, Bill, Schubotz, Dirk & Simpson, Audrey (2005) Sex education in Northern Ireland schools: a critical evaluation. *Sex Education*. Vol, 5, (3), pp. 217-234.

Rose, Damaris (2001) *Revisiting Feminist Research Methodologies: A Working Paper*. Canada: Status of Women Canada, Research Division.

Rubin, Herbert & Rubin, Irene (2005) (2nd ed.) *Qualitative Interviewing: The Art of Hearing Data*. London: Sage

Save the Children Fund and the Children's Law Centre (Northern Ireland) (2002) *The State of Children's Rights at the end of the 20th Century*. Belfast: SCF and Children's Law Centre

Schubotz, Dirk, Simpson, Audrey & Rolston, Bill (2003) *Telling it like it is! Young people's experiences of relationships and sex in Northern Ireland*. London: FPA.

Schubotz, Dirk (2005) *Young People's Attitudes to Politics and Elections: Report on the results of questions set by the Electoral Commission*. ARK Young Life and Time Survey. http://www.ark.ac.uk/ylt - accessed 26/11.05.

Schubotz, Dirk & Sinclair, Ruth (2006) *'Being part and parcel of the school': The views and experiences of children and young people in relation to the development of bullying policies in schools*. Belfast: NICCY/NBC.

Semple,John (2006) *Review into Affordable Housing in Northern Ireland*. Interim Report. Belfast:DSD

Sharpe,S (1976) *'Just Like A Girl': How Girls Learn to be Women*. London: Penguin

Sharpe, C., Aldridge, J. & Medina, J. (2006) *Delinquent Group Behaviour and Offending: Findings from the 2004 Offending, Crime and Justice Survey*. Home Office Online Report 14/06. London: Home Office.

Shucksmith, Mark (2004) Young People and Social Exclusion in Rural Areas. *Sociologia Ruralis*, Vol. 44, (1), pp.43-59.

Shucksmith, Mark (2000) *Exclusive Countryside? Social Inclusion and Regeneration in Rural Areas*. Findings 760. York: JRF.

Siegrist,J (2000) Place, Social Exchange and Health: Proposed Sociological Framework. *Social Science and Medicine*, vol 51

Sinclair,Ian; Baker,Clare; Wilson,Kate and Gibbs,Ian (2005) *Foster Children: Where they Go and how they get on*. London: Jessica Kingsley

Smith,Alan (2001) *Religious Segregation and the Emergence of Integrated Schools in Northern Ireland*. Oxford Review of Education, Vol.27(1) pp559-57

Smith, Alan and Montgomery, Alison (2001) *Values in Education in Northern Ireland*. Belfast: Northern Ireland Council for the Curriculum.

Smith, J. (1986) *Crime, Space and Society*. Cambridge: Cambridge University Press.

Smith, Roger, Monaghan, Maddy & Broad, Bob (2002) Involving Young People as Co-Researchers. *Qualitative Social Work*, Vol. 1, (2), pp. 191-207.

Spencer, Liz (2006) 'Analysing Qualitative Data' in A.Bryman *Integrating Qualitative and Quantitative Research. How is it done?*. London: Sage

Smyth,Marie (1998) *Half the Battle: Understanding the Impact of the Troubles on Children and Young People*. Derry/Londonderry: INCOR

Smyth, Marie (2000) *The Youthquest Survey 2000*. Derry/Londonderry/Incore

Stanley, Liz & Wise, Sue (1990) (2nd ed.) *Breaking Out Again: Feminist Ontology and Epistemology*. London: Routledge.

Stice, Eric and Whitenton,Kathryn (2002) *Risk Factors for Body Dissatisfaction in Adolescent Girls: A Longitudinal Investigation*. Developmental Psychology, vol.38, pp660-678

Storey, Pamela & Brannen, Julia (2000) *Young people and transport in rural areas*, Findings 750. York: JRF.

The Daily Mail (2005) 'Ladette' drinking to increase in next five years. 22/04/2005.

Thompson, T. (2001) Girls lead the pack in new gangland violence. *The Observer*, 15th April.

Todhunter, Colin. (2001) Undertaking Action Research: Negotiating the Road Ahead. *Social Research Update*, Issue 34.

Trimble, June (1991) *Equality of Opportunity: Provision for Girls and Young Women in the Full-time Sector of the Northern Ireland Youth Service*. Belfast: YouthAction Northern Ireland.

Viner,R and Barker,M (2005) *Young People's Health: the Need for Action*. British Medical Journal, 16 April, 330

Wade, Jim and Dixon, Jo (2006) Making a Home, finding a Job: Investigating Early Housing and Employment Outcomes for Young People Leaving Care. *Child and Family Social Work*, 11, pp199-208

Wiles, Rose; Charles, Vikki; Crow, Graham and Heath, Sue (2004) *Informed Consent and the Research Process*. Paper presented at the ESRC Research Methods Festival, University of Oxford, 2nd July 2004.

Wilkinson, R. (2001) *Mind the Gap: Hierarchies, Health and Human Evolution*. Yale: Yale University Press

Wilkinson, Sue (1998) Focus Groups in Feminist Research: Power, Interaction, and the Co-construction of Meaning. *Women's Studies International Forum*, Vol. 21, No. 1, pp. 111-125.

Witz, Anne (1997) *Introducing Women's Studies*. Hampshire: Palgrave

Women and Work Commission (2006) *Shaping a Fairer Future*. London: Women and Equality Unit

World Health Organisation (2000) Health and Health Behaviour Among Young People. *WHO Policy Series: Health Policy for Children and Adolescents*, Issue 1. Copenhagan: WHO

Young Life and Times (2006) Data on Attitudes to Politics – available on-line at www.ark.ac.uk

YouthAction Northern Ireland (2002) *Child Protection Policy and Procedures*. Belfast: YouthAction Northern Ireland.

YouthAction Northern Ireland (2006) *Working with young women with disabilities on the issue of employability: Challenges and strategies to effective practice*. Belfast: YouthAction Northern Ireland.

Youth Clubs UK & ASDAN (1997) *Youth Achievement Awards: Moderator Guide*.

Youth Council for Northern Ireland (1994) *Into the Mainstream: Equality of Opportunity, Gender Youth Work Curriculum Guidelines*. Belfast: YCNI.

Youth Council for Northern Ireland (2001) *Seen and Heard? Consulting with and involving young people within the public sector*. Belfast: YCNI

Youth Council for Northern Ireland (2004) *Barometer 2004: A Portrait of Young People in Northern Ireland*. Belfast: Youth Council for Northern Ireland.

YWCA (2002) *If Looks Could Kill: Young Women and Bullying*. London: YWCA

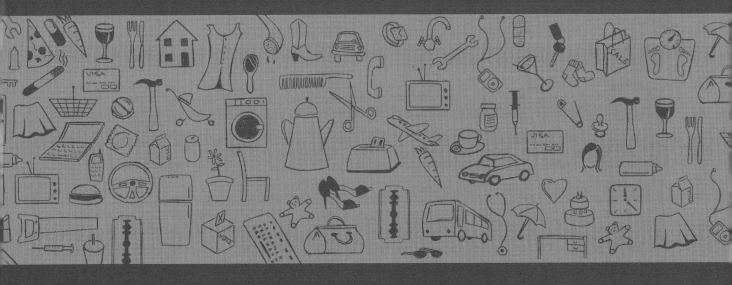

Appendix

Appendix

Membership of Research Steering Group

Rita Burke	Department of Education, Youth Service Inspectorate
Kate Campbell	Independent
Judith Cross	Equality Commission
Debbie Francey	Women Into Politics
Hilary Harbinson	OFMDFM
Claire Harvey	Youth Council for Northern Ireland
Louise Warde Hunter	Department of Education
Susan Kelly	Formerly Women Into Politics
Margaret Logue	Derry Women's Centre
Eliz McArdle	YouthAction Northern Ireland
Monica McWilliams	Former Chair – Human Rights Commission
Kate Moore	Formerly YouthAction Northern Ireland
Susan Morgan	University of Ulster @ Jordanstown
Dr Margaret Ward (Chair)	Women's Resource Development Agency
Etain O'Kane	Shout Project